DEATH IN THE HIGHLANDS

The Siege of Special Forces Camp Plei Me

J. KEITH SALIBA

STACKPOLE
BOOKS

Guilford, Connecticut

Published by Stackpole Books
An imprint of The Rowman & Littlefield Publishing Group, Inc.
4501 Forbes Blvd., Ste. 200
Lanham, MD 20706
www.rowman.com

Distributed by NATIONAL BOOK NETWORK

British Library Cataloguing in Publication Information available

Library of Congress Cataloging-in-Publication Data available

ISBN 978-0-8117-3881-1 (cloth: alk. paper)
ISBN 978-0-8117-6888-7 (electronic)

♾™ The paper used in this publication meets the minimum requirements of American National Standard for Information Sciences—Permanence of Paper for Printed Library Materials, ANSI/NISO Z39.48-1992.

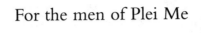

For the men of Plei Me

CONTENTS

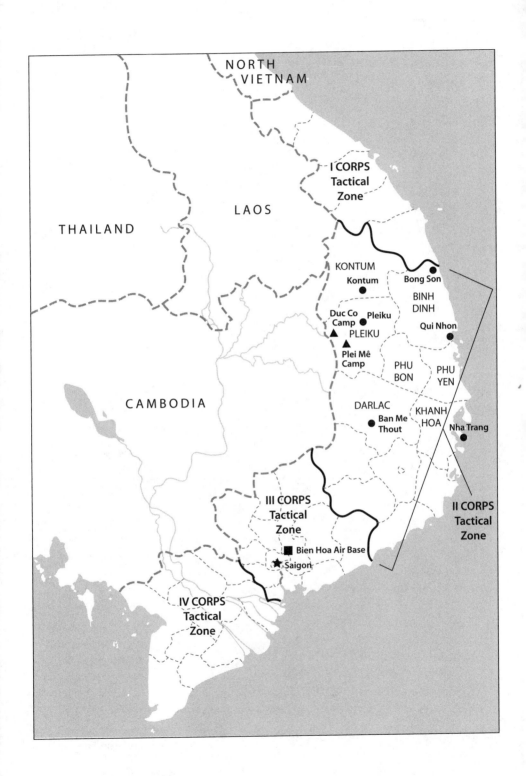

PROLOGUE

Better Lucky Than Good

The Western Highland's plateau swept to the horizon in a rolling expanse of green and brown. Through its center cut the thin line of Provincial Route 5, a single-lane dirt track that connected this remote corner of Pleiku Province with Highway 14 to the east. To the west, the enigmatic, mist-shrouded peaks of the Annamite Range could just be discerned. In quieter times, the view from Warrant Officer (WO) Dean Christensen's orbiting UH-1B helicopter gunship would likely have been pleasant, even serene. But these were not quiet times. In fact, all hell was raging below. The communists had besieged the Special Forces camp at Plei Me some twenty kilometers to the southwest, and II Corps had dispatched a relief force to save it. But this narrow dirt road was the only way to reach the camp. And the communists knew it. So they'd sprung the ambush that everybody knew was coming. Now, the rescuers needed a little rescuing themselves. Bright orange fireballs exploded skyward, as the communists unleashed 75mm recoilless rifle, B-40 rocket, and 82mm mortar fire along the length of the relief column. Still, the Army of the Republic of Vietnam (ARVN) armored task force was holding its own, pummeling enemy positions on both sides of the road with 76mm cannon shot and .50 caliber machine gun fire. All along the dirt track, red and green tracer rounds from friend and foe alike intermingled in a beautiful, deadly display.[1]

Tac-air had arrived to tip the scales in favor of the armored task force (ATF). Close-air support (CAS) strike aircraft roared overhead, laying into communist emplacements with a fusillade of rockets, 20mm cannon fire, and thunderous 500- and 750-pound bombs. Indeed, the airspace above Route 5 was crowded with a motley array of aircraft from the four corners of South Vietnam. There were World War II–era prop planes buzzing alongside supersonic F-105s, while helicopter gunships like Christensen's—call sign "Crocodile 3"—shared airspace with the tiny, Cessna-like O-1 Bird Dogs piloted by the forward air controllers (FACs). It was the FAC's job to marshal all the controlled chaos that is close air support. And today, he had his hands full.[2]

Christensen's headset crackled. It was the FAC circling overhead. The young warrant officer's two-ship flight of "Hog" gunships was cleared to start its gun run. Christensen felt the rush of an adrenaline surge. He'd already been in-country for almost a year now. In fact, his DEROS, or estimated date of return from overseas, was just two weeks away. This was nothing new to him. And yet the thrill was there every time. Christensen dipped the nose of his gunship and plunged to earth, wingman hot on his tail. Fast and low was the order of the day. Skimming nap-of-the-earth at better than one hundred knots made it that much harder for enemy gunners to draw a bead on him. The gunships flattened out at tree-top level, the forest on both sides nothing more than a blur through the Huey's Plexiglas. The trees crackled with bright orange flashes, as enemy gunners sought to drown the choppers in a tidal wave of antiaircraft fire.[3]

Suddenly, Christensen's headset came alive. "Break right! Break right!" his wingman screamed.

Christensen banked hard to starboard. No indecision. No second-guessing. Every bit of the gunship pilot's hard-won experience had taught him a simple maxim: He who hesitates . . . dies. A split-second later, a booming shockwave slapped the chopper like a sledgehammer, showering its underbelly with dirt, smoke, and fire. Below, high-explosive munitions gouged a flaming crater in the earth. Above, the silver visage of a B-57 Canberra thundered toward the horizon. The twin-jet tactical bomber had nearly plunked a 500-pounder right on top of Christensen's head. His wingman had saved him. But there was no time for thanks—or curses for the Canberra pilot. The enemy was still down there. As if on cue, arcing green tracers laced skyward along his flight path. As pilot, Christensen had the MK 4 "Mighty Mouse" rockets on his Hog's weapon system. His copilot controlled the 40mm grenade launcher mounted in the Huey's nose. The chopper shuddered as the 2.75-inch rockets, two at a time, screamed from the side-mounted pods, their 10-pound warheads exploding in cascading showers of dirt and fire all along the tree line. Below, he could see the tell-tale flashes of small-arms fire as communist gunners targeted his ship from inside a small house just off the road. Christensen rolled over and pumped two pairs of rockets through its front door. The side walls blew out in a geyser of flame and detritus as its thatched roof crashed down. The pilot swung around and hit it again for good measure.[4]

Just then, Christensen's door gunner howled. "What happened?" Christensen yelled. "Got hit in the foot," came the gunner's reply. "Ruined my new boot!" In one of those freak accidents of war, a small-arms antiaircraft round had struck one of the rockets just as it was leaving the pod. The bullet had somehow missed the rocket's warhead and struck the motor tube instead. But the ricochet had sent the round careening into the gunner's foot. Every man aboard—door gunner included—would take that outcome over the alternative any day of the week. A hit to the warhead would've blown the chopper from the sky. In war, it was always better to be lucky than good.[5]

They'd need a bit more of that luck before this day was done. Just as Christensen was about to peel off for Camp Holloway with his wounded man, the pilot felt a problem with the tail rotor. Something was off with the pitch change. Whether they'd been hit, he didn't know. The only thing for certain was that it had to be fixed—and right now. Christensen radioed an update to his wingman, then scanned the area for a suitable place to land. Most of the ground in this part of the Western Highlands was covered in low forest and sprawling patches of elephant grass, a ubiquitous regional species that could grow more than twelve feet tall. During more peaceful times, the big game hunters who came to stalk tigers in Vietnam would need to be wary of what lay hidden within that tall, thick grass. These days, it was very adept at concealing enemy troops, too. Just then, Christensen spotted a clearing nearby. The pilot radioed the FAC and told him he was going to set down. Was there anyone available to provide close air support while they got the tail rotor fixed? The FAC said he would see what he could do. Christensen muscled the chopper toward the opening, straining to keep the craft stable enough for a landing. No helicopter pilot relishes the idea of setting down with enemy lurking about. Indeed, if being blasted apart by one of his own rockets was Christensen's least favorite thing in the world, landing unprotected in the middle of Indian Country had to be second on that list.[6]

The warrant officer settled the chopper onto its landing skids and reluctantly cut the engine. It would make it that much harder to get the engine revved up in case they needed to get out fast, but there was no other choice. Dense vegetation bounded the little clearing on all sides. Christensen couldn't see more than a yard or two into the undergrowth. In his year in-country, he'd never felt more exposed than at this moment. The door gunner, heedless of the blood filling his boot where the ricochet had torn through, racked his M-60 and peered into the jungle, swiveling the medium machine gun back and forth on its bungee strap. Above,

Christensen's wingman orbited farther out, trying not to draw unwanted attention to his friends on the ground.[7]

Then, the FAC's disembodied voice over the radio. He'd spotted enemy troops moving toward the chopper. "Get your heads down," the voice warned. "I'm gonna bring 'em close." Moments later the jungle simply erupted in a wall of flame, as CAS strike aircraft roared in to deliver their ordnance at three hundred meters. Beyond the clearing, great billowing clouds of earth, fire, and smoke blasted skyward. Instinctively, the door gunner opened up with his M-60, the 7.62mm rounds sweeping the jungle like a scythe. After several tac-air passes, the crew chief leapt to the ground and scrambled up on to the chopper's tail boom to get at the rotor. There wasn't much time. If they couldn't resolve the problem with the tail rotor fast, the gunship crew would likely have to take their chances in the jungle until they could be extracted—a fate no one relished. "Come on, come on!" Christensen bellowed. "Get it fixed so we can get the hell out of here!"[8]

Anxious minutes ticked by. At any moment, thought Christensen, heart pounding, the communists would come swarming from that tree line in a human wave. Time slowed to a crawl. And just when he was sure he could stand no more, Christensen heard the crew chief throw himself through the side door. "Go! Go! Go!" the chief screamed. Christensen quickly ran through the Huey's startup procedure, winding up the chopper's Lycoming T53 turboshaft engine as fast as physics would allow. The pilot then pulled pitch and clawed for altitude, the door gunner spraying the tree line with wild abandon as the ship groaned skyward. Once they'd cleared small-arms range, Christensen banked the chopper northeast and thundered toward Camp Holloway. For the third time today, the men of Croc 3 had gotten lucky. Below, the fight on Route 5 raged on.[9]

Part I

THE ORIGINS

1

PRELUDE

As night fell on 19 October, the men from North Vietnam crept silently into their positions. Before them, nestled in a shallow bowl in western Pleiku Province, lay the American Special Forces camp they had come to eradicate. To reach this place, the soldiers—many of them untested conscripts in the North's war to reunify the two Vietnams under communist rule—had endured sickness, exhaustion, and hunger on their months-long trek down the Ho Chi Minh Trail. Once they had arrived, there was little time for rest, for the attack would commence in just ten days. So they were put through their training paces day and night. And when their officers were satisfied that they were ready, the men were ordered to dig their trenches and prepare their fighting positions quietly and under cover of darkness, for it was imperative that the Americans not know the assault was coming until it was too late. Yes, these men from North Vietnam were tired, sick, and hungry. But they were here, and they had trained for this. When the final signal was given, they would rush from their trenches and attack with all the ferocity they could muster.

The soldiers had traveled south as part of Hanoi's latest gambit to conquer South Vietnam. In late 1963, the communist high command had declared that the time had come to bring maximum pressure on their enemies to the south. That November, South Vietnamese president Ngo Dinh Diem had been overthrown and assassinated by a cabal of his generals. The "puppet" regime had been squabbling ever since and seemed on the brink of collapse. Hanoi resolved to help push it over the edge once and for all, so the high command had begun sending entire main force units south in 1964. The goal was simple: draw ARVN formations into large set-piece battles and destroy them. Once the people saw that the puppet army had

3

been crushed, they would rise up and join their communist brothers to the north. The focus would be the remote and sparsely populated Central Highlands, a massive, 67,000-square-kilometer region that dominated South Vietnam's midsection. The government of Vietnam's (GVN) influence was already weak there, and its isolated provincial towns and outposts could be cut off and overrun more easily than the population centers along the lowland coast. The Highlands' western reaches also ran adjacent to the Ho Chi Minh Trail, an ancient labyrinthine system of trails and footpaths snaking its way from North Vietnam down through Laos and Cambodia. This presented an ideal ingress point for infiltrating large bodies of men and materiel into South Vietnam.

By early spring 1965, North Vietnam had four main force NVA regiments operating in the Central Highlands. They had spent the last six months wreaking fear and chaos throughout the western provinces of the Highlands. By summer's end, the regiments had had their share of successes—and setbacks. But Hanoi wasn't done. After a two-month lull, the communist high command had settled on a new campaign to end the year. The B3 Front, the communist headquarters responsible for operations in the Central Highlands, would be given three full regiments to accomplish a new set of objectives: wreck what was left of ARVN's corps reserve, destroy the nettlesome Special Forces camps in the Western Highlands, and take effective control over Gia Lai—what the communists called Pleiku and Kontum provinces. One NVA regiment, having fought during the year's earlier offensives, was already in-country. The second would emerge from the trail in mid-October. The last would reach its western Pleiku base area by early November.

B3 Front commander Maj. Gen. Chu Huy Man had chosen the Plei Me Special Forces camp as his first victim. With two full regiments—some four thousand men—at his immediate disposal, Man would use one to lay siege to the camp, while the second would lie in ambush to destroy the relief force that would surely be sent to the rescue. Once both had been annihilated, the way would be clear to threaten the rest of Gia Lai—and even the all-important provincial capital of Pleiku City, the seat of government power in the Western Highlands. The offensive would mark the next evolutionary step in Hanoi's bid to crush the South. For the first time, multiple regiments would operate under a unified, division-level command. Indeed, the NVA regiments that had fought earlier in the year had been employed piecemeal, acting independently of one another in discrete operations. And they had sometimes suffered for it, often lacking sufficient firepower to strike the decisive blows so coveted in Hanoi. Division-sized commands required a greater level of administration, logistical planning, and coordination, but they also brought with them much more combat power. Division-level operations would make it that much easier to destroy large ARVN formations and thus hasten the collapse of South Vietnam. The eyes of the communist high command would be watching to see how this most-important test case played out.

Plei Me was indeed a ripe target. Located about thirty kilometers east of the Cambodian border in the untamed wilds of western Pleiku, it was a remote and isolated outpost on the fringes of GVN authority. Established in October 1963, Plei Me was tasked with monitoring and interdicting communist infiltration near the border and was one of many camps operating under the joint US Special Forces–South Vietnamese initiative known as the Civilian Irregular Defense Group (CIDG) program. The program had begun as a means of training rural villagers to fight Viet Cong activity near their homes, but it had quickly morphed into a more aggressive role. Twelve-man Army Special Forces "A-Teams"—experts in irregular warfare who specialized in organizing indigenous forces deep in hostile territory—were tasked with training company-sized CIDG combat elements in small-unit tactics like patrolling, setting ambushes, guerilla operations, and so on.

Designated as "Strike Forces," these CIDG units were largely comprised of Highland ethnic minorities known collectively as Montagnards, a moniker given them by the French that translated roughly as "mountain people." Ethnically distinct from the Vietnamese, the Montagnards were somewhat primitive by Western standards. But they could be fierce warriors—when they believed it was in their interest. Now, rather than remaining in static positions to defend their home villages, the Strikers were instead bivouacked in heavily fortified Special Forces–CIDG camps throughout the Highlands. There, under the guidance of American Green Berets, they would carry out offensive operations against communist guerilas in the area. A typical camp garrison consisted of three to five companies of Strikers totaling about 350 to 450 men, a twelve-man US Special Forces A-Team, along with a roughly equal complement of South Vietnamese Special Forces soldiers, known as the *Luc Luong Dac Biet*, or LLDB. While the LLDB were nominally in command of the camps, it was the American Special Forces troopers who actually ran the show.

The camps were purposely located in remote, largely ungoverned areas—what SF troopers satirically called "Indian Country." Indeed, the camps, with their palisades and battlements, were something like twentieth-century versions of the Wild West frontier forts of old. Now, as then, this scattered archipelago of strongholds deep in hostile territory was designed to gradually spread government authority throughout surrounding areas, ultimately eradicating enemy influence and activity. But these relatively primitive fighters, more accustomed to loincloths and crossbows than battle fatigues and rifles, had been trained and equipped to deal with local Viet Cong guerillas. Instead, secreted in the hills and trench works around Plei Me, were nearly two thousand disciplined, well-armed, and motivated soldiers of the North Vietnamese army. As dusk descended upon the western plateau, neither the Jarai Montagnards nor their handful of American Special Forces advisers had any inkling of the storm brewing just beyond the perimeter wire. They would all know soon enough. But what had led these men to this time and place? It is to that story that we first turn.

2

TO FREE THE OPPRESSED

The modern incarnation of US Special Forces (SF) began with the activation of the 10th Special Forces Group on 20 June 1952 at Fort Bragg, North Carolina's Smoke Bomb Hill, under the aegis of the Special Operations Division of the Psychological Warfare Center. But the army's special operations branch could draw its immediate lineage from a decade earlier. The 1st Special Service Force (SSF), a joint US–Canadian endeavor during World War II, was originally conceived as a means of attacking and disrupting German hydroelectric plants in Norway. The Nazis relied on the plants to help power their critical mining operations in the occupied country. Under American Lt. Col. Robert T. Frederick, 1st SSF operators were trained in demolitions, amphibious assault, rock climbing and ski techniques, and basic airborne fundamentals. Comprised of about 1,800 men, the unit was divided into three regiments of two battalions each and would see action in such far-flung locales as the Alaskan Aleutian Islands, France, Italy, North Africa, and beyond. The 1st SSF would go on to acquire its nickname, "The Devil's Brigade," from the captured diary of a German officer fighting in Italy. "The black devils are all around us every time we come into line, and we never hear them," he wrote. However, the end of World War II saw the disbandment of the 1st SSF—along with the Office of Strategic Services (OSS), formed to conduct operations behind enemy lines in occupied Europe and seen by many as the forerunner to the modern CIA—during the massive demobilization at war's end.[1]

But with the onset of the Cold War, marked by Soviet and Communist Chinese expansionism and support for subversive, guerilla movements in service of "national wars of liberation," some US Army planners argued that the hard-won lessons of irregular warfare developed during World War II needed to be relearned. As it stood, the Eisenhower administration's "New Look" strategy, relying primarily on massive nuclear retaliation as a deterrent against communist aggression, was the order of the day. The president and his advisers were committed to the cost-saving benefits of conventional demobilization and sought to build domestic prosperity at home while banking on the US atomic advantage abroad. Many conventional army officers, already facing dwindling funds and cutbacks on troop strength, viewed irregular warfare with great suspicion. In an era when every defense dollar counted, many saw any nonconventional pursuits—which seemed unlikely to impact any foreseeable superpower conflict anyway—as nothing more than an unwanted distraction. Still, the New Look approach seemed ill suited to confront the so-called low-intensity conflicts flaring throughout the Third World.[2]

Thus was born the 10th Special Forces Group under the command of former OSS agent Col. Aaron Bank. Some of those who volunteered were, like their commander, former OSS operatives. But most of the new recruits were simply highly trained and motivated conventional soldiers, many drawn from the ranks of airborne and Ranger units who'd seen combat in World War II and Korea. Officially, the US Army defined the 10th Group's primary mission as one designed "to infiltrate by land, sea, or air, deep into enemy-occupied territory and organize the resistance/guerilla potential to conduct Special Forces operations, with emphasis on guerilla warfare." Special Forces troopers had to be able to operate independently in small teams for extended periods of time behind enemy lines with little outside support. The Special Forces would adopt the Latin phrase *De Oppresso Liber*, "to free the oppressed," as their motto.[3]

Although the 10th Group began with just ten personnel—Bank, a warrant officer, and eight enlisted men—the unit in coming months soon ballooned to several hundred, as volunteer trainees streamed in from throughout the army. By 11 November 1953, the army was ready to try its new force in the field. With about half its personnel, 10th Group deployed to Bad Tolz, West Germany, to aid resistance movements operating behind the Iron Curtain, and if necessary, to prepare for behind-the-lines guerilla action in the event the Soviets' far larger conventional forces someday overran Western Europe. The Group's remaining soldiers stayed at Fort Bragg to form the nucleus of the new 77th Special Forces Group, eventually redesignated as the 7th Group. As the Special Forces' mission continued to grow worldwide, the army in 1957 added a third group, the 1st Special Forces. The Group was activated on Okinawa in June with the purpose of training and organizing host-nation personnel for irregular warfare missions on the Asian continent, including Korea, Taiwan, the Philippines, and throughout Southeast Asia.[4]

By 1958, the structure of the basic Special Forces unit had formalized into twelve-man teams known as Operational Detachment Alphas. Each team was comprised of two officers and ten enlisted men. Teams were normally commanded by a captain, with a first lieutenant serving as executive officer. Each team featured personnel extensively trained in five broad categories: intelligence/operations, weapons, demolition/engineers, medicine, and communications. Troopers were cross trained in at least two specialties, allowing twelve-man teams to be split into two, six-man units should the need arise. Such cross training also helped ensure that teams would retain full functionality should one or more of its troopers become incapacitated. Additionally, all members of an A-Detachment—commonly known as "A-Teams"—had to be airborne qualified. Once SF troopers had completed their basic skills courses, supplementary training followed. Because one of the fundamental tasks of the A-Team was to organize and train host-nation peoples to conduct unconventional warfare behind enemy lines, all Special Forces soldiers were required to develop language skills. It was mandatory that each man be familiar with at least one language other than English. Additional instruction might include underwater operations, high-altitude, low-opening parachute techniques, and so on. In general, the ideal Special Forces trooper was to possess natural leadership qualities, be physically tough enough to endure harsh conditions and privation, and be sufficiently intelligent and independently minded to operate deep in enemy territory for extended periods and with very little support.[5]

By 1961, Special Forces had attracted the attention and support of the newly elected president, John F. Kennedy. Eschewing the previous administration's New Look policy of massive nuclear retaliation as a means of deterrence, Kennedy and his advisers favored one of "flexible response." As the name implied, the approach was designed to offer policymakers a much wider array of military and nonmilitary options to confront communist expansionism. One option particularly favored by the Kennedy administration for dealing with low-intensity conflicts was that of counterinsurgency (COIN)—a comprehensive political and military effort to defeat guerilla or revolutionary movements. With its emphasis on working closely with indigenous elements to organize and train for the conduct of irregular warfare, Special Forces seemed a perfect component of the COIN approach. In his March 1961 message to Congress, Kennedy urged that Special Forces be expanded to further the mission of a counterinsurgency to combat communist aggression. By June, the army approved a three-thousand-man increase to various counterinsurgency forces. With the administration's backing, Special Forces expanded rapidly in the early 1960s. By fall 1961, the 5th Special Forces Group was stood up, followed by the activation of the 8th, 6th, and 3rd groups by the end of 1963.[6]

One area where the new flexible response doctrine might be applied was Southeast Asia. Indeed, following the May 1954 defeat of French forces by the communist Viet Minh near the northwestern Vietnamese town of Dien Bien Phu, US policymakers worried that the region was ripe for communist takeover. The Geneva Accords that summer dismantled France's Indochina colony, ultimately resulting in the emergence of four successor states: the Democratic People's Republic of Vietnam; the State of Vietnam; the Kingdom of Cambodia; and the Kingdom of Laos. While Laos and Cambodia were granted outright independence under the agreement, Vietnam was temporally divided along the 17th parallel. From its capital city of Hanoi, Ho Chi Minh's communist government was to control the northern portion of the country. Former emperor Bao Dai, who'd abdicated his throne in 1945 but remained the nominal head of state, would hold sway in the south. The Accords, which neither the United States nor Bao Dai signed, nevertheless called for nationwide elections to reunify the country by 1956. Still, the nascent governments of South Vietnam, Cambodia, and Laos almost immediately came under pressure from North Vietnamese–backed revolutionary movements.[7]

US SPECIAL FORCES IN LAOS

The situation in Laos offered one of the earliest tests of Special Forces doctrine and tactics. The fledgling country had been threatened by the North Vietnamese–backed Pathet Lao from the outset. The group had begun in 1945 as the Lao Issara, a noncommunist, anti-French nationalist movement. But by 1950, it was renamed the Pathet Lao under its leader, Prince Souphanouvong. The revolutionary leader had worked closely with the communist Viet Minh during the First Indochina War against the French. His Pathet Lao had aided the Viet Minh when they invaded the northeastern portion of Laos in 1953. The combined force of nearly seven thousand troops would eventually go on to capture the strategically impor-tant Laotian Panhandle. The Viet Minh had also carved out a portion of the country's southeastern region as well. The 1954 Geneva Accords officially established Laos as a neutral country, with nominal leader Prince Souvanna

Phouma—half-brother to Souphanouvong—tasked with unifying the country under a coalition government from the capital in Vientiane.

But the agreements planted the seeds of ongoing conflict. The negotiations permitted the Pathet Lao to retain their territory in the country's two northern provinces, effectively establishing the group as a rival ruling regime there. Further, although the accords required that all foreign forces leave the country, the Viet Minh refused. Together with its Pathet Lao clients, Hanoi solidified its hold on Laos's eastern regions with a two-pronged goal in mind: the installation of a communist government in Vientiane and the dramatic expansion and improvement of its Duong Truong Son infiltration network along the country's eastern spine. The network, which in the West would come to be known as the Ho Chi Minh Trail, was a vital thoroughfare for the infiltration of men and materiel into the southern portion of Vietnam.[8]

The Trail actually began as a primordial web of trails and footpaths that had for centuries been used by hunters, travelers, and traders traversing the rugged, jungle-swathed mountains of the Annamite Range. The Viet Minh had used the trail system to some extent during the First Indochina War. But in anticipation of renewed war against the anticommunist government of South Vietnam, Hanoi embarked upon a dramatic expansion of the Trail. In May 1959, the NVA established Group 559, a logistics and transportation unit tasked with improving and expanding the trail system and with overseeing the movement of troops, weapons, and other war materiel south. The ultimate purpose was to aid the southern Vietnamese communist insurgency—known colloquially as the Viet Cong—fighting to overthrow the government of South Vietnam. Over the ensuing years, the ranks of Group 559, which began with only a few hundred troops, would swell to nearly thirty thousand personnel. The unit would take the Trail from a series of foot and bicycle paths through rugged mountains to a full-on network of roads and base areas that could accommodate all manner of mechanized traffic. In addition to the tens of thousands of NVA troops that would march south on the Trail, Soviet- and Chinese-built trucks would eventually haul everything from small arms, medicine, and men to heavy artillery and antiaircraft weapons. The Trail would one day even feature a fully functional fuel pipeline, complete with various relay pumping stations down its length.[9]

By 1959, the Laotian Civil War had simmered for years, periods of relative calm punctuated by occasional flareups. But five years after independence, it was threatening to boil over. It was into this fray that US Special Forces entered. Since the activation of the 1st Group on Okinawa in 1957, Special Forces had been active in the region, conducting training missions with host-nation forces in Thailand, Laos, and South Vietnam. The United States, who'd established a presence in Laos as early as 1955, had a strategic interest in maintaining the country as a buffer state between its ally Thailand and communist North Vietnam. While Laotian national defense continued to be administered by the French, the United States agreed to pick up the tab on most of the materiel costs associated with bolstering the poorly organized and trained Royal Laotian Army. Normally, the United States would have established a Military Assistance Advisory Group in-country to coordinate such an aid effort. But because the Geneva Accords prohibited the presence of foreign military forces in Laos, the United States instead set up the Programs Evaluation Office (PEO). Established in December 1955, the PEO was meant to track and evaluate how US resources were being used, but it was never able to effectively oversee how American materiel was being used in the field. That, along with mounting pressure from both the Pathet Lao and Viet Minh, eventually made it clear that more would need to be done to stave off a communist victory. After consulting with their French and Laotian allies in May 1959, US planners directed the 77th Special Forces Group to launch Project Hotfoot.[10]

Commanded by Lt. Col. Arthur "Bull" Simons, the covert effort called for the secret insertion of eight-man field training teams—essentially pared-down versions of the standard A-Team—to instruct the Royal Laotian Army in fundamental battalion-level conventional tactics. At first glance, the training of conventional forces appeared to conflict with the stated raison d'etre for Special Forces. But because the mission required teams to develop rapport with indigenous troops and operate in remote areas with little support, SF was nevertheless deemed the most appropriate option. Despite the NVA's open violation of the Accords' prohibition on foreign military presence in Laos, the United States nevertheless presented the Hotfoot teams as nonmilitary contractors, who dressed as civilians and carried civilian identification. By July 1959, the first twelve teams were on the ground. However, ongoing conflict with French advisers, along with the general lack of motivation among Laotian troops, hampered progress. The Pathet Lao and their North Vietnamese patrons continued to make headway, aided by a supposedly "neutralist" coup—backed by Soviet aerial resupply and North Vietnamese artillery—that saw Vientiane temporarily fall to the plotters before being retaken by anticoup forces five months later.[11]

As the fortunes of the Laotian Civil War ebbed and flowed, the United States, on 19 April 1961, finally established the Military Assistance Advisory Group Laos. Project Hotfoot was officially renamed Operation White Star, and Special Forces presence ramped up dramatically. Special Forces troopers were now permitted to wear their uniforms and operate openly, and teams were brought up to their full-strength complement of twelve men each. By September 1962, Special Forces would reach a peak strength of forty-eight White Star Mobile Training Teams in Laos. Teams performed many and varied tasks. Some served as instructors in the newly established Laotian military schools. Others moved into the field to act as advisers to conventional combat units. These combat advisory roles provided the opportunity for Special Forces operators to hone the essential skills that would serve them well in future conflicts: combat medicine, coordinating artillery support, aerial resupply missions, maintaining communication nets, and so on. But it was those teams that moved deep into the jungled mountains to live with and train various ethnic minorities that would prove most portentous for the future of Special Forces operations.[12]

Two tribes would become central to the Special Forces training program: the Hmong and Khmu. The Hmong, at the time more commonly known by the pejorative "Meo," were a mountain-dwelling people of Chinese extraction. The tribespeople were highly resentful of Laotians and Vietnamese, both of whom largely disdained the ethnic minority as primitive savages. Special Forces, with the help of the CIA, hoped to leverage the Hmong's antipathy by arming them against the communists. By 1962, six White Star teams had organized and trained more than eight thousand Hmong warriors. The mountain people proved especially hardy and capable and were used to great effect throughout the Laotian highlands to ambush and harass Pathet Lao and NVA forces.

Similarly, the Khmu people in the south proved very effective fighters. Under Operation Pincushion in late 1961, ten White Star teams trained the Khmu and organized them into one-hundred-man shock companies that were used primarily to attack and cut into Hanoi's operations in the Bolovens Plateau, which represented the southern tip of the Ho Chi Minh Trail in Laos. In just six months, some sixty Special Forces troopers and six hundred Khmu tribesmen were able to clear the plateau of Pathet Lao forces. Simons planned to expand the program and recruit up to ten thousand Khmu to break Hanoi's hold on the Laotian Panhandle as well. But while both programs showed signs of real long-term success, they also generated a great deal of animosity among their Laotian hosts, who viewed arming and training the hated minorities with alarm. This state of affairs—much to the chagrin of Simons and others who'd put so much effort into bringing the projects to life—led to the eventual closeting of one program and the complete abandonment of the other.[13]

The matter would prove moot for US Special Forces, at least in the short run. Following the May 1962 catastrophic defeat of Royalist troops by four NVA battalions near the Chinese border at Luang Namtha, Laos's power brokers agreed to form a neutralist, coalition government. Signed at yet another Geneva conference that July, the International Agreement on the Neutrality of Laos called for the withdrawal of all foreign troops by 6 October. The United States was forced to disband its Military Assistance Advisory Group, and all White Star teams and control elements were evacuated by the deadline. However, some Special Forces elements, with the help of transport planes and helicopters from the CIA's covert transportation airline—Air America— continued to secretly work with the Hmong to conduct guerilla operations against communist forces in Laos. The Hmong commandos would over the next ten years grow to nearly forty thousand strong and continue to be a highly effective guerilla force against Pathet Lao and occupying NVA forces. As before, North Vietnam ignored the Geneva agreement's so-called neutralist decree and instead kept an estimated ten thousand troops in Laos in the short run. That number would steadily increase in coming years. Together with its Pathet Lao client, Hanoi would use its base areas in eastern Laos to devastating effect in the war with South Vietnam.[14]

While the results were certainly less successful than hoped for, the experience in Laos had provided much-needed training, logistics, and combat experience for the Special Forces. The teams had gained valuable experience working in the sort of mountainous jungle terrain and climate that they would deal with for nearly the next decade in Vietnam. Troopers also had ample opportunity to test operational systems and techniques from communications, artillery support, and aerial resupply to weapons, logistics, and irregular warfare tactics. Finally, while the teams demonstrated that they could operate independently to train and advise host-nation forces, it was their ability to effectively organize, train, and lead remote ethnic tribes that would prove especially helpful in coming years. For the Special Forces would soon become inextricably linked to another hardy and remote hill people: the tribes collectively known as the "Montagnards" of Vietnam's Central Highlands.[15]

US SPECIAL FORCES IN VIETNAM

To the east, South Vietnam presented yet another challenge for US policymakers. Even before the Geneva Accords had partitioned the country in 1954, the United States in February 1950 had extended formal recognition to Bao Dai's regime in the South. Five months later, President Harry S. Truman granted $15 million in military aid to combat the Viet Minh, and by August had opened the Military Assistance Advisory Group Vietnam to train and advise aid recipients in the use of American military resources. American assistance to the French and their anticommunist clients continued to grow over the next four years. While US policymakers favored the dissolution of the colonial system following World War II, the need to bolster its war-weakened French ally—especially in light of the threat posed by the spread of communism—prompted Washington to hold the line in Vietnam. As noted, the French were nevertheless compelled to sue for peace following their defeat at Dien Bien Phu in May 1954. But neither former emperor Bao Dai nor the United States were signatories to the "Final Declaration of the Geneva Conference" that summer.[16]

A month prior to the agreements, Bao Dai, living in France at the time, had handpicked Ngo Dinh Diem as his new prime minister. Diem, who himself had been in exile for four years, returned to his country on 26 June and assumed the office of premier. Diem had a reputation for being both a committed nationalist and anticommunist. Diem argued that South Vietnam would not sign any agreement that the country's leadership had not had a hand in negotiating. A particular sticking point for both Diem and Washington was the Final Declaration's mandate that elections be held to reunify the country within two years. Both would eventually contend that the totalitarian nature of the North Vietnamese regime made the prospect of free and fair elections unlikely. Regardless, Diem himself began the process of ruthlessly consolidating power upon his return. On 6 October 1955, he announced a nationwide public referendum for the purpose of deposing Bao Dai as head of state and replacing the erstwhile emperor with himself. The referendum, widely seen as fraudulent, was held on 23 October and supposedly showed a 98.2 percent majority in favor of ousting Bao Dai in favor of Diem. Three days later, Diem proclaimed the formation of the Republic of South Vietnam, with himself as president, prime minister, defense minister, and supreme commander of the armed forces. The government was immediately recognized by the United States, France, and other Western allies throughout the world. Diem's power, at least for the time being, was secure.[17]

During its early years, South Vietnam's nascent military had no Special Forces capability. Given the guerilla warfare nature of the conflict, US Special Forces first turned its eye toward instructing the South Vietnamese in basic irregular warfare tactics like long-range patrolling and harassment operations. In early 1957, seventy officers and sergeants from the ARVN were selected for parachute and communications training at the coastal town of Vung Tau, southeast of the capital city of Saigon. The fifty-eight most promising soldiers were then sent to Nha Trang to await further training. On 24 June 1957, 1st Special Forces Group was activated on Okinawa and tasked with training and organizing host-nation forces for irregular warfare missions on the Asian continent. The Group's first action in South Vietnam was to dispatch the 14th Special Forces Detachment to what would eventually become the South Vietnamese Commando Training Center in Nha Trang. The detachment's two officers and ten sergeants assumed responsibility for training the fifty-eight ARVN troops in special warfare tactics over the next four months. Forty-four of the trainees would go on to form the foundation of the Vietnamese 1st Observation Group, forerunner to the *Luc Luong Dac Biet*, the South Vietnamese Special Forces that would be officially formed 15 March 1963.[18]

Another thirty SF troopers arrived from Fort Bragg in May 1960 to establish an official training program for Special Forces in South Vietnam. But it wasn't until the inauguration of President John Kennedy in January 1961 that the counterinsurgency effort in Vietnam would ramp up dramatically. Indeed, the Special Forces had found an enthusiastic patron in the young president. As noted, Kennedy preferred a policy of "flexible response" to deal with Third World insurrections supported by the Soviets and China. The new president had a great deal of faith in the counterinsurgency capabilities of the Special Forces. In March, Kennedy had asked Congress for a dramatic increase in the nation's irregular warfare capability. A large part of that would come in expanding the Special Forces, whose total numbers had never exceeded 2,500 personnel. Kennedy would go on quadruple that number. In May, another four hundred troopers arrived in Nha Trang to bolster counterinsurgency training for the South Vietnamese military. By late summer, some seventy ARVN companies had received training in basic tactics and commando methods. On 21 September, the 5th Special Forces Group was activated at Fort Bragg. The Group would eventually deploy to Nha Trang to take charge of all Special Forces operations in Vietnam. Also that fall, Kennedy made a personal visit to inspect the Army Special Warfare Center at Fort Bragg. Standing in the center that would one day be renamed in his honor, Kennedy approved the Green Beret as the official headgear of the Special Forces. The Army Special Forces was well on its way toward becoming the foremost instrument of US counterinsurgency policy.[19]

3

THE CIVILIAN IRREGULAR
DEFENSE GROUP PROGRAM

One of the hallmarks of the French defeat during the First Indochina War was that government influence rarely extended very far outside the larger cities and towns. This put a great deal of territory and population at the mercy of the Viet Minh insurgency. Now, as the Second Indochina War heated up, it seemed that the Diem regime faced much the same problem. Saigon's regular ARVN was simply not large enough to maintain an effective presence throughout the villages and hamlets of South Vietnam's vast backcountry. As before, the dearth of government presence resulted in a relatively unchecked flow of enemy infiltration and activity. One by one, southern villages and hamlets fell under Viet Cong (VC) control, providing the guerillas with both supplies and fresh conscripts for the insurgency. To stem the tide, Diem in 1955 created paramilitary forces that he hoped would fill the governmental void in the countryside and help guard against the loss of further villages. The Civil Guard and Self-Defense Corps were the government militias designed for that purpose. The hope was that their presence would not only protect the population from falling under the sway of the VC but also free up ARVN manpower to pursue the communists. Later renamed the Regional Forces/Popular Forces—known colloquially as "Ruff Puffs"—the poorly trained and equipped peasant paramilitaries never proved a match for the battle-hardened Viet Cong. By the end of 1961, the South Vietnamese government had effectively lost control over many rural provinces, and contemporary CIA estimates asserted that perhaps 50 percent of the country's western highlands villages could be classified as Viet Cong supporters.[1]

Enter the CIA's Combined Studies Group. Beginning in 1961, the clandestine organization had experimented with a pilot program to organize the isolated tribal minorities of South Vietnam's Central Highlands, a vast, sparsely populated mountain region of nearly 67,000 square kilometers. Stretching through the country's central-western reaches, the region shared a long, rugged, and largely untamed border with neighboring Laos and Cambodia to the west. Therefore, it represented a natural ingress route for communist men and materiel from the North. Due to the area's isolated nature, North Vietnamese and Viet Cong cadres could usually take control of villages with little fear of government intervention. The CIA-sponsored program to have Operation White Star Special Forces teams train and arm Hmong tribesmen in Laos was already paying dividends, so the spy agency once again turned to Special Forces to organize and train yet another ethnic minority, this time an assortment of Central Highlands' tribes collectively known as Montagnards.[2]

The moniker was a holdover from the French colonial period and translated roughly to "people of the mountains." The Montagnards were not ethnic Vietnamese but rather of Mon-Khmer or Malayo-Polynesian extraction. Like the Hmong and Khmu of Laos, the Montagnards were generally despised by the Vietnamese, who regarded them as backward and uncivilized. Over the centuries, the more numerous lowland Vietnamese had steadily pushed the Montagnards inland from the fertile coastal regions to the less-desirable interior. And like the Laotians, the Vietnamese elite viewed any effort to train and arm such people as a dangerous proposition indeed. For their part, the Montagnards heartily returned the Vietnamese's disdain and wished only to be left alone in their mountain redoubts. But US advisers argued that the rapidly deteriorating situation in the country-side demanded that the GVN leverage every bit of manpower—even the despised Highlanders—in order to prevent the VC from completely domi-nating the rural population.[3]

There were fifteen major Montagnard tribes residing in Vietnam's interior, with the Jarai and Rhade the most numerous. To be sure, the Montagnards were unsophisticated by First World standards. They lived a rudimentary life of subsistence hunting and farming. Villagers dressed in simple loincloths and wore homemade bracelets of copper and brass, along with colored glass beads to indicate status and wealth. The Montagnards were animistic and had a profound belief in the spirit world and its in-teraction with their own. Consequently, they were very superstitious and dependent upon various religious rituals to cleanse evil spirits and otherwise guide their lives. Animal sacrifice during such rituals was common. While the Montagnards had little love for the Vietnamese, they were nevertheless fairly welcoming of Westerners. Under the French, the tribes had generally been left to their own devices, residing on protected land reservations and largely shielded from Vietnamese enmity. Many of the Montagnards had combat experience, as the French had organized some of them into gue-rilla units they called Montagnard "Maquis," a nod to the French resistance fighters of World War II. The possibilities for employing the Montagnards as an anticommunist force were there, but the CIA and Special Forces would need to overcome several obstacles to make it happen.[4]

BUON ENAO

The origins of this effort can be traced to Buon Enao, a village of approximately four hundred tribespeople about six kilometers outside the Darlac provincial capital of Ban Ma Thuot. While the Central Highlands provinces of Kontum and Pleiku were most threatened by communist activity in 1961, Darlac had come under considerable pressure in its own right. Directly south of Pleiku Province, Darlac shared a long, untamed border with Cambodia to the west, a region where the Saigon government had exercised very little control. CIA intelligence suggested that a major branch of the Ho Chi Minh Trail fed directly into the area. Travel outside of Ban Ma Thuot was both difficult and dangerous. There were large swaths of the province where government officials simply refused to go.

The ongoing danger was punctuated by two spectacular attacks that year. On 24 July, the Viet Cong ambushed and massacred a government convoy, including two members of the National Assembly who had been inspecting a village development project about 25 kilometers south of the capital. And in September, the communists had mounted a two-battalion offensive to plunder supplies from several villages, easily swatting aside the Civil Guard and Self-Defense Corps units charged with their defense. The Viet Cong occupied and terrorized the villages for several days before elements of the ARVN's 23rd Division in Ban Ma Thuot could arrive. Government troops reached the area only to discover that the communists had already melted back into the mountains. US embassy officials worried that such incidents, along with a general lack of contact between the government and its people, would lead more and more of the province's isolated villagers to conclude that their only hope for safety was to accept Viet Cong dominance.[5]

It was amid this cauldron of danger and uncertainty that the CIA in late 1961 attempted a bold plan to turn things around. Agency Director Allen Dulles, at the behest of President Kennedy, had in October ordered the spy agency to enact a major new counterinsurgency initiative in the Central Highlands. Col. Gilbert B. Layton, head of the agency's Military Operations Section in Vietnam, was just one of many CIA officers in search of a new plan. He would eventually team with a young aid worker, David Nuttle, to conceive of a project that would lead to one of the Agency's—and Special Forces'—most successful contributions to the Vietnam War: the Civilian Irregular Defense Group program. Nuttle, an official with International Voluntary Services (IVS), a nongovernmental organization and forerunner of the Peace Corps, had been working with members of the Montagnard Rhade tribe to improve an agricultural project near Ban Ma Thuot. Nuttle eventually formed a close friendship with tribe members, and his amity was heartily returned. His new friends soon warned him that he'd been marked for assassination by the local Viet Cong. The Rhade confided that they were not fond of the Viet Cong but feared that alienation at the hands of the Diem government threatened to drive more of their people into communist hands. Nuttle realized something had to be done before it was too late to save not only the Rhade—which constituted the largest ethnicity in Darlac—but the rest of the province as well. The aid worker also happened to be dating Layton's daughter at the time, so the two came into frequent contact. Nuttle confided what the Rhade had told him, and over the course of some weeks, the men developed a pilot program to help the Rhade help themselves.[6]

The project would involve training and arming Rhade villagers to defend themselves against the communists. The men believed the Rhade were ideal for several reasons. First, the tribe was generally averse to the Viet Cong and resented their demands for supplies, labor, and taxes. Indeed, the Viet Cong were yet another in a long line of Vietnamese groups bent on exploiting the Rhade. Secondly, while the tribespeople likely wouldn't fight for the Diem government, Nuttle believed that they *would* fight for their own families and villages. Finally, the Rhade were seen as the most advanced of the Montagnard tribes. Several tribe members had served effectively in high positions throughout the South Vietnamese government. In fact, one of the National Assembly members killed in the 24 July ambush was a member of the Rhade tribe, as was the chief of Montagnard education in Darlac, who also died in the attack. And after a long and relatively productive relationship with the French—which sometimes included military service against the Viet Minh—the Rhade had come to see the value brought by Westerners, namely, education, modern medicine, and agricultural improvement. For these reasons, both Nuttle and Layton believed the tribe offered the best chance of success.[7]

Convincing the South Vietnamese government was another matter. Diem and ARVN leadership viewed training and arming Highlanders with deep suspicion. Aside from the long-festering racial enmity that existed between the Montagnards and Vietnamese, there was also the question of the former's drive for semi-independence. Indeed, following 1958's short-lived Bajaraka autonomy movement, whose Montagnard leaders had agitated for more political freedom for the Central Highlands' ethnic minorities, Saigon had arrested the ringleaders and even confiscated the tribes' crossbows and spears. The GVN was unlikely to look kindly on putting weapons back into the hands of Highlanders. Nevertheless, Layton pushed the idea up the chain on 5 May to William Colby, CIA chief of station in Saigon. Seeing the program's potential value, Colby then followed up by meeting with Ngo Dinh Nhu, brother to South Vietnamese president Diem. Nhu had taken a keen interest in the counterinsurgency effort, but like his brother, he was wary of arming the Montagnards. Colby helped sell the idea, however, by suggesting that South Vietnamese Special Forces (VNSF) act as a highly involved government watchdog as the project unfolded. Diem, through his Presidential Survey Office, exercised a great deal of personal control over the nascent VNSF, employing it at least as much to root out potential coup plotters as he did for counterinsurgency purposes. Indeed, since its inception, its officers had been appointed much more on the basis of their loyalty to Diem than for their military effectiveness. Still, Colby surmised, the group's direct involvement would likely smooth over lingering doubts as to the wisdom of arming the Highlanders.[8]

And he was right. Nhu was receptive, but it still remained unclear if his brother would give his assent. Over the ensuing months, the strange bedfellows of the CIA, Nhu, and even Ambassador Frederick E. Nolting, worked to convince Diem to give the project a try. Finally, Colby enlisted the aid of Sir Robert Thompson, a widely respected counterinsurgency expert whose most recent success had been the defeat of the communist insurrection during the Malayan Emergency. Thompson was now serving as a special British adviser to Vietnam. Once Thompson threw his support behind the effort, Diem at last gave the go-ahead—with certain caveats. The program would initially be restricted to just one village. Rhade defenders would be issued only traditional spears and crossbows to start. Tribesmen would be given firearms and trained in their use only after they'd erected a fence around the village and posted signs of allegiance to the government. The signs also had to contain a warning that any communists trying to enter the village would be killed.[9]

Nuttle, who had since resigned his IVS post and signed on with the CIA, was placed in charge of spearheading what was to become the Village

Defense Program (VDP) in Darlac. Nuttle and Layton soon settled on Buon Enao as the program's pilot village for several reasons. First, Nuttle knew the village chief, Y-Ju, well and considered him a close friend. Additionally, the fact that the village was not presently under Viet Cong pressure should give the project some breathing room to grow. Finally, Buon Enao's proximity to the government resources and protection offered by Ban Ma Thuot was a definite plus. But friend or no, Y-Ju and other village elders had their own list of conditions before agreeing to become the program's test village. After all, erecting fences and displaying signs of allegiance to the government would surely mark Buon Enao and its people as targets for Viet Cong violence. Village elders insisted that all government attacks on Rhade villages must stop, that any Rhade tribesmen who'd been forced to cooperate with the VC must be granted amnesty, and that the government must guarantee the Rhade medical, educational, and agricultural assistance as part of the deal. After a minor back-and-forth, the deal between the government and Buon Enao was sealed in early November 1961.[10]

Recruits were drawn from the village itself and carefully screened for Viet Cong affiliation. Part of the vetting process involved having tribal leaders vouch for the recruits' loyalty. The few that didn't pass muster were referred for political "reeducation" to get them to come around to the government's point of view. Shortly thereafter, a squad of VNSF arrived and commenced training the thirty-man village defense force. This ten-man team, along with Nuttle and a few others, were the only ones authorized to use firearms and were therefore responsible for village defense during the training period. In the meantime, work began on the fencing, bomb shelters for villagers, and a medical dispensary. Per the agreement, the villagers displayed progovernment placards and even flew the South Vietnamese flag. A few weeks later, Layton and Col. Le Quang Tung, the head of the Presidential Survey Office (PSO) and the man charged with ensuring that the program was serving Diem's interests, flew in to inspect progress. They discovered that the villagers had indeed fulfilled every aspect of the agreement. The men authorized the distribution of firearms, a shipment of which arrived a few days later. While the 1903 Springfield bolt-action rifles and Madsen M-50 submachine guns were quite antiquated, they were still a most welcome upgrade to the Rhade's traditional crossbows and spears.[11]

In early December, soldiers with Special Forces Detachment A-35 arrived to begin training the village's "Strike Force" unit. Unlike village defenders, Strikers were paid, full-time soldiers and were generally much better armed and trained than the Village Defenders. Strikers were usually equipped with machine guns, mortars, and grenades. Rather than relying strictly on static defense, the Strike Force, usually accompanied by Special Forces troopers, conducted regular patrols in its area of operations. The sweeps were intended to provide an added measure of village security by adopting a more proactive posture and were also helpful in gathering intelligence about potential enemy activity in the area. While the VDP was overwhelmingly defensive in nature, Strike Force patrols also set occasional ambushes, lending a small degree of offensive capability to the program. Eventually, the Strike Force would be centrally located among a cluster of program villages and act as a rapid response force should one of them come under attack. Village Defenders were tasked with holding the line until the Strike Force could arrive to help. A third type of force, the Information Team, was raised a short time later. Like the Strike Force, the IT was composed of full-time, paid soldiers. The thirty-man team was well armed and trained and comprised entirely of Montagnards, most of them Rhade. Its primary responsibility was recruitment, with its members gradually pushing farther and farther out to proselytize on the program's behalf and convince other villages to join. As the program expanded, the pattern of these unit types was replicated.[12]

By the middle of the month, another government contingent arrived to inspect the program's progress. Among the dignitaries were Layton, Colby, and even Nhu himself. The president's brother was reportedly so impressed with what he'd seen that he authorized the program's expansion to other Rhade villages throughout Darlac. Colby renamed the project the Civilian Irregular Defense Group (CIDG) program, although in Darlac it continued to be known as the Village Defense Program. Buon Enao was soon designated the first CIDG Area Development Center (ADC). It would be used as a base for training Rhade defenders, for expanding the program to other villages throughout the province, and for coordinating their defense. The ADC's dispensary also became a de facto hospital for Montagnards throughout the area. Not long after Buon Enao's Village Defenders and Strike Force had completed their training, the program simply exploded. Forty nearby villages opted into the program in the ensuing weeks. One reason that the VDP may have been popular, especially when compared with the GVN's Strategic Hamlet Program (SHP) that began a few months later, was that it was *voluntary.* Unlike the SHP, which involved the forced relocation of villagers—often to new fortified hamlets far from their native lands—the VDP placed the agency for action in the villagers' hands. They could decide whether they wanted to defend their *own* villages from the VC or not. When given the choice—along with training, weapons, and other support—the Rhade villagers overwhelmingly chose to stand and fight to protect their homes and families.[13]

As each new village was added, it raised its own cadre of Village Defenders. The area Strike Force would defend the new village while its recruits were then trained by Vietnamese Special Forces. By April 1962, nearly one thousand Village Defenders had been armed and trained at the Area Development Center to protect about fourteen thousand people in the villages. A three-hundred-man Strike Force was also based at Buon Enao to add muscle to the program. Over the next six months, five more ADCs were created in the villages of Buon Ho, Buon Krong, Ea Ana, Lac Thien, and Buon Tah. Each ADC contained a small contingent of Special Forces soldiers. By October, some two hundred Rhade villages comprising about sixty thousand tribespeople were defended by some 10,600 Village Defenders and 1,500 Strike Force soldiers. This conglomeration of Rhade villages would become known as the Buon Enao Complex. Communist activity within its area of influence fell to almost nothing. Indeed, by any objective measure, the CIDG program had so far proven to be an unqualified success.[14]

OPERATION SWITCHBACK

Unfortunately from the anticommunist perspective, the program almost immediately became a victim of that success. By summer 1962, the Diem regime was already having serious second thoughts about a program it had authorized less than a year before. From Diem's perspective, the Americans had placed an awful lot of weapons in the hands of a people who made no secret of their animosity toward the Vietnamese, had agitated for autonomy, and who had no demonstrable allegiance to the GVN in Saigon. The Highlanders also showed little inclination to use their newfound training and weapons to pursue the Viet Cong beyond the areas around their villages. Ultimately, Diem wanted the program brought under tight control—or better yet, eliminated, with the Rhade disarmed, inducted into the ARVN for use against the communists, and their villages rolled into his Strategic Hamlets Program.[15]

Another problem with the CIDG's rapid expansion was that it was already threatening to become too large and unwieldy for the CIA to handle alone. The program had pushed beyond Darlac's provincial borders, bringing into the fold various other Highland tribes in the process. In May 1962, Military Assistance Command Vietnam (MACV), established that February, acquired joint jurisdiction over CIDG with the CIA. Just two months later, the Department of Defense ordered that all Special Forces activity in

Vietnam be placed under MACV's command. The transfer would take place under the codename Operation Switchback, with nominal control over the CIDG villages and defense forces gradually handed over to the province chiefs. Within a year, the CIA would be squeezed out entirely, and MACV would in practice control both the Special Forces and the CIDG program. Under this new regime, CIDG would take a decidedly militaristic turn. Out was the culturally holistic program of Montagnard self-defense birthed by Nuttle, Layton, and Colby. In was the much more aggressive posture of border surveillance, interdiction, and VC hunting.[16]

By November 1962, Special Forces had on the ground a headquarters element based in Saigon, one Operational Detachment-Charlie serving in a support role for headquarters, and three B-Teams commanding and assisting some twenty-six A-Detachments operating in-country. The A-teams came from the 1st Group in Okinawa and from the 5th and 7th Special Forces groups based at Fort Bragg. While the teams served their six-month tours, they were under the control of US Army Special Forces (Provisional) Vietnam, commanded by Col. George C. Morton, former head of MACV's Special Warfare section. Morton, who'd taken over in September, was the first unified commander of all Special Forces activity in Vietnam. In February 1963, he moved Special Forces headquarters from Saigon to the more centrally located Nha Trang along the South China Sea coast. On Morton's watch, Operation Switchback was officially completed 1 July 1963. By December, Special Forces and their LLDB counterparts had trained some eighteen thousand Strike Force troops and just over forty-three thousand Village Defenders, who were now simply referred to as village militia.[17]

But under MACV and Special Forces, CIDG had become a very different program indeed. The focus had moved away from establishing networks of mutually defended villages working to expand their influence outward, as had been the case at Buon Enao. Instead, new camps were being built primarily as bases from which Strike Forces could mount offensive operations against the Viet Cong. Thus, campsite locations were often chosen more for their potential to interdict enemy activity than for any affinity received from local villagers. An increased focus on interdicting communist infiltration from the North meant that many of the new camps were located in remote areas where South Vietnam's borders intersected with those of Laos and Cambodia. By mid-1964, twenty-four CIDG camps had been built in the triborder area alone. But because these areas were isolated and had been the scene of largely unchecked VC infiltration and activity, communist influence tended to be relatively high. The new SF-CIDG camps truly resembled frontier forts of America's Old West: heavily fortified redoubts in the midst of hostile "Indian Country." CIDG camps in such locations were especially vulnerable because their isolation from other friendly bastions meant that they were on their own during hours of darkness. If the VC attacked, the earliest camp commanders could count on reinforcements was the next morning—and sometimes not even then.[18]

Then there was the problem of communist infiltration into the camps themselves. As before, Strikers and village militia were recruited from the local population (although Strike Forces sometimes had to be relocated from other areas). But the rapid expansion of the CIDG program rarely afforded the time and deep tribal affiliations needed to thoroughly vet recruits as was done at Buon Enao. That, coupled with the program's push into areas where VC influence was high relative to Buon Enao, meant the greater likelihood of communist infiltrators slipping through and serving in Strike Forces and village militia. This was a dangerous state of affairs and obviously raised the specter that villagers trained and armed under the program might one day turn those weapons against their benefactors.

That is precisely what happened at the CIDG camps at Plei Mrong on 3 January 1963, Hiep Hoa on 23–24 November 1963, Polei Krong on 4 July 1964, and Nam Dong two days later, on 6 July, to name just four. The Nam Dong attack was particularly brutal, with VC infiltrators reportedly slitting the throats of some of the loyal defenders while they slept. It was later estimated that as many as one hundred of the supposedly loyal Montagnard Strikers were actually Viet Cong. Detachment A-726 commander Capt. Roger H. C. Donlon would earn the Medal of Honor as he and the survivors fought a desperate battle to hold the camp until daylight. More than fifty camp defenders, including two American Special Forces troopers, were killed. Another sixty-five were wounded.[19]

In the wake of such attacks, and with the loyalty of CIDG forces in serious question, new standard operating procedures were announced for US detachment commanders assigned to the camps. Among the provisions was the use of small contingents of Nungs as personal security details for Special Forces soldiers. The Nungs, who had already fought side by side with Americans during various attacks on CIDG camps—including with Donlon at Nam Dong—were yet another of South Vietnam's ethnic minorities. Emigrating from China in the seventeenth century, Nungs had a well-earned reputation as exceptionally fierce fighters. Special Forces would go on to employ the Nungs in many roles, including as scouts, ambush specialists, and bodyguards. The men quickly became known as trustworthy and highly effective warriors for the American side, in the process becoming the highest-paid non-American soldiers in Vietnam.[20]

With the rapid growth of CIDG, so too came a precipitate expansion of South Vietnam's irregular forces. By late 1962, Diem's anxiety over the mushrooming CIDG program had reached its apex. The president had already decreed earlier in the year that all but a few of the weapons provided to the Rhade tribesmen in the Buon Enao Complex be confiscated and that Village Defenders and Strikers be subsumed into ARVN for use against the Viet Cong elsewhere. Still, if any version of CIDG were to continue, he wanted it tightly monitored and controlled. The president ordered that a roughly equal number of personnel from his 77th Observation Group be stationed alongside the Special Forces A-Teams at each CIDG camp. A Vietnamese officer would command the camp, with the Americans serving as advisers. The 77th had thus far remained a relatively small paramilitary force, but Diem's orders necessitated a rapid influx of new personnel to meet increased demand.

A new 31st Observation Group was established but was soon merged with the 77th. On 15 January 1963, the combined force was formally renamed the Vietnamese Special Forces. But men capable of flourishing in the high-pressure world of irregular warfare didn't grow on trees. Inevitably, this hurried addition of new personnel brought with it a diminution of quality among the ranks. While some of Diem's LLDB had performed well in the early days of CIDG, the paramilitary organization generally enjoyed a fairly poor reputation among their American colleagues. The infusion of even less qualified personnel in early 1963 only exacerbated Special Forces' low opinion of the LLDB.[21]

By late summer 1964, the long-simmering resentment of the Montagnard Rhade finally boiled over. While the overthrow and subsequent assassination of Ngo Dinh Diem and his brother Nhu in November 1963 might have caused the Rhade some reason to hope for better treatment from Saigon, those hopes were soon dashed. Indeed, while Diem certainly perpetrated his share of mistreatment upon the Highlanders during his nine-year reign, the Montagnards quickly discovered that not much changed once he was gone. And in some ways, things had become worse. The Highlanders generally worked better with individual province chiefs rather than the central government in Saigon and had even built up a level of trust and something approaching loyalty toward some of them. But Diem's assassination had ushered in a volatile carousel of government officials in the Highlands, as provincial posts continually changed hands depending on which way the winds of postcoup Saigon blew. Aside from the humiliating disarmament program undertaken by Diem in late 1962, the usual racial discrimination at the hands of Vietnamese officers, officials, and even civilians continued largely unabated. Food supplies for Highland war refugees were slow in coming, and medical care, when it could be obtained at all, was usually only reluctantly extended by ARVN dispensaries.[22]

At some point during the year, remnants of the still-alive Montagnard Bajarka autonomy movement, which had gone to ground following Diem's 1958 crackdown, decided the time had come for an uprising. The group now called itself the United Front for the Struggle of the Oppressed Race. On 19 September, troops from two CIDG camps in Quang Duc Province and two from Darlac Province took control of their respective camps. After restraining, but not harming, their US Special Forces advisers, the mostly Rhade contingent fell upon some of the Vietnamese and LLDB troops and commanders in the four camps, murdering about fifty-five of them. The various rebel CIDG forces, a total of between two thousand and three thousand troops, then converged on nearby Ban Ma Thuot in an apparent attempt to take control of the provincial capital. The town, however, was garrisoned by the ARVN 23rd Division, and the revolt's momentum was soon halted. Other than a brief firefight at an ARVN roadblock that resulted in ten rebel casualties, more bloodshed was avoided. Still, ARVN and American forces prepared assaults in case the rebels, who had taken some sixty Vietnamese hostages, didn't surrender. Only a week of tense negotiations that saw the personal intervention of American advisers and high-level ARVN officers—and even Gen. Nguyen Khanh, who had himself taken power in January after yet another Saigon coup—brought about a relatively peaceful end to the uprising. The rebellious Rhade released the hostages unharmed and laid down their arms. Remarkably, and in spite of the rebels' initial killing spree, no Vietnamese reprisals were forthcoming. Both sides pledged renewed commitments to peaceful coexistence. But for the Montagnards, there would be no autonomy. And for the GVN, the fear that further Highland revolts might be forthcoming continued to color the way it viewed both the Highlanders and their role in fighting the Viet Cong.[23]

4

HIGHLANDS IN THE CROSSHAIRS

Although 1965 dawned relatively quietly in the Central Highlands, it was merely the calm before the storm. Certainly, the year would see the most intense fighting of the war by far in South Vietnam's high country. Following Diem's assassination in November 1963, Hanoi's leadership decided the following month at its Ninth Plenum of the Party Central Committee that the time had come for an all-out push to win the war quickly. The plan was the brainchild of the Party's First Secretary Le Duan, second only to Ho Chi Minh as the most influential man in North Vietnam. Together with his deputy, Le Duc Tho, the men pushed through their strategy of "General Offensive/General Uprising," often abbreviated as GO-GU. The idea was to first infiltrate large, conventional units into South Vietnam and then draw out and destroy ARVN forces in pitched battle. The emphasis would shift away from offensives in the Mekong Delta, where communist leadership had traditionally focused, and instead concentrate on big-unit clashes in the Central Highlands. This represented the strategy's "general offensive" phase. According to the plan, the destruction of main force ARVN units would demoralize the South Vietnamese populace. With help from the Central Office for South Vietnam, the communist headquarters that coordinated the southern insurgency, the strategy's second phase— the general uprising—would see the civilian population rising against the GVN. The combined military and political pressure would, according to the plan, bring about the collapse of South Vietnam's government. Ultimately, it was hoped that all of this could be accomplished quickly enough to prevent the United States from stepping in and saving the regime.[1]

Hanoi's focus on the Central Highlands as a crucial theater under Le Duan's GO-GU strategy was demonstrated in May 1964 when the North

Vietnamese Politburo established the B3 Front, also known as the Central Highlands Front. The new command would be responsible for directing the war in the South Vietnamese provinces of Kontum, Pleiku, and Darlac, and the western areas of Binh Dinh and Phu Bon. Essentially, B3 was to serve two main functions: (1) to build and coordinate communist main force units in the Central Highlands in order to bring to battle and annihilate large South Vietnamese military formations, and (2) to help maintain and protect the regional sections of the Ho Chi Minh Trail to ensure that communist infiltration could continue flowing into the South. B3 would work under the close supervision of Military Region 5, which had been established three years earlier to coordinate the war throughout the northern regions of South Vietnam.[2]

By fall 1964, the first large NVA main force units began moving south. The first to depart was the 32nd Regiment from its base in Na Nam Province, North Vietnam. The communists' supply corridor that snaked its way through Laos and Cambodia, known colloquially as the Ho Chi Minh Trail, was at this stage in its development unable to accommodate regiment-sized units. Therefore, the 32nd was forced to send its battalions south one at a time. Its 334th departed in September, with the 635th following shortly thereafter. By the end of October, its third and final battalion, the 966th, began its journey. All three battalions would reach northern Kontum Province by the end of January 1965. The three regiments of the powerful 325th Division, along with several attached battalions and companies, would also be sent, making the journey from November 1964 to February 1965. The combined forces of the 32nd Regiment and 325th Division represented a massive surge in communist firepower destined for the Central Highlands.[3]

Unfortunately, from the anticommunist perspective, this massive influx of enemy combat power would come just as South Vietnamese military force in II Corps was stretched precariously thin. In October 1964, the ARVN 25th Division was redeployed from II Corps to a new base area west of Saigon in III Corps to help deal with serious enemy pressure in the northern Mekong Delta. Although the division's 51st Regiment remained in II Corps as a standalone element, the departure of the 25th left II Corps—the largest of South Vietnam's four tactical zones and constituting nearly half of the country's total land area—with just the 22nd and 23rd divisions to defend it. II Corps commander Brig. Gen. Nguyen Huu Co predicted that his weakened corps tactical zone was ripe for a communist offensive. He therefore decided that consolidating his modest forces would be his best hope of preventing large-scale defeat in II Corps. This would, however, involve the necessary abandonment of some areas—and their people—in order to hold on to others.[4]

THE MONSOON OFFENSIVE

Consequently, by the beginning of the communists' summer Monsoon Offensive in June 1965, such consolidation, and its commensurate reduction in village-level counterinsurgency efforts, had already exposed vast stretches of the countryside to communist influence. Many villagers, no doubt sensing the growing power of the Viet Cong, began to cast their lot with the insurgency. A particularly disturbing trend for the anticommunist side was the increase in peasant recruitment for communist military units during this period. Most of these effects were the result of normal insurgent activity simply filling the void left as ARVN units vacated some areas. To be sure, the first half of 1965 saw several sharp fights in II Corps that contributed to this state of affairs, including the devastating 7 February attack on both MACV's II Corps Headquarters and Camp Holloway airfield outside Pleiku. The attacks killed eight Americans and wounded another 126. Then came a series of clashes along Highway 19 near the Mang Yang Pass that claimed heavy casualties on both sides. And finally, there was the communist attack on Special Forces Camp Kannack in March. Although communist forces were defeated at Kannack, the enemy still managed to seize control of the northern portions of both Kontum and Binh Dinh provinces, with government authority relegated to scattered enclaves. And yet, the hardest fighting of North Vietnam's main force offensive still lay ahead.[5]

From Hanoi's perspective, the summer monsoon season in the Central Highlands offered a propitious opportunity to launch their GO-GU strategy full bore. While ARVN's forces were reeling and spread thin, the communists knew that the vaunted air power of the Americans stood poised as a deadly equalizer. They hoped the poor flying weather of the monsoons would mitigate that. The southwest monsoon usually began in late May and often lasted into the early fall. Warm air from the Gulf of Siam regularly blanketed the highland plateau of Central Vietnam in thick cloud cover, rain, and heavy fog. Raging tropical thunderstorms, some lasting for days, were common. Operating in the Highlands under such conditions presented unique problems for pilots. Such weather along the coast could be flown around, but in the hills and mountains of the Highlands, pilots were confronted with a choice: fly high and risk plowing into a fog-shrouded peak, or fly low and run the gauntlet of enemy ground fire. Requirements for "good" flying weather included at least a thousand-foot ceiling with a minimum two and a half miles of visibility. Springtime in the Highlands normally yielded about twenty-five good flying days a month. During the summer monsoon, that number plummeted to just six. While the complete grounding of American and Vietnamese airpower was unusual, these conditions added yet another layer of danger and complexity to the task of close air support and resupply.[6]

The communists kicked off the offensive in late May by ramping up their systematic effort to isolate the Central Highlands from the rest of South Vietnam. Land communications to outlying areas was cut, bridges blown, and trenches dug across major roadways, including Highway 19, the main thoroughfare linking the Highlands to the seaport at Qui Nhon. Once the few major land routes into the Highlands had been severed from the supply centers on the coast, even secondary roads were targeted by local force VC. The result was the further isolation of already-remote district towns and other outposts from the provincial capitals. Soon, GVN control in the Highlands began to resemble an ever-shrinking archipelago of government strongpoints caught in a rising tide of communist influence. Resupply of even the provincial capitals soon depended almost completely on airlift alone, which necessitated several costly ARVN operations to temporarily open road traffic and allow supply convoys into the Highlands, with mixed results. The civilian population was understandably shaken by this new turn, and their morale was not improved as local Viet Cong stepped up a terror operation of assassination, intimidation, and plunder against government-aligned villages and hamlets.[7]

Meanwhile, the NVA set their newly infiltrated main force units upon towns, outposts, and Special Forces camps throughout the Highlands. Over the next few months, the attacks came fast and furious, as four NVA regiments from the North, with help from at least two more recruited south of the 17th Parallel, unleashed a series of assaults and sieges across the northern Highlands provinces of Kontum, Pleiku, and Phu Bon. The NVA launched several attacks in Phu Bon and Kontum in May, but ARVN counteractions managed to blunt any overwhelming communist success. This was not the case, however, at the town of Le Thanh in Pleiku. Beginning on 31 May, the NVA's 32nd Regiment, along with the 925th Sapper Battalion, first annihilated the district capital, then in the immediate aftermath managed to spring *two* separate ambushes on the convoy of Pleiku province chief Lt. Col. Vo Van Ba. Ba had been making his way to Le Thanh for a routine visit when the town had been overrun. Before he could be warned of the danger, his convoy stumbled into the first trap. Only the stout defense of his Regional Force escorts, along with timely close support air strikes, allowed Ba and a few surviving vehicles to escape back toward Pleiku. But en route, the remnants of his convoy, along with a small rescue force that had linked up with Ba, were caught in yet another carefully prepared kill zone. The convoy was cut to shreds in a hail of 57mm recoilless rifle and B-40 rocket fire. Gunships from the 52nd Aviation Battalion at Camp Holloway arrived to buy time for the survivors, but two were shot down. Miraculously, Ba and a few stragglers escaped into the jungle and were picked up a few days later by friendly troops. But the attack was a clear-cut NVA victory. An Airborne task force was dispatched to recapture Le Thanh but found that the communists had already pulled out. Le Thanh would nevertheless be abandoned some weeks later after it was deemed too vulnerable to defend.[8]

Another ARVN defeat quickly followed on the heels of Le Thanh when a battalion of the 40th Regiment was effectively destroyed in an ambush along Highway 7 in southern Phu Bon. After suffering heavy casualties, the survivors simply fled in disorder. This defeat was the last straw for government control of Phu Tuc District, which fell under communist dominance over the ensuing weeks. Meanwhile, following a 9 June bloodless coup that brought Air Marshal Nguyen Cao Ky and Gen. Nguyen Van Thieu to power in Saigon, a new command structure was ushered in at the top of II Corps. Gen. Co was recalled to Saigon to assume the role of Joint General Staff chairman, and Maj. Gen. Nguyen Phuoc Vinh Loc was appointed commander of II Corps. Born in Hue in 1929, Vinh Loc was the cousin of Vietnam's final emperor, Bao Dai, who'd been pushed out as Head of State by Diem in 1955. He was seen by some as a larger-than-life character but was nevertheless generally respected at the time among the ARVN officer corps. Vinh Loc necessarily adopted at least one of Co's strategies for dealing with the NVA's main force Monsoon Offensive in the Highlands—that of a largely defensive posture marked by a consolidation his forces. But the new II Corps commander also undertook a review of the military value of the region's outposts and towns. He settled on a plan of reinforcing key positions that were deemed vital to the overall defense of II Corps, while abandoning those of lesser importance. According to the plan, ARVN was to fight tooth and nail to defend these key points, holding on as long as possible to exact upon the enemy the highest number of casualties and materiel losses.[9]

The communists continued to launch attacks of varying success for the remainder of their Monsoon Offensive—including the capture of two northern Kontum district towns, Toumorong and Dak To, in late June and early July. But Vinh Loc's strategy began to pay real dividends during the NVA's siege of the Duc Co Special Forces camp in late July and early August. Because it sat astride infiltration routes from Cambodia into Pleiku, Duc Co had been marked as an outpost worthy of defense. Indeed, located in northern Kontum Province along Highway 19, Duc Co was just thirteen kilometers from Cambodia. The outpost was one of a spate of new CIDG camps opened in 1963 whose primary mission was border surveillance and interdiction of communist infiltration. Special Forces Detachment A-215, commanded by Capt. Richard B. Johnson, occupied the camp with a roughly equal number of Vietnamese LLDB, about two hundred Jarai Highlanders, and another two hundred Nung mercenaries. Duc Co truly was a tiny island in a sea of hostility. Since the loss of nearby Le Thanh in June, area villages had been steadily lost to communist control. So it was that the NVA's 32nd Regiment, fresh off the Le Thanh attack, coiled around the camp to deliver the final blow to GVN influence in the area.[10]

Effectively besieged since late June, the camp by mid-July couldn't even be resupplied by air, as NVA gunners gradually tightened a ring of murderous antiaircraft fire around Duc Co. With the supply situation critical and no way to evacuate the wounded, Vinh Loc tapped Brig. Gen. Cao Hao Hon and his 24th Special Tactical Zone (STZ) to organize the camp's rescue. The 24th STZ, based in Kontum, had been established in March to assume responsibility for military operations throughout Pleiku, Kontum, and Phu Bon provinces. Hon initially chose for the duty the 2nd Airborne Task Force, advised by Maj. Norman Schwarzkopf, who would one day go on to lead US Central Command during Operation Desert Storm. After some delay caused by infighting, the task force, consisting of the 3rd and 8th Airborne battalions, was air assaulted into Duc Co on 3 August with the intent of breaking the siege from within. Despite the added effect of devastating close air support strikes, however, it quickly became apparent that the NVA's investment was too powerful to make such a breakout possible. In fact, the additional soldiers inside the camp only worsened the critical supply shortage and crowded conditions at Duc Co.[11]

II Corps planners then cobbled together a more formidable array consisting of Task Force Alpha and its two Marine battalions, along with the 3rd Armored Task Force, commanded by Lt. Col. Nguyen Truong Luat. The idea was to catch the encircling NVA in a vice, hitting them from both within and without. But Vinh Loc initially balked at the commitment of what amounted to II Corps' entire remaining strategic reserve. After the II Corps commander's request for reinforcements was turned down by his own government, Gen. William Westmoreland, commander of US forces in Vietnam, stepped in to commit the newly arrived 173rd Airborne Brigade to act as the corps reserve. Vinh Loc then gave the go-ahead on 8 August to unleash the rescue force. While the communists put up a stiff fight in several sharp actions over the next few days, they were now perilously outnumbered—and the continued target of murderous close air support strikes. By 11 August, the NVA's 32nd Regiment had taken a terrible beating, and the remnants of its battered and beleaguered battalions slinked away to lick their wounds. The siege of Duc Co was over.[12]

While fully reliable casualty tallies are hard to come by—partly out of the communists' practice of carrying away their dead, partly out of the South Vietnamese penchant for over-counting enemy casualties—it seems clear that the combined ground fighting and air attacks during the long siege had killed the North Vietnamese by the hundreds. And those who'd survived had their morale badly shaken. According to Col. Theodore Mataxis, senior adviser for II Corps, captured NVA soldiers lamented the pounding they had taken at the hands of South Vietnamese firepower and American air support. The men also bemoaned the hunger, sickness, and privation that had plagued the regiment since it began its journey south the previous fall. Meanwhile, ARVN morale received a much-needed boost. Its casualties, while not inconsequential, were nevertheless a fraction of NVA losses, and it heartened the government troops to know that they'd taken the vaunted NVA's best and were still standing in the end. It seemed that Vinh Loc's strategy of holding the line at key points—at least at Duc Co—had paid off.[13]

Duc Co defeat or no, the communists managed to fire off one last salvo before their summer offensive, like the rain and fog that gave it cover, finally petered out. On 18 August, the NVA 101A Regiment launched a simultaneous assault on the district town of Dak Sut in northern Kontum and its nearby CIDG training camp. Beginning in early June, the regiment had invested the area around Dak Sut and had steadily tightened the noose in preparation for an all-out attack. Though the town was almost immediately overrun, the CIDG camp continued to hold its own. But it was only delaying the inevitable. The camp would finally succumb as dawn broke on 19 August. Camp defenders, which included Special Forces Detachment A-218, were forced to break into small groups, slip through the communist net, and escape into the surrounding countryside. Over the next several days, groups of the bedraggled and hunted men crept from the jungle and made their way to friendly positions. Of the 474 CIDG garrisoned at the Dak Sut camp, only about half managed to get out alive.[14]

In the end, the communists' summer Monsoon Offensive, which featured at least nine major clashes and assaults, had yielded mixed results for Hanoi. On the plus side, NVA units had captured five Highlands district towns, four of which remained in communist hands following the offensive. Road traffic and most land-based communication throughout the northwest Highlands continued to be severely disrupted—if not completely cut off. This resulted in the further isolation of district towns, outposts, and

CIDG camps, necessitating resupply largely by air. In general, communist influence had grown significantly in Kontum and Pleiku, and Phu Bon Province had been nearly lost in its entirety. Indeed, in many areas, government control did not exist outside the towns it still controlled. In the wake of these communist gains, morale in government-aligned villages and towns was seriously damaged.[15]

On the negative side of the ledger, all provincial capitals remained in GVN hands, as did the vast majority of district towns. Perhaps most tellingly, the offensive failed in its primary objective: luring in and destroying large ARVN formations. Such victories, according to Le Duan's "win-the-war-now" GO-GU strategy, were designed to destroy the South's ability to continue the war and spark a general uprising as the people abandoned the failing GVN. Both, it was hoped, would ultimately prevent the United States from sufficiently reinforcing South Vietnam before it capitulated. But none of these things happened. In fact, other than the routing of a single battalion of South Vietnam's 40th Regiment, the bulk of ARVN forces not only remained intact but had fought well in several engagements. This despite Hanoi's commitment of four NVA main force regiments to the effort, while drawing upon a fifth that had been recruited from the Highlands' coastal plain. Certainly, the North had allocated an unprecedented number of well-trained and equipped regular army troops to its Central Highlands gambit but had come up short. Part of the reason surely stems from the unseasonably clear skies that prevailed during parts of the monsoon season. This allowed the anticommunist side to more fully exploit its advantage in close air support and airlift capabilities. And the NVA regiments suffered for it. Yet, the summer monsoon season, with its thick blanket of clouds, rain, and fog, had still been the most likely period for Hanoi to realize its ambitious goals.[16]

It soon became clear that communist leadership was neither satisfied with the results of its Monsoon Offensive nor finished trying to achieve the larger goals of GO-GU in the Highlands. Indeed, the B3 Front, like II Corps, had come under new leadership when Maj. Gen. Chu Huy Man assumed command in July. Powerful and widely respected in Hanoi, Man's military and political bona fides were impeccable. He'd joined the revolutionary movement in 1930 and subsequently been imprisoned by the French at Kontum. He later joined the Viet Minh's army during the 1945 August Revolution, rose to regimental commander, and fought in nearly every campaign during the First Indochina War. At Dien Bien Phu, he served as political commissar of the 316th Division, instrumental in the attack on the French stronghold. Man would go on to achieve the rank of "senior general," a rare honor and the equivalent of a five-star general in the US Army. Man's appointment to head the B3 Front was yet another indication that the communist high command continued to see the Highlands as a pivotal theater in the war. While the 95A, 18A, and 101A regiments would be withdrawn from the Highlands—possibly because they were urgently needed elsewhere due to the American buildup—Man would soon have two fresh, newly infiltrated NVA regiments at his disposal. Along with a rested and refitted 32nd Regiment, the general would have a powerful force to wield in yet another effort to smash ARVN forces in the Highlands: Hanoi's Tay Nguyen (Western Plateau) Campaign.[17]

THE TAY NGUYEN CAMPAIGN

The Tay Nguyen Campaign was the brainchild of Gen. Nguyen Chi Thanh, overall commander of the Central Office for South Vietnam (COSVN), which had been established in mid-1961 in Tay Ninh Province along the Cambodian border and was responsible for the conduct of military and political operations in the southern portion of South Vietnam. But since the adoption of Le Duan's GO-GU scheme in late 1963, COSVN had also become integral to executing his "win now" strategy in the Highlands. Le Duan's go-for-broke strategy had never been universally accepted among either Hanoi's senior leadership or the communist operation in the South. Opponents in the North wanted to continue the more cautious protracted-war approach, while those in the South were wary of risking units and infrastructure they'd spent years building, only to see them squandered in reckless head-on confrontations with the American-backed ARVN. While Le Duan and his supporters had managed to marginalize such opponents, communist high command apparently believed some foot-dragging was still taking place, especially in the South. By September 1964, Hanoi decided a change in COSVN's leadership was in order. Despite being a Le Duan protégé himself, COSVN's longtime leader Nguyen Van Linh was out, and Thanh was in. North Vietnam's leadership may have believed that as a Politburo member and head of the NVA's General Political Department, Thanh possessed the gravitas to overcome any lingering resistance and fully implement GO-GU.[18]

The exact objectives of Thanh's Tay Nguyen Campaign are debatable. Some analysts argue that the offensive was merely the first step in Thanh's larger Long Xuan (Winter-Spring) Campaign of 1965–1966, a multidivisional offensive designed to destroy large ARVN and even American units and ultimately capture the five northern-most provinces of II Corps. According to this analysis, the offensive would effectively cut South Vietnam in half and, in the process, inflict so many US casualties that public outcry would force the Americans out before they could become fully invested in the war. Set to begin in September and be completed by spring 1966, Tay Nguyen's piece of Long Xuan was to seize all of Kontum and Pleiku provinces, along with parts of Binh Dinh and Phu Bon.[19]

Other observers contend that Tay Nguyen's objectives were more modest. Under this interpretation, the campaign was likely no more than an impromptu effort to recapture, after a two-month lull, the strategic initiative in the Highlands following that summer's Monsoon Offensive. Large-scale American intervention, according to this analysis, would surely cause Hanoi to proceed more cautiously. A postwar interview with Man in 1990 seems to support this perspective. Man testified that, although an audacious winter-summer offensive had indeed been in the works, the US buildup—especially the 173rd Airborne Brigade's introduction into the Central Highlands—had prompted the communists to rein in their ambitions, at least in the near term. The Vietnamese senior general asserted that the plan to cut South Vietnam in half was therefore postponed for ten years and was completed only during the final phases of the North's victorious drive south in 1975. Accordingly, said Man, the Tay Nguyen Campaign was scaled back as well. One of its revised objectives was to draw newly arrived American units into combat to learn the best ways to fight them. A North Vietnamese history published in 1990 adds further weight to the "modest goals" thesis, asserting that Tay Nguyen was merely designed "to destroy a portion of the U.S. armed forces, to continue to cause the puppet army (ARVN) to disintegrate, to defeat the enemy's dry-season campaign, to expand our base areas, and to gain control of most of the mountain jungles and rural areas, focusing especially on those mountain jungles which are of strategic importance."[20]

At any rate, it seems clear that communist planners at the very least hoped Tay Nguyen would bring considerable pressure to bear on the northwest Highlands and were willing to invest large and powerful main force units to do it. Indeed, the communist high command would commit three NVA regiments to the effort, two of which—the 33rd and the 66th—began their southward march well before the Monsoon Offensive ended in late August. While the effort appeared to reflect a continuation of GO-GU's objective of luring and destroying as many ARVN—and now American— main force units as possible, it seems self-evident that high command would also welcome the capture of the strategically vital provincial capitals of

Kontum and Pleiku. Both represented important symbols of GVN power and resources in the Western Highlands. Kontum was home to the 24th Special Tactical Zone headquarters, responsible for coordinating military operations in the northwestern Highlands. Still more valuable was Pleiku. Home to II Corps headquarters and its corps reserve, the US Army airfield and MACV headquarters at Camp Holloway, and the US Air Force base at New Pleiku Airbase, Pleiku was the last line of defense in western II Corps. Its loss—even if only temporary—would be not just a strategic catastrophe for the anticommunist side but also the kind of worldwide propaganda victory that might finally usher in GO-GU's long-desired general uprising among the South Vietnamese people.[21]

As commander of the B3 (divisional) Front, Man was tasked with planning and executing Tay Nguyen. As noted, he would have three NVA regiments at his disposal, along with a 120mm mortar battalion, a battalion of 14.5mm antiaircraft guns, and the newly formed H-15 Viet Cong Main Force Battalion. The H-15 battalion was locally recruited and had just been created that October and drawn entirely from Gia Lai—the communists' name for Pleiku and nearby parts of Binh Dinh and Phu Bon provinces. Its 375 personnel were split into four companies that would provide coordination and support during the campaign. Additionally, Man would also have logistical and labor support from several sources. The southern sector of the Rear Services branch of the Central Highlands Front would be responsible for requisitioning, purchasing, or otherwise seizing the necessary supplies to support the first stages of the campaign. Meanwhile, local laborers—either communist sympathizers or conscripts—were drawn from local villages to act as guides and recon elements; transport food, medicine, ammunition, and other supplies into the battlespace; and aid with casualty evacuation, burial details, and so on.[22]

While multiple regiments had participated in the Monsoon Offensive, they had not operated as a divisional unit. Tay Nguyen would in fact be the first time an NVA force would operate in South Vietnam under a unified divisional command. The first of his regiments to infiltrate was, of course, the 32nd under Lt. Col. To Dinh Khan, whose lead elements had departed North Vietnam's Na Nam Province in September 1964. By the time of the Tay Nguyen Campaign, the regiment had been thoroughly combat-tested after nine months in the Central Highlands, recording actions at Polei Kleng in March, Le Thanh in June, and most recently at Duc Co in July and August. Still, while the 32nd was certainly battle hardened and intimately familiar with the Western Highlands, its troops had suffered mightily over the past year. Sickness and hardship during the long march south on the Ho Chi Minh Trail had cut into its strength, and the casualties exacted throughout the campaign—especially during its protracted siege at Duc Co—had further enervated the regiment. The 32nd had spent the intervening months since Duc Co fortifying itself for the next hard fight in the Highlands.[23]

Meanwhile, the 33rd Regiment under Lt. Col. Vũ Sắc was completely untested. Its green troops had spent the life of the regiment in the North and had only begun their infiltration from North Vietnam's Quang Ninh Province in late July. But their education was about to begin. Indeed, the 33rd's route was long and onerous, marked by the suffering and privation that afflicted all units infiltrating down the Trail. The journey began innocuously enough, as the men moved by truck and even train while still in North Vietnam. But once in Laos, the misery began. All travel was then by foot, as the men tramped over rugged mountain trails, across rivers, and through dense jungle. Group 559, responsible for maintaining the Trail, had set up some fifty way stations along the route from the 17th Parallel down to the regimental staging area in the 450-square-kilometer Chu Pong mountain complex straddling the Pleiku-Cambodia border. But while these posts might offer some meager assistance, food, medicine, and other essentials were nevertheless scarce. The troops supplemented what little they got by foraging for edibles in the jungle. If they were lucky, some might occasionally pull a fish from one of the rushing mountain streams that crisscrossed their path. Inevitably, hunger and the arduousness of the march soon wrought sickness. Many fell out from malaria and other jungle diseases along the way. According to one estimate, 40 percent of the men in the 33rd's rifle battalions were still sick when Tay Nguyen began. Still, the Trail wound on and eventually led them into Kontum Province, only to veer back west into Cambodia. It wasn't until 10 September that the 33rd's lead elements would finally arrive in western Pleiku. By 2 October, the entire regiment had settled into the staging area near the communist-controlled village of Anta at the eastern foot of the Chu Pong Massif in the Ia Drang Valley.[24]

The region had long been a Viet Minh sanctuary and staging area and saw extensive use during the First Indochina War. Indeed, it was a nearly perfect natural military hideaway. Its deep jungle valleys and dense forest canopy provided excellent cover from aerial observation, allowing even large formations to camp, move, and train freely even during daylight. Ample water for drinking, cooking, and medical care was easily accessible from the area's many streams and river tributaries. Several large supply depots of weapons, ammunition, medicine, rice, salt, peanuts, and even cooking grease were secreted within the mountains. Perhaps as important was the sanctuary's proximity to Cambodia—an official no-go for the anticommunist side—allowing NVA and VC units to easily slip beyond the reach of their enemies should a fight not go their way. Since at least the start of the Second Indochina War in 1954, no ARVN forces had encroached upon the sanctuary. Thus unmolested, the Viet Cong and NVA had enjoyed years of refuge and respite among the forested mountains. The region was the destination of Man's third regiment, the 66th, under Lt. Col. La Ngoc Chau, as well. It was the last to depart, leaving North Vietnam's Thanh Hoa between 10 and 18 August. The 66th would not reach the regimental base area until early November, and the 120mm mortar and 14.5mm antiaircraft battalions would not arrive until mid-November. Still, if all went well in the campaign's early stages, these late-arriving units would then be used in conjunction with the 32nd and 33rd regiments to further press the advantage against the remnants of ARVN in II Corps— along with its American benefactors.[25]

Every one of Man's regiments had a total authorized strength of 2,200 troops. Each featured three battalions of 550 men apiece, along with a 75mm recoilless rifle company, an 82mm mortar company, a 12.7mm antiaircraft machine gun company, and additional company-sized elements of medics, engineers, transportation personnel, and signal troops. Of course, the hardships endured on the march south almost certainly meant that none of Man's regiments would begin the campaign at full strength. Aside from the 33rd's woes, some contemporary estimates put the average attrition rate for all of Man's forces as high as 20 percent, though troop replacements were constantly filtering down the Trail. Man's infantry was outfitted with 7.62x39mm assault rifles, likely the Chinese Type 56, an identical copy of the Soviet's vaunted AK-47. Like the rifle that inspired it, the Type 56 was known for its powerful cartridge, 30-round magazine capacity, and the rugged reliability that allowed it to operate even under the dirtiest and wettest conditions. Other standard infantry armaments included the Soviet RPD 7.62mm light machine gun. Its 50-round drum magazine and lighter weight made it a more mobile and effective light machine gun in the offense than the substantially heavier, belt-fed US M-60. Units were also equipped with the RPG-2 rocket launcher, initially intended as an antitank weapon but which proved highly effective against fortified infantry positions as well. Known by anticommunist forces as the B-40 rocket, the launcher could fire an 82mm or 90mm warhead and had an effective range of approximately 150 meters. All infantrymen carried from three to five Chinese Type 67 stick grenades, similar in appearance to the "potato mashers" used by World War

II's German Wehrmacht. Finally, each man hauled some sort of entrenching tool. These pick axes or shovels saw significant use, as NVA commanders usually ordered their men to dig fighting positions for any marching halt lasting longer than two hours.[26]

The Tay Nguyen Campaign's first target would be the Special Forces–CIDG camp at Plei Me. Established in October 1963 with the primary mission of border surveillance and interdiction, Plei Me was isolated deep in "Indian Country," about thirty kilometers east of the Cambodian border in the rolling hills and scrub of Pleiku Province's southwest corner. The nearest friendly town was Pleiku City, about forty kilometers north and slightly to the east. The CIDG camp was situated on a single-lane dirt track known as Provincial Route 5 (also known as the Phu My–Plei Me Road) that intersected at two points with Highway 14, the Central Highland's main north-south thoroughfare connecting Kontum in the north with Pleiku City and Ban Ma-Thuot further south. Plei Me's garrison consisted of a four-hundred-strong CIDG Strike Force of local Jarai tribesmen trained by American Special Forces. While the Strikers were billeted in barracks within the camp, their wives and children lived in a cluster of Montagnard long-houses just outside the main gate on Plei Me's east side. Unlike the NVA troops they would soon face, the Strikers were relegated to the antiquated weapons of World War II: the M1 Garand, M2 carbine, and the Browning Automatic Rifle. A contingent of fourteen Vietnamese Special Forces soldiers commanded by Capt. Tran Van Nhan was also stationed in camp. Technically, the VSNF were supposed to be in command of both the Strike Forces and CIDG camps, but this was rarely the case in practice. Instead, they usually acted as Saigon's watchdogs, ever wary of the next Montagnard revolt. Plei Me was no exception. Instead, command responsibility fell to Nhan's "adviser," twenty-four-year-old Special Forces Capt. Harold M. Moore, of Pekin, Illinois. Moore had arrived at Plei Me only about two weeks earlier, having just taken over command of Detachment A-217 from Capt. Kenneth E. Short.[27]

The camp sat at an elevation of about 320 meters, with higher ground to the northeast and south. From the air, Plei Me cut the form of an equilateral triangle, each side about 160 meters long. A helipad sat just to the east of camp, and a 450-meter-long dirt airstrip, capable of accommodating C-123 Provider transport planes, stretched just to the south. Two rows of barbed and concertina wire bounded its outer perimeter. Inside the wire was a bulldozed and cleared no-man's-land seeded with interlocking webs of tangle-foot wire, Claymore mines, and trip flares. Finally, a smaller triangle, roughly half the size of the first and bounded by yet another barrier of concertina, lay within and delimited the camp's livable space. Here, a four-foot-deep gun trench with rifle positions spaced along its periphery marked the camp's outermost line of active defense. This was backed up by a series of sandbagged bunkers, each housing an M1919 Browning .30 caliber machine gun with interlocking fields of fire. The camp's grounds were crowded with personnel and more than a dozen low, wooden buildings with corrugated metal roofs. These included A-217's team house and a heavily fortified tactical operations center in the middle of camp, ammo and communication bunkers, the medical dispensary, CIDG living quarters, and so on. A reinforced blockhouse equipped with an M2 Browning .50 caliber machine gun sat at each of the triangle's three corners, a specific strength of the triangular layout. Heavy machine guns positioned at the apexes provided fully interlocking fields of fire, allowing two emplacements at a time to sweep positions forward of a single wall with murderous fire. For this reason, communist assault teams were usually very keen to knock these positions out as quickly as possible. Several interconnecting communication trenches crisscrossed the camp, making it possible for defenders to move between positions without exposing themselves above ground. Plei Me's defenses also boasted two 81mm mortars, along with an M30 "Four-Deuce," a 4.2-inch heavy mortar with a maximum effective range of up to 6,800 meters. Both mortars could fire various munition types, including illumination rounds. This capability often proved a godsend for the isolated Special Forces camps, which were usually hit at night. The ability to light the darkness beyond the wire could sometimes spell the difference between life and death.[28]

The Plei Me operation was to be a classic example of the "lure and the ambush" tactic that the communists had so often employed, most recently at Duc Co in August. The idea was simple: place an isolated enemy unit or outpost in dire straits, then lie in wait to ambush the inevitable reaction force that would be sent to its rescue. The Viet Cong had played the game for years. Now it was the NVA's turn. Still, the tactic had not been particularly successful at Duc Co. Ironically, the various successes the NVA had enjoyed since the beginning of the year probably contributed to their failure at that CIDG camp. After nine months of aggressive communist assaults—which saw the loss of several district towns and CIDG outposts during the Monsoon Offensive—24th STZ planners were taking no chances on losing Duc Co. They had responded with such overwhelming force that the NVA's 32nd Regiment simply couldn't cope. Nevertheless, Man apparently believed this time would be different. The fact that he would have a substantially more powerful force this time around—two full regiments, along with attachments—made it unlikely that the ARVN response would be something his men couldn't handle. And that force was to be employed against a better-chosen target. Indeed, Duc Co was located along Highway 19, the major east-west thoroughfare running from the Central Highlands all the way to the South China Sea. The paved, two-lane highway had allowed ARVN's mechanized Duc Co relief force ease of movement and maneuver. By contrast, Plei Me was isolated along Route 5, a single-lane provincial dirt road that marked the only likely route that a rescue force could take. The narrow track would work to stretch out any relief column, making it easier to chop up and destroy. The several hills overlooking the road could also be utilized to canalize the enemy into a number of ideal kill zones. Finally, the shoulders of Route 5 were choked with thick foliage that not only precluded off-road maneuvers but would help conceal ambush positions as well.[29]

The date of attack was set at 19 October. The plan was to unfold in three phases: During phase one, the 33rd Regiment would surround the camp and then unleash a ferocious attack. Meanwhile, phase two would see the experienced and battle-hardened 32nd Regiment lie in wait in carefully chosen and prepared ambush positions along Route 5 to destroy the II Corps relief force. That accomplished, the regiment would join forces with the 33rd to overwhelm and destroy what was left of Plei Me during phase three. Communist planners believed the final phase would take no longer than an hour to accomplish. Success would of course mean the destruction of an important enemy outpost—the western-most island of GVN influence in Pleiku—and what was sure to be a substantial portion of ARVN's II Corps reserve. But it would also demonstrate that NVA regiments could indeed operate effectively under a unified field front headquarters. To be sure, all eyes of the communist high command would be watching to see how the siege of Plei Me played out. If successful, it would of course be an auspicious start to the Tay Nguyen Campaign. But in the longer run, it would pave the way for just the sort of multiregiment, division-controlled operations that could finally bring Le Duan's GO-GU strategy to its full fruition.[30]

It was a simple plan, and indeed one that communist troops and planners were well familiar with. But success still depended upon thorough preparation. The 32nd had the advantage of already being in-country when the plan was devised. Its commanders and men began preparing as early as 19 September. By 10 October, the battalions of the 32nd had completed their operational rehearsals and moved out to prepare their ambush positions northeast of Plei Me along Route 5. The 33rd, however, had just spent the previous months coming down the Trail. While its lead elements would reach Anta Village by 10 September, the rest of the regiment would not settle into its base area until 2 October. This meant that the regiment's untested troops would have just ten days of tactical exercises to rehearse its part of the attack. Regimental commander Lt. Col. Vũ Sắc was understandably concerned that this would not be enough time for his inexperienced men. But he would do his best to get them ready. The men of the 33rd spent the next several days conducting drills and rehearsals under the relative safety of Anta Village. For operational security, no one other than the regimental staff, battalion commanders, and reconnaissance element knew that the target was Plei Me until 15 October. For the next four days, the 33rd's troops were put through their final paces, as they set about constructing assault positions and trench works and making other last-minute preparations. Of course, all of this had to be completed under the cover of darkness so as not to alert the camp and give away the element of surprise. Fortunately, from the communist perspective, the dense vegetation and creek beds surrounding the camp provided natural cover and made for excellent avenues of approach. The communists had also had Plei Me under close observation for several weeks. By the time of the attack, the NVA had assuredly developed an understanding of the camp's standard operating procedures, its defenses, the comings and goings of patrols, etc.[31]

Meanwhile, the 17th Company, the regiment's transportation element, worked feverishly to carry in the necessary stocks of food, water, ammunition, and medicine from nearby supply caches that had themselves been hauled in from the Chu Pong base areas to the west. The regimental medical company, the 18th, was broken up into three aid stations: the first was intended for immediate casualties, the second for the seriously wounded, and the third to care for the sick and injured. The medical company would have its work cut out for it, as nearly half of the 33rd's infantry battalions were sick. On 20 October, a third support unit, the 19th Transportation Battalion, would also arrive in Pleiku to help keep the 33rd Regiment supplied. His logistics taken care of, it was time for Lt. Col. Sac to get the regiment into its final assault positions. The plan was clear in his mind. He would deploy the three rifle companies of his 2nd Battalion in well-prepared positions southwest of camp, less than three hundred meters from its outer perimeter. The regimental mortar company would be positioned farther south. To maintain complete coverage of the camp, Sac wanted his two 81mm and seven 82mm mortar tubes positioned at no greater distance than six hundred meters from Plei Me's perimeter. His 75mm recoilless rifle company was to be held in reserve to the southwest. Sac understood his enemy's ability to land troops by helicopter, so he would also detach

one company of his 1st Battalion to act as a blocking force against heliborne assault. Sac would then position the remainder of his 1st and 3rd
Battalion rifle companies west and northeast of camp. His men, with help
from local laborers, had managed to dig well-fortified trench works—
especially to the northeast—as close as fifty meters from the camp's outer
wire. And so the table was set, the designated hour had at last arrived. The
men of the 33rd Regiment were moving to their places. How would they
acquit themselves? It was time to find out.[32]

Part II

THE SIEGE

5

THE STORM BREAKS
(19–20 OCTOBER)

There had been rumblings that something was afoot in Western Pleiku for weeks. As early as 27 September, MACV's J2 intelligence sector began receiving periodic agent reports that battalion-strength Viet Cong units had been spotted operating from ten to fifteen kilometers north and northwest of Plei Me. Another agent report in early October asserted that the Special Forces–CIDG camp at Plei Me had been targeted for attack. That initial trickle of reports soon became a flood. Between 1 and 20 October, MACV J2 received eighteen separate reports that enemy units up to regiment size were operating in Western Pleiku. There were also indications that a communist training center had been established about ten kilometers north of Duc Co. The NVA's 32nd Regiment, identified as the enemy unit involved in August's Duc Co attack, was believed to be in the Chu Pong vicinity, along with the Viet Cong local force H-15 Battalion. The existence of the Chu Pong base area was well known to MACV intelligence, and J2 had begun studying options for hitting the area with B-52 strikes in September. A communist defector claiming to have been with the 20th Transportation Battalion of the 325th Division had reported on 13 September that an NVA regiment was at Chu Pong and that supply depots and a hospital were located between the mountain complex and Duc Co.[1]

Yet, despite the warning signs, little credence was paid to such reports. One reason may have been pure desensitization. American and South Vietnamese intelligence had since the end of the communists' Monsoon Offensive in August received numerous warnings that the Viet Cong were planning to attack virtually *every* Special Forces camp within the 24th Special

Tactical Zone. None of those admonitions had come to pass. Further, Plei Me had not had any notable enemy contact since June. The camp regularly sent out patrol sweeps of its area, but none had uncovered anything other than the usual local force Viet Cong harassment. Still, the reports had to be checked out. Capt. Harold M. Moore, twenty-four, of Pekin, Illinois, had assumed command of the US Special Forces Detachment A-217 from the outgoing Capt. Kenneth Short just two weeks earlier. On 17 October, Moore had ordered his executive officer, 1st Lt. Robert H. Berry, twenty-two, and Sgt. 1st Class Jimmie Beech, an intelligence and light weapons specialist, to take an eighty-five-man company of Jarai CIDG and investigate the reports of Viet Cong activity. Officially dubbed Operation Chương Dương 40, the mission was to last six days. Berry's company was to first sweep about fifteen kilometers northwest of camp, then turn east toward Highway 14. The patrol was then to swing south along the highway, before turning west along Route 5 toward Plei Me. The company was equipped with a Korean War–era PRC-10 radio, whose limited range meant the patrol would be out of radio contact with the camp for most of the mission.[2]

Now, as darkness fell on 19 October, Moore took stock of his defenses. The young captain had been sure to maintain all-around security. He had five, eight-man CIDG security ambush patrols deployed in the areas around the camp, along with two regularly maintained twenty-man outposts farther out. The first was about one kilometer northeast of Plei Me, near an old French fort. The other was located atop Chu Ho hill about two thousand meters to the south. Both outposts were in radio contact with the camp. Subtracting the Jarai Strikers on Berry's sweep and clear mission, the ambush patrols, and outposts, there were about 250 CIDG troops remaining in camp, along with a fourteen-man contingent of South Vietnamese LLDB. Finally, with Berry and Beech gone, Moore was left with only eight other Special Forces troopers. They were as follows: Spec. Dan Shea, the team medic; SFC Robert "Poncho" Navarro, a communications specialist; Staff Sgt. Robert Sloan, heavy weapons; Sgt. Eugene Tafoya, light weapons specialist; Staff Sgt. Cornelious Clark, demolitions; Staff Sgt. Joseph Bailey, intelligence specialist; Sgt. Ron Maddox, light and heavy weapons; and Spec. Nick Walsh, demolitions.[3]

At about 1915 hours, the distant crackle of gunfire drifted over the parapets of Plei Me's south wall. Somewhere out in the gathering gloom, the lead elements of the NVA's 2nd Battalion had run into one of the camp's eight-man squad pickets. Then the night was quiet again. But about three hours later, the blazing orange flashes of gunfire once again split the darkness, this time atop Chu Ho hill farther south. A forty-man NVA assault

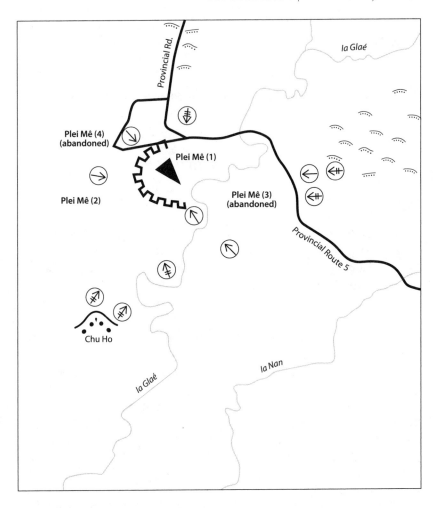

force had taken Plei Me's southern outpost by surprise. The Jarai tribesmen fought desperately, but radio contact with the outpost was soon lost. It was later discovered that the CIDG had held out until their ammunition ran dry. And then the NVA had rolled over the little outpost like a terrible wave. None of the Jarai would escape Chu Ho alive. Then, at about 2300 hours, Plei Me itself began to feel the wrath of the encircling NVA. The camp was rocked by 57mm recoilless rifle fire, while 82mm mortars crashed down. Sloan ran to the 4.2-inch mortar pit at the center of camp. Soon, the heavy weapons specialist was sending his own rounds downrange. Nearby, the CIDG mortar teams had fired up their 81mm mortars as well. In the rifle pits and bunkers lining the camp, their fellow Jarai gripped their weapons and peered into the black void beyond the wire. The SF troopers dispersed themselves along the line, shoring up the Montagnards' courage. Soon, the air above Plei Me was alive with the snap and pop of small-arms and the staccato rhythm of machine gun fire. Somewhere out in the darkness, Sac's first assault troops crouched in their positions, steeling themselves for the trials to come. The siege of Plei Me had begun.[4]

20 OCTOBER

Capt. Robert K. Wright

Forty kilometers to the northeast, Capt. Robert K. Wright was just set-tling in for what he hoped would be a quiet night. As commander of the 119th Aviation Company's 3rd Platoon (Guns), Wright, thirty-two, always made sure to carry his own weight. He'd chosen on this late 19 October evening to remain on standby while others slept. Based at Camp Holloway near the provincial capital of Pleiku, the 119th's standard operating pro-cedure required that a two-helicopter flight of gunships, known by their "Crocodile" call sign, be kept at the ready at all times. And with good reason. The company had been getting almost daily contact with local force Viet Cong units. The rest of the company's 24 UH-1B "Hueys," including its transport slicks known as "Alligators," were set to lift off for Bong Son at first light to add airlift support for Operation Than Phong 6, a weeks-long, multiunit II Corps mission to root out enemy troop concentrations along the coast. The men would certainly be busy enough in coming days. Let the rest of them get some shut-eye, Wright thought. His fire team would stand watch tonight.[5]

Commanding the second Crocodile gunship was WO Ron Macklin, twenty-seven, of Glendale, California. Macklin sat in the right pilot seat and controlled the chopper's 2.75-inch rocket pods. As Wright's wingman, it was Macklin's job to flank and cover the flight leader wherever he went. Communication was key, especially when it came to calling out antiaircraft fire. Each man kept the other apprised of enemy fire so he could either return his own or at least dodge the incoming. Wright had worked with Macklin before and found him to be solid and dependable. "If he's following me on my wing, and I say, 'I'm getting it from my right rear,' the words are about out of my mouth, and there are already rockets hitting that area," says Wright. "We worked well together because we were getting shot up about every day anyway. It was just pretty much a normal day for us."[6]

Macklin had been known to put fire on Holloway's prodigious rat population, too. One night the warrant officer was awakened to the telltale scratching of one of the rodents scurrying across the rafters of his hooch. In a flash, Macklin came up with a 12-gauge shotgun and began blasting away at the beast, easily the size of an eight-pound cat. While he didn't hit home that night, he did manage to blow several holes in the roof—and scare the hell out of his hooch-mates, who thought the camp had come under attack. One of those roommates was WO Dean Christensen, a gunship pilot. While he described Macklin as one of his closest friends in the unit, Christensen said that his fellow warrant officer was plagued by the conviction that his tour in Vietnam would end tragically. "From the first day he got there," Christensen recalls, "he was always telling everybody about how he was going to get shot down and killed." Macklin always carried several pistols and a rifle whenever he flew. If he were ever to be shot down and managed to survive, the aircraft commander was determined not to be taken without a fight.[7]

To Macklin's left was his copilot and hooch-mate, Don G. Knowlton, a quiet and professional twenty-four-year-old warrant officer from Minneapolis. He fired the ship's 7.62mm machine guns and stood ready to take control should Macklin become incapacitated. In the back, Spc. 5 Franklin D. Racine, twenty-three, served as the crew chief. Racine, friendly and well liked in the company, was seen as a standout chief known for taking the initiative and keeping his ships in tip-top shape. The young Midlothian, Illinois, native and his wife, Jackie, were expecting their first child any day now. But despite his amiable demeanor, Racine, like Macklin, was haunted by premonitions that he wouldn't survive Vietnam. He frequently confided to friends that his only hope was to live long enough to see his son born. Rounding out the crew was Spc. 5 Wesley McDonial, thirty, from the 25th Infantry in Hawaii. The Chicago native had volunteered to come over on temporary duty status to ride "shotgun" as an M-60 door gunner. The standby crews had bedded down in Holloway's "firehouse," a small ready station on the flight line. But if they slept at all, it would be in their flight gear, ready to get airborne on ten minutes' notice.[8]

They wouldn't have to wait long. Just after midnight, the duty officer called the alert—trouble was brewing down at Plei Me. For the past several hours, the camp had come under a steadily intensifying barrage of mortar, machine gun, and recoilless rifle fire, and had lost contact with its twenty-man outpost located about two thousand meters to the south. As the command and control element for all Special Forces operations in II Corps, C2 had just called down from the unit compound a few miles up Highway 14 to relay Plei Me's appeal for flare and gunship support. Camp commander Moore suspected that a powerful Viet Cong force was lurking somewhere in the darkness, and he needed flare ships to augment his own mortar-fired illumination. More light was needed to keep the beast at bay. It would fall to Wright and company to hold the line until additional Air Force assets could arrive on station.[9]

The 52nd Aviation Battalion, parent unit to the 119th, was no stranger to flying support for Special Forces. Since its arrival in Vietnam in August 1963, the battalion was based primarily at Camp Holloway and was the principal aerial lifeline for the remote SF-CIDG camps scattered throughout the Central Highlands. With subordinate units stationed at Ban Ma Thuot and Qui Non, the 52nd flew everything from routine "ash and trash" resupply and mail call runs to medevac, airlift, close air support, recon, and other missions. Although Wright had landed at Plei Me only a few times since arriving at Holloway that spring, he remembered the camp's young commander. Moore was, in Wright's words, a "stand-up guy" who always seemed to have "everything under control." If Moore and his SF troopers were calling, then Wright and the 119th would be there to answer. And so the crews scrambled to their choppers and prepared to lift off into the dark night and whatever awaited.[10]

For as long as he could remember, Bob Wright had wanted to fly. Not that his family's humble means allowed for such a pricey pursuit. He'd have to find a more creative way to make it happen. So, at just fourteen, Wright began taking odd jobs at Northway Air Park near his hometown of Columbus, Ohio. There, he scrubbed planes or did just about any other job the mechanic could dream up in exchange for flight training. When his bosses decreed that he'd built up enough labor capital, young Wright would earn himself an hour's flight time in a Piper J-3 Cub. Before his school-age peers were able to drive the streets below, Wright was soaring through the clouds above. And so it went for years, learning to fly one piece at a time. By the time the Army came calling with his draft notice, Wright had already earned his pilot's license. Not that it mattered much for an enlisted man. It would be a long and winding road before he'd see the inside of an Army cockpit. After basic training, Wright did a stint with the 82nd Airborne before being tapped to attend electronics repair school in Augusta, Georgia. He was the only soldier in his unit with high enough test scores. Then it was on to Fort Rucker, Alabama, after being selected as an avionics technician.

And it was there that his commanding officer spotted something special in the young soldier. After a bit of prodding, the colonel simply took it upon himself to submit Wright's application for Officer Candidate School (OCS). He even signed his name for him.[11]

But pilot's license and potential aside, he would have to bide his time a while longer before returning to the skies. After graduating OCS in 1960, Wright learned that he'd first have to spend three years in an artillery unit in Germany. When that duty was finally discharged, he applied and was accepted to flight school back in the States. After finishing in December 1963, it was on to Fort Campbell, Kentucky, and the 101st Airborne. Then back to Fort Rucker for the Army's Advanced Graduate Flight Training to further hone the skills he'd need as Vietnam loomed. By spring 1965, Wright had arrived at Camp Holloway, his home away from home for the next year. The camp was named for Chief Warrant Officer (CWO) Charles E. Holloway, a chopper pilot who'd been killed in 1962 on an air assault with the 81st Transportation Company, which had established the base in August of that year. The 81st would later morph into Wright's unit, the redesignated 119th Aviation Company.[12]

From its beginning, the army airfield had proven a thorn in the side of communist ambitions in the Central Highlands. Holloway not only provided badly needed airlift and support throughout II Corps, but its proximity to Pleiku made it especially nettlesome for North Vietnamese aspirations. The city was strategically vital to both communist and allied interests. For Hanoi, the provincial capital was the main impediment to its plan of eventually splitting South Vietnam in two from the Cambodian border all the way to the South China Sea. For the US and its South Vietnamese allies, Pleiku represented the government's western-most island of influence in the Highlands and an important endpoint for logistics moving from the populated coasts inland along Route 19. The isolated, sparsely populated region, with its proximity to the Ho Chi Minh Trail and communist sanctuaries in neighboring Laos and Cambodia, was a near-perfect ingress point for infiltrating war-fighting materiel and regular army soldiers from the North. Indeed, the Holloway-Pleiku complex was akin to a rock in the middle of a rapidly swelling river of communist influence. The Viet Cong had for some time maintained a sizable presence in the area around Holloway, frequently targeting the camp with mortars, harassing fire, and the occasional probe. But in February 1965, the communists launched a battalion-strength attack that would mark a turning point in America's growing involvement in the war. The assault on Holloway and the MACV compound killed eight Americans and wounded another 108. Two days later, President Lyndon

Johnson ordered Operation Flaming Dart, a series of limited retaliatory airstrikes against North Vietnam. But Holloway, along with a similar attack on US service members at Qui Non a week later, would serve as the catalyst for a dramatic escalation of US involvement—the much more substantial Operation Rolling Thunder bombing campaign unleashed in the following weeks. Now, nearly eight months later, Camp Holloway and its 52nd Aviation Battalion would once again stand athwart communist aims in the Highlands.[13]

Capt. Richard G. Shortridge

At about the same time that Wright and his fire team were climbing into the night sky above Holloway, Major Howard Pierson was taking off in his C-123 Provider fixed-wing flare ship from Da Nang Airbase about 225 kilometers to the east. He too had gotten the call that Plei Me was in trouble. But first, he'd need to make a pit stop and pick up Forward Air Controller Capt. Richard Shortridge at Pleiku. The twenty-nine-year-old was a senior FAC with the 21st Tactical Air Support Squadron based just outside the city at New Pleiku Airbase. It would be Shortridge's job to direct the first close air support strikes from the right seat of Pierson's Provider.[14]

Just after midnight, Shortridge was sound asleep in the barracks when he was called out. "We need to have a FAC in a C-123," he was told. "Plei Me's getting mortared." As the sleep-woven cobwebs began to clear, Shortridge thought the name sounded familiar. After all, he'd visited nearly all of the remote Special Forces camps dotting the Highlands. The FAC had established a friendly, symbiotic relationship with the troopers. He was their lifeline to civilization; they were his eyes and ears into the barely glimpsed world beneath the jungle canopy. Shortridge knew that life was hard for the twelve-man A-teams in their remote, jungle redoubts. Air Force pilots could at least come home to a reasonably secure air base at night, with hot showers, food, and even a drink at the officer's club to help ease the strains of war. But the Special Forces troopers lived Spartan existences, isolated and alone in Indian Country. And it was a dangerous existence, too. On any given night, all that stood between survival and annihilation were a few sandbagged bunkers, themselves, and their primitive Montagnard allies. So the FAC tried to do whatever he could to make the guys a bit more comfortable. Oftentimes he'd fly in and drop off their mail, extra supplies, or even a few cold beers. They always seemed to appreciate it. Some nights, he'd stay for dinner; land crabs and rice was a favorite. Invariably, table talk turned to what the VC were up to these days. And that was good. For without reliable intel, he had no targets. And without targets, he wasn't doing his job.[15]

But even as he gathered his gear for the mission, the first pangs of anxiety set in. Not that he was a stranger to running FAC ops. He'd been in several skirmishes throughout II Corps since that July. But this one felt different somehow. For one thing, he'd never been rousted out of bed for a middle-of-the-night pickup before. Normally, he ran FAC ops out of his little 0-1 Bird Dog, a two-seat prop plane resembling a civilian Piper Cub. And preferably during the day. Nighttime FAC missions were tricky business, indeed. But all of that seemed to be thrown out the window on this one. They needed him right *now.* No, he thought. This is something else. Something . . . *bigger.*[16]

A jeep sat rumbling quietly on the street outside. Shortridge climbed in for the short ride over to base operations and a quick briefing. When he arrived, he received yet another clue that something big was afoot. Hollywood actress and comedian Martha Raye, who'd been doing a USO show nearby, had gotten wind that something was going on. She'd showed up with an Air Force major, and they both wanted to tag along. Raye was well-known in military circles for her willingness to entertain—and often drink with—service members in far-flung locales, from World War II to Korea and now in Vietnam. President Johnson would even go on to make her an honorary lieutenant colonel in the Army the following year. That, plus her willingness to go wherever the troops were, earned her the affectionate nickname "Colonel Maggie of the Boondocks" among the men. But friend of the soldiers or no, having her ride along on this mission was the last thing Shortridge needed tonight. After a fair amount of cajoling from Raye and the major, Shortridge finally had to give it to them straight. "No, Martha, you can't go along. It's my job to go fight the war, and your job to stay with the USO. You do your job, and I'll do mine." The major said they were going anyway. Exasperated, Shortridge finally called the 21st's air liaison officer, Lt. Col. Ed Manning. Manning's Air Force Support Center (AFSC) at II Corps had for a few days been receiving sketchy intel from various sources that something big was brewing around Plei Me. Warnings about impending attacks on CIDG camps were common. But the AFSC had quietly called in FACs from surrounding areas just in case. Like Shortridge, Manning was in no mood for shenanigans on this night. He issued a direct order that neither Raye nor the major would be flying that night. The message finally received, Shortridge walked alone on to the tarmac. Outside, he stood silently in the cool night air of the Highlands, scanning the skies for sign of the C-123 that would take him into the unknown.[17]

Ironically, it was love that had brought Shortridge to this moment. Shortridge's childhood had been a rough one, poor and in and out of foster homes, so when his mother could no longer care for him, a teen-aged Shortridge had been forced to leave his native Willamette Valley near Portland and move in with family friends in Joseph, Oregon. There, he met Beverly, and the two teens fell in love and married right out of high school. "Then you realize just how poor you can be," he says with a chuckle. If he wanted his new wife to live with him, he'd need more money. And like so many young men before him, the eighteen-year-old Shortridge decided that the steady paycheck offered by joining the military would solve the problem. He quickly settled on the Air Force. Living conditions in the Army were not good, he reasoned, and the Navy was at sea far too much for a newlywed couple in love. But the Air Force, they went home at night, and he'd heard the food wasn't half bad either. That, thought Shortridge, was the only way to fly.[18]

And fly he did. Shortridge began his career as an airborne radio op-erator and later worked as an electronic countermeasures tech aboard the Air Force's strategic bomber at the time, the Convair B-36 Peacemaker. The ten-engine Peacemaker was built to deliver two MK-17 thermonuclear bombs on targets in the Soviet Union as part of the newly formed Strategic Air Command and could remain airborne for more than a day and a half. Fifteen crewmembers worked in shifts of four hours on, four off. Enlisted men didn't have bunks to sleep on, so they were forced to hit the sack— literally. Shortridge often slept on piled-up equipment bags. But there were upsides, too. Peacemaker duty brought an extra $65 a month to augment Shortridge's meager $36 monthly pay. That came in handy now that their first child, Richard, had come along. Being on a B-36 was also something of a prestige assignment and good duty for an enlisted man. "Being a two-striper on this plane was as good as being a staff sergeant on the ground," he would later say.[19]

Still, the duty kept him away from his family for lengthy stretches. Shortridge's longest flight was just over thirty-six hours, a surveillance mission up to the Arctic Circle, down along the coast of Far East Russia, and finally to Tokyo. On one of those long flights, one of the Peacemaker's engines caught fire over the Pacific. Shortridge and the navigator, fearing that the plane would go down, drank an entire case of grape juice believing they'd need the hydration if they were stranded at sea. Luckily for them, the plane landed safely without further incident.[20]

Shortridge soon decided that he wanted to make the Air Force his career, but he didn't want to do it as a striper. He knew officers had it far better than enlisted and came to relish the idea of having that big eagle on his flight cap. But while the treatment and prestige officers enjoyed was good, the extra money was even better. His and Beverly's little family continued to grow when Caprice was born. An officer's pay rate would certainly help there. Trouble was, he had to come up with $500 before applying to Officer Training School (OTS) to cover the cost of the new uniform and other sundries, As usual, the Shortridge's were tight on money, so he re-enlisted just in case and then used the bonus to pay his way into OTS.

And if he were going the officer route, Shortridge figured he'd go all the way. He wanted to be a pilot. Indeed, he'd already been bitten by the bug on those long, monotonous trans-Pacific flights. Rather than racking out during his four-hour respite, Shortridge would instead climb up to the cockpit and watch the pilots. The aircraft commander would sometimes even let the young enlisted man take over the controls. Soon, Shortridge had learned all the instruments and calls. By the time his tour on the B-36 was over, he had already racked up some fifty hours of flight time at the controls.[21]

After OTS in San Antonio, Shortridge headed for flight training at Graham Airbase in Marianna, Florida. There, all that control time on the B-36 paid off. Fledgling pilots first needed to qualify on the Beechcraft T-34 Mentor before moving on to more advanced training at Webb Air Force Base in Big Springs, Texas. Normally, it took about eight hours to solo on the T-34. Shortridge was able to do it in just over half that and finished third in his class at Webb. That meant he would have his choice of planes to fly after graduation. Shortridge decided he had seen enough of bombers. The life of a fighter jock was calling. He'd fallen in love with the sleek new F-100 Super Sabres but heard that all those who specialized in the "Hun" were being relegated as flight instructors. This wouldn't do, Shortridge thought. He wanted action, so he chose the venerable F-86 instead. After all, it had been the Air Force's frontline air superiority fighter during Korea. Wouldn't it be for the next war, as well? The best laid plans, as someone once said. Ironically, it was Sabre pilots like Shortridge who ended up as flight instructors, while the F-100 became the frontline fighter-bomber during the early years of Vietnam. "It just goes to show that you can never outguess the services," he would later say with chagrin, so in 1962, he trudged back to Texas once more, this time as a trainer at Randolph Air Force Base.[22]

No, Shortridge's dream of becoming a supersonic fighter pilot was not to be. Instead, he would land at the controls of a tiny prop plane that was lucky to see triple-digit airspeed on a good day. Enter Cessna's O-1 Bird

Dog. "I went from going about 500 miles an hour down to 80," he quipped. While undeniably slow, it was an exceptionally versatile and agile single-engine prop plane first used in Korea for observation and liaison duties. As America's involvement in Vietnam grew in the early 1960s, so too did its need for a reliable spotter aircraft capable of flying low and slow enough to spy enemy activity in the jungle below. The 0-1 filled the bill perfectly. Designers placed its wing assembly atop the cabin to provide largely unobstructed sight lines, and this, along with oversized Plexiglas windows that could be opened, helped pilots get a clear view of everything around and below them. The wing assembly placement also provided the 0-1 with superlative lift capability and handling at slow speeds. Yes, its 213-horsepower engine produced less-than-stellar top-end airspeed, but the Bird Dog's unique design allowed for an impressive climb rate of a thousand feet per minute. In fact, one of the requirements set by the military during the design phase was that the 0-1 be able to take off and land in six hundred feet or less while clearing a fifty-foot obstacle—all at its maximum allowable weight of 2,800 pounds. Of course, such short takeoff and landing capability was just the ticket for getting the 0-1 in and out of tight spaces in Vietnam's backcountry. The Bird Dog would eventually be used for everything from target acquisition and reconnaissance to artillery spotting and as a FAC platform for coordinating tactical air strikes.[23]

Of course, this last one was to be Shortridge's *raison d'être* in the burgeoning war in Vietnam. After getting trained up on the 0-1 at Florida's Hurlburt Air Field in early 1965, Shortridge and Beverly returned home to Joseph. Better to have Beverly and their *three* kids now—Tammy had come along by then—in a familiar place with family nearby, he thought. Beverly's father had died three years before, and now her mother lived alone on their small family farm just outside town. She'd invited Beverly and the grandkids to come and stay. Beverly would help around the farm, and her mom would help with the kids. It made them all feel a little bit better. At least everyone but young Richard. At just twelve, he was a sensitive boy but old enough to know that his father might not come home from that faraway place. While the girls were younger and still largely oblivious, Richard would be left to worry along with his mother over the next year. Shortridge worried a bit, too, though not for himself. He knew the perils of poverty better than most. Shortridge dreaded to think of what might become of his young family should he not make it home, so he made sure to buy extra life insurance before he left, just as they'd advised back at Hurlburt. He knew he might very well need it. Then, like so many before him, Shortridge kissed his wife and children goodbye, and headed off to war.[24]

When he arrived in Vietnam in July 1965, he discovered a nascent FAC operation in disarray. His ostensible base, Bien Hoa Air Base outside Saigon, didn't even have quarters for him. Instead, he was forced to check in to a Saigon hotel to sleep at night. And it wasn't just sleeping accommodations that were in short stock. In those first weeks, Shortridge and company didn't even have office supplies. Instead, they were reduced to "foraging" for the basics, stealing a pencil here, a pad of paper there. Finally, the unit commander arrived about two weeks later, and things marginally improved. Shortridge and his fellow FACs soon settled into a routine. New 0-1s would arrive disassembled in crates. The FACS would then assemble the aircraft and ferry them throughout South Vietnam, depositing the Bird Dogs at other bases where they were needed.[25]

While a tedious process, it wasn't without its upsides. Flying all those 0-1s around Vietnam was like extended flight training for Shortridge. By the end of those first weeks, he had ferried between ten and twelve Bird Dogs to their new homes, in the process becoming much more proficient with the aircraft. After all, he'd gotten only about five or six hours on the 0-1 while qualifying back at Hurlburt. Ultimately, a FAC had to have complete mastery over his aircraft. Indeed, all the Bird Dog's design innovations counted for little without a skilled and experienced pilot to take full advantage of them. This meant knowing its capabilities like the back of his hand. It meant the ability to take off and land in incredibly tight spots. It meant the capacity to maneuver and avoid enemy fire—all while coordinating and directing multiple aircraft in a combat zone. It meant, in the end, the difference between life and death. And with the storm now gathering around Plei Me, Shortridge would need every bit of that extra training.[26]

Capt. Russell L. Hunter

It was past midnight when Capt. Russell L. Hunter, twenty-nine, felt someone shake him awake. In the dim light of his sleeping quarters, he could see the silhouette of a man standing over him. "Colonel Patch wants you in the commo shack," said the noncommissioned officer (NCO). Hunter, the unit surgeon, shook off the cobwebs, quickly dressed, and made his way to C-detachment's communications bunker. Inside, he found Patch and the other C2 officers gathered around the single-side band, listening intently to a voice on the radio. "We have mass casualties," said the voice, "and we need a medevac now." It was the Special Forces camp at Plei Me, and they were under heavy attack. Lt. Col. William Patch, a 1948 West Point grad and combat-wounded veteran of Korea, was C-detachment's commanding officer. Despite their differences in age and rank, he had become something of a friend and mentor to Hunter. Patch had shepherded the young captain through his first combat operation against a reinforced Viet Cong battalion near Ban Ma Thuot earlier in his tour. The CO often treated Hunter as a respected colleague rather than a junior officer. The two spent the next forty-five minutes in the dark of the commo shack hashing over their options. From the sound of things, this was a fairly substantial attack, and camp defenders couldn't be left to fend for themselves. But how best to support them? The two eventually agreed that Hunter would fly into Plei Me at first light to augment the camp's enlisted medics, while Patch explored further options with Col. William McKean, the overall commander of 5th Special Force Group in Nha Trang.[27]

The rationale was straightforward. The action at Plei Me sounded too hot to risk an air train of medevacs. The best bet would be to instead insert Hunter and let him care for the wounded onsite. The physician was the first to admit that because of the limitations of combat medicine, he could often do no better than an accomplished medic. But he also understood that he could sometimes do a great deal more. The reasons were threefold: first, his trained medical eye allowed him to more effectively triage the wounded, knowing with precision which casualties should be prioritized and when a medevac should be risked. Second, as a medical doctor, Hunter's skills were simply superior, with far more tricks up his sleeve to keep even the most egregiously wounded man alive until more substantial care could be rendered. Lastly was a notion that was more intangible but no less important— what Hunter called the "mystique" of the physician. The men simply *believed* that he could do more. Having a surgeon in their midst was a powerful morale-booster, even an inspiration. It was the faith that, should the worst happen and they be wounded, Hunter would be there to save them. In some ways, that faith was misplaced. But cold reason rarely makes an impression on such certitude.[28]

So Hunter packed up his gear and made his way to the helipad outside the C2 compound. It wasn't so much fear that he felt as he stood alone in the dark waiting for the chopper to arrive. Sure, there was always a bit of anxiety going into combat, but he'd seen this movie before. Indeed, he'd been on many such missions since arriving in July. There would be casualties to treat, perhaps a great many of them from what he'd heard over the radio. But it was almost always the same: the VC liked to hit isolated Special Forces camp in the dead of night and inflict as many casualties as possible. Sometimes, the guerillas even managed to overrun a camp during a night attack—a worst-case scenario, to be sure. This left the SF troopers and CIDG to escape and evade until they—if very lucky—could reach safety. That's what had happened up at Dak Sut near the Laotian border in August. Detachment A-218 and its complement of about 475 CIDG were overwhelmed by a superior Viet Cong force. The communists managed to overrun the camp in just over four hours, and only about half of the garrison had escaped to tell the tale.

But such events were few and far between in his experience. Usually the VC would hit and run. And with good reason, for once daylight arrived, so too would the punishing tac-airstrikes. The communists nearly always preferred to slink away to fight another day. Then Hunter would be called to chopper into the camp in the early morning hours, stabilize the situation, and be back at C2 after a few hours' work. There were, of course, exceptions. He himself had been caught up in the siege of another Special Forces camp at nearby Duc Co in August. The VC had stubbornly refused to quit, even under the relentless pounding of American artillery and airstrikes. It eventually required eight ARVN battalions, including support from two battalions of the US 173rd Airborne Brigade, to break the forty-eight-day siege. While that may have been a rather grim aberration, perhaps Duc Co had been the start of something new, a sea change in VC tactics. Perhaps Plei Me was just the next in line. Waiting for his chopper to arrive as he gazed up into the night sky, the C2 surgeon figured he would find out soon enough.[29]

Hunter was the first to admit that he didn't fit the caricature of the gung-ho, snake-eating Special Forces trooper. If anything, the Kansas native likened himself more to the quintessential citizen-soldier, a man—not unlike the prototypical Minute Man of the American Revolution—who without fanfare stepped up to do his duty when his country asked. Isn't that what John F. Kennedy had called on all Americans to do in his 1961 Inaugural? "Ask not what your country can do for you," and all that? Hunter had come from a long line of citizen-soldiers who'd answered the call. Family members on both sides had fought in every major American war, from the Revolutionary War to Vietnam. Ten of his uncles had served in World War II alone, and it was that war that had made the biggest impression on a young Hunter. His first memories were of Japan attacking Pearl Harbor in December 1941. He had begun kindergarten that fall. Over the next four years he followed as the Nazis ravaged Europe, and Japan the Pacific. And when the United States ended the war in 1945 by dropping two atomic bombs on Japan, it did so by launching the B-29 Superfortresses that carried them from the same Tinian airstrip that his uncle Roy, a Seabee, had helped build. Indeed, the war against fascism and Nazism had not just been a family affair for Hunter, it was also deeply formative and would serve as the script of his youth.[30]

In the years that followed, a new evil—communism—had risen to take the place of the old. This, too, profoundly imprinted Hunter's view of the world and his responsibility within it. From his teens into his twenties, the Cold War ran across his mind's eye like a series of deeply disturbing images: the Iron Curtain; the Berlin airlift and later the Wall; the Soviets as a nuclear power; the loss of China to the communists; Korea; the Vietminh's defeat of the French at Dien Bien Phu; Fidel Castro and the Cuban Revolution; the Cuban Missile Crisis; China and its atomic bomb. Everywhere, communism seemed to be on the march, with half the world already living under the totalitarian boot of the Sino-Soviet bloc. And the beast seemed ever hungry for more. Indeed, hadn't Soviet Premier Nikita Khrushchev in 1956 vowed to "bury" the West, even while pledging to support "wars of liberation" around the globe? Communism had declared itself the enemy of his country and creed, so when the time came for him to do his part, Hunter resolved that he would be ready to meet the challenge.[31]

A young man of deep Christian faith, Hunter graduated Abilene Christian College in 1958. That's also where he met and married his wife, Carolyn. The two set about building a life together. Hunter dreamed of becoming a physician, but it was a long, demanding, and expensive endeavor. Carolyn worked as a teacher to supplement the couple's income in the meantime, but even with Carolyn's help, they knew that the debts would mount. By 1963, Hunter had finished his training at the University of Kansas Medical School and been accepted for an internship at Ben Taub General Hospital in Houston. It was while finishing up there in spring 1964 that the newly minted physician received his country's call. He'd been caught up in the "doctor draft," a provision that had been created under the Selective Service Act of 1948. This authorized the government to compel health care professionals to serve in the military. For many—especially those who'd just spent years working to become physicians—such news would be vexing, to say the least. But Hunter welcomed it, for by then, he had become in his words a "True Believer": in his Christian religion, in his country, and in the just cause of defeating communism.[32]

But if he were going to do this, he didn't want to waste two years "treating the clap at Fort Riley," while leaving others to hold the line against his country's enemies.[33] So where, Hunter wondered, could he be most useful in this new war? He wrote the Surgeon General of the United

States to find out. Volunteer for the Special Forces, he was told. They needed doctors very badly. He and Carolyn hashed over his different notions of service—service to his family and service to his ideals. Going Special Forces probably meant Vietnam and at least a year away from his wife and their eleven-month-old daughter, Wendy. On the other hand, just about any regular Army assignment would keep him stateside and offer a comfortable billet more suited for family life. Volunteering also meant further delay to the long-awaited payoff of finally becoming a medical doctor. It had been a long and grueling course of study, and the debts had indeed piled up. Why not just do his two years, then slip into a lucrative private practice that would finally offer his family the financial stability they deserved? And, of course, there was the very real possibility that serving in Special Forces—at the "tip of the spear"—might mean Hunter would be killed in action, leaving Carolyn without a husband and Wendy without a father. For all these reasons, she tearfully begged him not to do it. But for Hunter, the True Believer, there really was no choice in the matter. He was powerless to resist the formative experiences of his youth. Like so many of the citizen-soldiers his family had produced over the years, it was now his turn to step up, and so he said goodbye to his wife and baby daughter and embarked on the road to war.[34]

First came the Basic Officer Leader Course, and then the three-week Basic Airborne Course, at Fort Benning, Georgia. It was there, known colloquially as "Jump School," that in October 1964 he earned his silver jump wings and was even selected as the course's outstanding officer graduate. From Benning, it was on to Fort Bragg, North Carolina, and six months of Special Warfare School. Upon graduation from SWC, Hunter and his newly minted SF troopers faced their final test: Cherokee Trail. Twelve-man teams were required to make night jumps into the swamps of the Florida Everglades and then spend the next three weeks being pursued by the 82nd Airborne Division. This allowed the green troopers to put all their training into practice: escape and evasion, survival, hit and run raids on "enemy" positions, and so on. By the time Hunter had completed the operation, he had become a full-fledged trooper of Fort Bragg's 7th Special Forces Group (Airborne). And yet, he soon discovered that "full-fledged" merely meant that he had met Special Forces' minimum training requirements. There were two distinct castes within Special Forces. Newbies like himself who, while young and physically capable, had light to nonexistent combat résumés. And then there were the grizzled hard-chargers of old. Those men who'd jumped into France and Korea, who wore Purple Hearts, Silver Stars, and Combat Infantryman Badges upon their chests. Who, wizened and gray, still stood on the front lines of their nation's wars every day. In short, these were the professionals, the men who'd dedicated their lives to soldiering.[35]

Although he had donned his crisp new Green Beret that bore the Special Forces' flash, Hunter had no illusions about his place in this new universe. He was a temporary citizen-soldier, with one foot in the world of medicine and the other in combat arms. He would need to watch, learn from, and lean on these professionals if he were to survive the coming year in Vietnam. Yes, he was technically a member of the SF brotherhood, but he knew in reality that he was a man apart, so it was perhaps fitting that when he embarked for Vietnam in July 1965, he did so alone. A solitary figure in the cavernous belly of a C-130 transport plane, bound for what, he did not know.[36]

Wright

By the time Wright's flare ship mission had climbed into the gloom and headed south for Plei Me, they could already see the battle glowing on the horizon. Distant flashes, like heat lightning, flickered in the night sky. Wright's enhanced "Hog" gunship was an especially heavily armed variant of Bell's standard UH-1B Iroquois Huey, featuring the XM-3 Subsystem, four 2.75-inch rocket pods mounted in pairs along the chopper's sides, normally twelve rockets to a pod. There was also a pair of flex-mounted 7.62mm machine guns on each side, twin M-60s for the door gunners, and a nose-mounted 40mm grenade launcher. The "Blooper," as it was known, was housed in a power-operated flexible turret and boasted a potent anti-personnel fragmentation projectile. It was rare at the time for a Hog to be outfitted with both the launcher and rocket pods, but it offered added punch to a gunship. Unfortunately, the launcher's low rate of fire and muzzle velocity left a lot to be desired. Getting the Blooper's slow-moving projectiles on target involved a steep learning curve. The copilot, who controlled the sighting mechanism and fired the weapon, needed to lead his target by a considerable margin to have any hope of hitting home. Wright and his fellow pilots often joked that the Blooper's projectiles were so slow that the choppers risked outrunning them and being shot down by their own rounds. What's worse, the original 40mm ammo trays were designed to carry only twenty or thirty rounds. Luckily, Wright's door gunner Jim Varney worked with the crew chief to rig up a 75-rounder. But the added weight of the larger tray and all that extra ammo—not to mention the Blooper itself—cut in half the number of rockets his Hog could carry. For Wright, the tradeoff was far from worth it. And he would need every bit of firepower he could get on this night.[37]

The same went for Plei Me's defenders on the ground below. At about 0030 hours, the communists launched their first big push to breach the camp's outer perimeter. Aside from the limited gun support that Wright's two-ship fire team would soon provide, the first heavy close air support strikes were still hours away. Camp defenders were on their own. The initial thrusts came from the north and northwest, but soon nearly every section of the camp's perimeter was under heavy pressure. NVA sappers, armed with satchel charges and Bangalore torpedoes, stormed the wire along with communist infantrymen of the 2nd Battalion, 33rd Regiment. From well-prepared positions as close as 275 meters from the outer perimeter, battalion gunners laid down withering small arms and machine gun covering fire.[38]

A long metal pipe packed with explosives, the Bangalore was a simple but highly effective weapon for blowing holes through defensive positions—if enemy soldiers could get close enough to use them. Indeed, many sappers were cut down well before they reached their mark, their torn and blasted bodies piling up by the score beyond the wire. The camp's own machine guns were literally melting under the strain of cyclic fire, as bullets tumbled wildly from the red-glowing barrels. But communist soldiers seemed to be in good supply this night, as they came in wave after wave, clad in khaki and pith, the uniform of the North.

Soon, the Bangalores began to strike home, as whole sections of concertina wire simply disappeared in great cascades of fire, mud, and shrapnel. By 0110 hours, NVA troops had clawed their way inside the camp's wire barriers to the south, east near the main gate, and to the northwest near that section's heavy machine gun corner bunker. Two attempts were made to blast through the camp's main gate. Both were thrown back, but the communists were especially keen to overrun any and all of Plei Me's .50 caliber machine gun emplacements situated at the corners of the camp's triangular layout. Having pushed closest to the northwest corner bunker, the communists for the moment concentrated their efforts there. NVA gunners blasted away with B-40 rockets and 57mm recoilless rifles, pummeling the fortified position into a smoldering wreck. Still, the defenders rallied and held on, inflicting grievous losses in the process. At last, the onrushing wave of NVA troops broke and rolled back.[39]

But even though the northwest corner bunker had held for the moment, the NVA's first concerted attempt to overrun the camp had left Plei Me's defenders battered and bruised. The medical dispensary, communications bunker, and ammo storehouse had all been knocked out during the early barrage of Soviet-made 82mm mortars and other enemy fire. Everywhere, the evidence of incoming was plain to see. Shredded sandbags and blasted ramparts intermingled with those pockmarked buildings that still stood. And it wasn't just NVA bodies that were stacked up like cordwood. While Moore and his handful of SF troopers had so far managed to escape injury, the first hours had taken a terrible toll on the Jarai-Montagnards manning the trench lines. Dozens had already been killed and wounded, both inside the camp and in the outlying pickets and the southern outpost. And the NVA were just getting started.[40]

Wright's team had arrived on station at about 0050 hours and set up orbit northeast of the camp where enemy ground fire seemed the lightest. He then contacted Plei Me and asked where he was most needed. "We sure could use some ammo down here," crackled a voice over his headset. But Wright couldn't help them there. There would be no slicks into Plei Me tonight. But he could rain down a torrent of fire and steel on advancing NVA troops. As the flare chopper began sprinkling illumination flares from on high, casting the camp in flickering pale light, Wright made several passes to get the lay of the land. He quickly spotted at least three particularly hot spots, the muzzles of .51 caliber machine guns flashing white-orange as NVA gunners poured fire into the camp. The worst seemed to be coming from south of Plei Me, near the camp's 1,500-foot-long dirt airstrip. Wright banked hard and began saturating NVA positions with 2.75-inch rockets and 40mm fragmentation shells, homing in on the enemy muzzle flashes. The dark earth below erupted in billowing fireballs as Wright made his gun run, but still the communist gunners blazed away from their slit trenches, glowing streaks of green tracers raking the camp's defenders. Plei Me was going to need more firepower.[41]

The first step came at about 0340 hours when Howard Pierson's C-123 flare ship finally appeared overhead. Pierson set up orbit and got a situation report from the camp as he began deploying his own magnesium flares. About ten minutes later, the first flight of A1-E fighter-bombers arrived on station. Now the tac-air effort would really ramp up. Indeed, the Douglas A1-E Skyraider was uniquely suited for its close air support role in Vietnam. Affectionately nicknamed the Spad in "honor" of the old French biplane of the same name, the moniker was a tongue-in-cheek nod to the flying anachronism that was the Skyraider: a prop-driven, World War II relic still clinging to life and purpose in a supersonic age.[42] But prop plane or not, the Skyraider was no dud. Originally designed as a carrier-based torpedo/dive bomber for the US Navy in the waning days of World War II, the Skyraider was a powerful workhorse. It was built around a massive 2,500-horsepower radial engine—the same Wright R-3350 Duplex-Cyclone used to power Boeing's colossal B-29 Superfortress. At the time, this ranked the Skyraider as the most powerful single-seat, propeller-driven combat plane on earth, capable of hauling up to twenty-seven thousand pounds of fuel and ordnance. This was roughly equivalent to the capacity of the storied—and much larger—four-engine B-17 Flying Fortress.[43]

Typical armaments for a Skyraider in Vietnam included four under-wing 20mm autocannons; four 250 or two 500-pound bombs that could be arrayed in a combination of napalm and cluster ordnance; and two under-wing 2.75-inch rocket packs, nineteen shots apiece to complete the ensemble.[44] And while its 321-miles-per-hour top speed was less than impressive for the jet age, the Skyraider's potent, torque-filled engine ensured that a skilled pilot could turn the aircraft on a dime. Finally, its enormous fuel tank and 1,500-mile range meant that the Spad could linger "low and slow" over a target for hours, not an option for fast-movers like the F-100 or F-105 Thunderchief. Indeed, it was just this combination of heavy weaponry, maneuverability, and staying power that rendered the Skyraider such a deadly threat to enemy ground forces.[45]

Shortridge got on the radio and coordinated with the incoming Skyraider pilots, with the first tac-air strikes commencing about twenty minutes later. But the situation was dicey. A blanket of low, heavy cloud cover had settled over the area, requiring Pierson to orbit the camp at a lower-than-normal altitude as he rained flares to light the way for the A1-Es. Often, the Skyraiders and Pierson couldn't even see each other in the murk as the fighter-bombers cut through the clouds to make their attack runs. Below, the NVA were still pushing hard against the southern leg of the camp. Shortridge directed the Skyraiders to bring down their ordnance as close to the perimeter wire as possible to staunch the flow of enemy assault waves. He radioed a warning to the base. "Get some cover, get in the bunkers. We're gonna put some stuff in close," he said, as the pair of Skyraiders, engines roaring like buzz saws, dove to unleash a torrent of napalm and cluster munitions all along the southern edge of the camp. But as good as the coordination was between Shortridge and the A1-Es, it was still night and the weather conditions poor. Concern for the safety of those in the camp meant that tac-air could bring its airstrikes only so close. The NVA knew this, so they resisted the all-too-human instinct to flee the murderous rain of fire and steel from on high and instead pushed even closer to the camp. While this tactic of "hugging the belt" of defenders may have spared the assault teams the worst of the airstrikes, the corpses still piled up. Here and there, body parts clung to the wire in burnt and bloody chunks. Beyond, the reserve elements of Lt. Col. Vũ Sắc's 33rd NVA Regiment had it even worse. Held a little farther out, they suffered egregious casualties at the hands of US airpower.[46]

Nevertheless, the appearance overhead of flare and tac-air assets had attracted the attention of communist gunners. The Skyraiders, who'd so far dealt out serious punishment, were now drawing their own share of fire. On one gun run, an A1-E was met by heavy machine gun fire from prepared positions near the camp. As the NVA gunner's green tracers arced toward him, the pilot pivoted and dove on the .51 caliber nest, unleashing a hail of 20mm cannon fire. But each time the Skyraider dove, he was met by return fire. It took four gun runs to finally silence the big NVA weapon.[47]

Thus, the fight ebbed and flowed over the next two hours, each side delivering its blows, neither giving an inch. Then, at about 0600 hours, the NVA decided to give the northern bunker another go. This time, they brought the heavier fire of the 75mm recoilless rifle, likely a Chinese-made Type 52, to bear on the position. Originally designed as an antitank weapon in World War II, the recoilless rifle was experiencing new life in Vietnam as a superlative bunker buster. But despite the bigger gun's more powerful punch, the partially destroyed corner blockhouse continued to hold, as defenders in nearby trenches poured fire into the NVA position. At some point during the previous few hours, the CIDG families that normally resided in the Montagnard long houses just east of camp flooded through the main gate during a lull in fighting. The women and children moved right into the gun trenches with their husbands and fathers and would continue to live there throughout the siege. It was a good thing they moved when they did, for about two hours later, NVA sappers once again made an all-out effort to blow the main gate on the camp's east side. And as before, the beleaguered Special Forces troopers and Montagnards stiffened, throwing back the latest assault with heavy small-arms and machine gun fire. More NVA bodies stacked up beyond the wire. While Moore had had his doubts, it appeared that both he and Plei Me would survive its night under siege. But what would the day bring? Would the VC, as they had so many times in the past, simply melt away in the light of day and its promise of ever-more-punishing close air strikes? Or would they stay and fight? The answers were not long in coming.[48]

Hunter

The sun was not yet up when Hunter heard the *whump whump whump* of the Huey's rotor blades pounding the early morning air. The chopper, piloted by Maj. Louis Mizell of the 2nd platoon, 498th Medical Company out of Camp Holloway, settled onto its skids, and Hunter heaved aboard his medical bag and M16 rifle. Mizell had gotten word that Plei Me was surrounded and had casualties that needed immediate evacuation. Platoon commander Maj. Steven N. Kash balked, insisting that Plei Me was too hot at present to risk a medevac. Mizell eventually won the argument but quickly wondered whether that was such a good thing. There were, after all, very good reasons for not trying to land a chopper in the middle of a firefight. "I can still remember the knot in my stomach as we were on the way out to the helicopter," he later wrote. "I think if I hadn't been walking, my knees would have probably said 'hello' to each other." Still, he had a plan for getting in and out, and it was as bold as it was simple. A few miles outside Plei Me, he would drop his Huey to tree-top level, then skim nap-of-the-earth at full throttle to avoid enemy fire. At the last possible second, Mizell planned to throw his ship into a radical flare to bleed off airspeed and hit his landing target. All of this, he hoped, would minimize the time enemy gunners had to target his chopper.[49]

Hunter climbed inside and saw that the medevac was rigged with three casualty litters. Supply bundles, probably ammunition and additional medical stores, were stacked here and there. It looked like the medevac would double as a slick transport this morning. Good, he thought. Make every trip count. The crew chief handed him a headset so he could hear what was going on over the deafening, high-decibel whine of the chopper's Lycoming T53 turboshaft engine. And then they were up and off into the lightening sky. Over the headset, the C2 surgeon could hear snippets of the usual stuff. Pilots chatting about the flight. Armed Forces Radio and Tony Bennett crooning, *"I Left My Heart in San Francisco."* Hunter settled in for the flight. A short while later, with the sun now peaking over the horizon, the Special Forces doctor looked out the open side hatch and saw that two gunships had suddenly appeared alongside the medevac. He hadn't expected a gunship escort today. It was the Crocodiles from the 119th.

Wright and Macklin had returned to Holloway at about 0430 hours to refuel and rearm. Wright's ship had also taken several hits from ground fire and had to be switched out. That left the crews a few minutes to catch a hurried breakfast at the commissary before heading back to Plei Me. The cafeteria was already a beehive of activity as the crews prepared to depart for their mission to the coast. Early morning flights meant even earlier breakfasts. You ate fast—if you had time to eat at all. Knowlton, the copilot on Macklin's ship, found a seat and hunkered down for a quick bite. He was joined a few minutes later by 1st Lt. Jerry Riches, a section leader in command of four Huey slicks bound for Bong Son.

"What do you have going today?" Riches asked, pulling up a chair.

"Gotta link up with a medevac going into Plei Me and run escort," Knowlton replied. The pilot said that the camp had been under attack but didn't mention that he'd already been flying gun support for the last several hours. After all, it was nothing special. That was simply the job when you were on the standby fire team.[50]

Riches, who'd been with the company since April, knew all about the Special Forces camps. For the most part, the Viet Cong had cut the roads out to the remote outposts, so resupply by units like the 119th was really the only option for maintaining the camps. The pilots and SF troopers had built a sort of friendly, symbiotic relationship. Slick pilots' ash-and-trash missions kept the camps stocked with just about everything they needed. The troopers repaid the favor whenever they could. For example, when Riches first arrived at Holloway, he'd reported to the unit armorer for weapon issue. He was handed a .45 caliber pistol and seven rounds of ammunition. Riches knew that he would be operating in Indian Country, and that crash landings in hostile territory were very likely.

"Well, where's my rifle?" Riches asked, incredulous.

"Sorry, lieutenant," came the reply. "You don't get one. We don't have enough to go around."

"You gotta be kidding me," Riches said. "I can throw this thing better than I can shoot somebody with it." The enlisted man could only shrug. It was the best he could do. The next time Riches knew he'd be flying out to one of the isolated SF camps, he made it a point to take along a little something extra. Aside from the usual mail and supplies, his crew chief had managed to scrounge up three or four cases of cold beer from the mess hall. Later, the chopper settled onto its skids at the SF camp. After he'd handed over the beer, Riches told the trooper, "If you happen to find an extra rifle out here, pick it up for me, will you?" The sergeant grinned. "I've got one right now." He disappeared and came back a few minutes later with a .30 caliber M1 carbine. Not the shiny new M16 everybody was using, but it was still a lot better than a pistol. Riches would later acquire a .45 caliber M3 "grease gun" before finally being issued an M16 some months later.[51]

Back in the Holloway commissary, Riches and Knowlton said their goodbyes and were off just as quickly as they'd met, each with a mission to accomplish this morning. Now, rearmed and refueled, and with a fresh ship for Wright, the Crocodiles lifted off once more, this time for the rendezvous point with their medevac.[52]

⸙

The camp came into view about a half an hour later. It was about 0730 hours, and the sun was now up. Long, wraith-like columns of black smoke curled into the skies above Plei Me and the surrounding hills. Hunter heard the pilot get on frequency with the camp, their escorts, and Shortridge. As dawn broke, Pierson's flareship was no longer needed, so he'd dropped Shortridge back at Pleiku. The FAC then simply climbed into his 0-1 Bird Dog and headed back to Plei Me. But it wasn't easy. Shortridge, call sign "Baron 15," had never experienced heavy combat, and this was already shaping up to be his first big battle since arriving earlier that summer. Ground fire ebbed and flowed from desultory to death-dealing. It had been bad enough in Pierson's mammoth C-123, but now he was in his slow-moving, thin-skinned Bird Dog, with no armaments to shoot back except a few white phosphorous rockets used to mark targets. The enemy, even in full daylight and at the mercy of US airpower, was not slinking away as usual. If anything, their attacks had become even more determined over the last few hours. It was, in Shortridge's words, "scary."[53]

But he'd been the first on station. He was a senior FAC at Pleiku, so Plei Me really was becoming *his* battle. Technically, Shortridge controlled only Air Force assets, but every service that entered his airspace coordinated with him, finding out where the heaviest enemy fire was coming from, what airstrikes had been laid on, etc. Using a simple grease pen, the FAC jotted down on his Bird Dog's Plexiglas windows the various aircraft and sorties he had lined up. Daylight had brought many more CAS options into play. Now, Shortridge had at his disposal F-100 Super Sabers, more advanced F-105 Thunderchiefs, B-57 Canberra tactical bombers, and more. As the battle wore on, he'd sometimes have strike planes "stacked up" as high as forty thousand feet. And this didn't include all manner of helicopters and fixed-wing resupply aircraft moving through his airspace. It was a life-and-death balancing act of controlled chaos. Give the green light to a C-7 transport plane to make his supply drop at the wrong time, and Caribou and crew might be roasted alive in a friendly napalm strike. Indeed, this was becoming his fight, his trial by fire. And he intended to meet the challenge. If the communists wanted to stay and take a beating, he would be more than happy to oblige them.[54]

But first he had to get the medevac in and out safely. It would be the first into Plei Me since the siege had begun some fifteen hours earlier. Having already used up his white phosphorus rockets, Shortridge would have to find another way to mark the targets for the F-105 fighter-bombers loitering overhead. Then he remembered the dozen or so smoke grenades he carried. Not optimal, but there was no time for a trip back to Pleiku and more Willie Pete. "Hold up," Shortridge's voice crackled over the headsets in the medevac and escort choppers. "We're bringing in napalm. Wait for the planes to clear before making your run into the camp." And with that, Shortridge banked his Bird Dog and careened laterally across the camp's axis, lobbing smoke grenades from the side window to mark targets surrounding the camp. White puffs of smoke began dotting the landscape, and Hunter felt Mizell pull back on the throttle. Moments later, a flight of Thunderchiefs screamed in like silver bolts from on high, canisters of napalm erupting in a two-thousand-degree deluge of jellied fire all along NVA positions ringing the camp. Mizell's voice piped over the headset. "When they make their last run, we'll follow the fighter-bombers in."[55]

The Thuds made two more flaming passes before rocketing away in a swirling vortex of jet wash and afterburner. Over his headset, Hunter could hear the voice from Plei Me. "Whatever you do, don't come in from the South. It's murder." Wright, who'd been flying support for the camp all night, had relayed roughly the same instructions when his fire team had rendezvoused with Mizell earlier. They would approach from the northeast and avoid at all costs the antiaircraft hornets' nest southwest of the camp. Mizell spotted his target ahead. The troopers had popped an M18 smoke grenade, its yellow smoke curling upward to mark the landing zone (LZ). Normally, they'd use the helipad near the front gate or the dirt airstrip along the camp's southern leg. Both were out of the question today. Instead, Moore's troopers had chosen a makeshift landing zone between two buildings on the camp's north side. It was the best they could do. The medevac's door gunners on each side racked their M60s. Hunter felt the chopper throttle up. Suddenly, the medevac and escorts swooped to the deck like birds of prey, as Mizell poured on the speed. Hugging the earth, the pilot knew that the lower you were and the faster you went, the harder it was for enemy gunners to draw a bead on you.[56]

For Hunter, time seemed to compress and expand simultaneously, as the next several seconds played out in both slow motion and fast forward. A series of vivid snapshots. Through the open door, the greens and browns of the Central Highlands rushing past in a blur, the chopper no more than fifty feet off the ground. Over the headset, one of the pilots let loose with a raucous, *yeeee-haaww!* as the chopper raced between two lines of trees, rotors chopping away at branches on either side, inches away. Above the whining din of the engine, Hunter suddenly realized that they were taking fire, as the faint snaps and pops of enemy rounds ripped the air around them. A split second later something walloped the chopper's Plexiglas windshield like a hammer, but neither pilot was wounded. Several more small-arms rounds punched through the Huey's skin near the door. Both door gunners blazed away with their M60s. Hunter tried to make himself small. He wasn't wearing a flak vest. He never did. An unspoken ethos of the Special Forces. But he envied the door gunners' vests on this day. The escort gunships, a little above and behind, were laying down a wall of suppressive fire. The ships' rocket pods flickered and smoked as they saturated the surrounding hills.[57]

All at once, the medevac was over the camp. Per his plan, Mizell pulled the ship into a violent flare to slow the chopper and not overshoot the LZ. The medevac pilot had intended his low, fast approach to reduce his exposure time prior to landing, but the radical, last-second flare had brought his chopper up too high, perhaps as much as two hundred feet, an engraved invitation for NVA gunners. Wright instantly knew that something had gone wrong. "He was just a standing target there," Wright recalls. "He just ballooned up and was hovering there all by himself and trying to get down. He was very, very fortunate that he didn't get knocked out of the sky."[58]

One reason he didn't may have been the actions of his escorts. Normally, Wright's Hogs would've broken off their pattern and turned east once the medevac was safely on the ground. It was a pattern they'd already run several times over the previous hours. But with Mizell up so high, Wright knew he'd have to overshoot the camp to draw away enemy fire and keep him covered. And for the flight leader, there was never any question. The very reason his Crocodiles were out here this morning was to see the medevac safely into camp. He wasn't about to break off and leave him exposed, so Wright thundered past to the southwest—and right into the teeth of the NVA's heaviest antiaircraft fire. Macklin, his wingman, followed. Both pilots poured suppressive fire to cover Mizell, then banked sharply to the left, desperate to get to the east of camp and relative safety. Several rounds of small-arms fire peppered Wright's ship, but none hit anything vital. Macklin, trailing to the left, wasn't so lucky. He'd run right into the path of a 20mm cannon.[59]

"I'm taking heavy fire from the right rear!" Macklin radioed, as the massive rounds tore baseball-sized holes through his ship. Reflexively, Wright tried to lay down some suppressive fire, but by now he was pointed in the wrong direction. He leaned into his left turn, straining to muscle his chopper even tighter to get back to Macklin. It was too late. By the time he'd gotten around, Wright saw to his horror that his wingman's ship, shredded and burning, was already careening to earth. It exploded in a terrible plume of flame and smoke upon impact, just off the runway south of camp.[60]

For a split second, Wright could only look on in mind-numbed shock. Then he snapped to and swooped down, frantic to see if any of his friends had survived. As he drew near, he could see scores of khaki-clad NVA boiling out of their trenches and swarming the burning chopper, already eager to get at what was inside. He unleashed a torrent of 2.75-inch rockets and 7.62mm machine gun fire on the gathering throng of NVA troops. In desperation, Wright made three passes, sometimes as low as twenty feet and less than sixty miles per hour, flames from the burning wreckage scorching his chopper's underbelly. Again, his ship was riddled with holes but miraculously remained viable. But there were no signs of life. His ammunition spent, he finally had to relent and peel off to the northeast and Camp Holloway. The entire tragedy had taken mere minutes to unfold.[61]

Wright was deeply shaken. Four of his comrades-in-arms, his *friends,* gone in an instant. He didn't blame Mizell. One of the unit's most experienced pilots, Wright knew better than most that coming in fast and low represented your best chance of not being shot down. "You go as fast as you can," he said. "It's what you do when you're getting your butt shot off." But he didn't blame himself, either. Shortridge had come on the radio in a fury, incensed that the escorts had gone where he told them not to go. But to Wright, he'd had the better vantage point than the FAC, who was circling at more than two thousand feet above. It was clear to the flight leader that Mizell was vulnerable. Breaking off his pattern and leaving the medevac uncovered was unthinkable. "There's not much else you can do if you're going to cover the dust-off," Wright said. "We weren't going to just let that aircraft go unprotected."[62]

But the toll had been a heavy one. Macklin, twenty-seven, left behind a wife, Margaret, and two children, Jennifer and Jim. Knowlton, twenty-four, and McDonial, thirty, would see their young lives snuffed out far too soon. Making matters worse, Wright had grown especially close to the ship's young crew chief, Racine. They'd known each other prior to Vietnam, when the two had spent time ferrying choppers around the States. Wright knew of Racine's grim apprehension that he would die in Vietnam, and the two had even prayed over it just the day before. "It's in God's hands," Wright told him. "You'll get through it." And yet here they were. Racine, who'd just turned twenty-three in August, would never get to meet the son, whose birth he'd so hoped he would live to see. His baby boy, Mark Allen, was born five days after a father he would never know was shot down and killed in the skies above Plei Me.[63]

Wright keyed his mic. He had to let Maj. Charles W. Mooney, the 119th's commander, know that they'd just lost four of their brothers.

Mooney, who'd taken over command in August, was with the rest of the company over the Mangyang Pass on the way to Bong Son. Wright briefly recounted what had just happened.

"Any survivors?" asked Mooney.

"No, we lost them all," Wright said.

Like the rest of the unit, twenty-six-year-old 1st Lt. Charles Oualline, who commanded a four-ship section of slicks and was the company's intelligence officer, was listening in to the communication. Through the Plexiglas windshield he could see the choppers of the 119th flying a tight "V" formation, rotor blades as close as five feet apart. The pilots always prided themselves on keeping a rock-steady pattern, even under the heaviest of enemy fire. But when Wright's words came across the radio net, they hit like a sledgehammer. And it was in that instant that Oualline saw the entire formation waver and ripple, like it had been buffeted by some foul wind. It was a visible manifestation of what they all felt at that moment. "It was a shock to all of us," he said. Oualline would later fly one of the choppers in a "missing man" formation at Holloway to honor the fallen Croc gunship crew. To be sure, it had been a tough year for the 119th. The company had lost five men during the Viet Cong's 7 February attack on Camp Holloway—including commanding officer Maj. Seyward N. Hall. Nine others had been killed during separate actions in April and June. Such losses always took their toll. And it was especially hard for Oualline, who'd only arrived in July. Until now, none of his comrades had been killed or even seriously wounded, but now they'd lost an entire shipload of his friends at once. This was something very different, indeed.[64]

Minutes earlier, Mizell had managed to wrestle the medevac to earth. Now, waiting for the wounded to be on-loaded, he kept the chopper at full throttle. Anxious seconds ticked by. Being on the ground was a most unnatural place for a helicopter pilot, a period of maximum vulnerability. Every moment brought death that much closer, and few things inspired the "pucker factor" more for an earth-bound pilot than mortars. Sure, a stray bullet could always find its way home, but at least here there were buildings and parapets around for cover. But mortars? They were a different beast altogether. There was a certain capriciousness to them. A feeling that at any given moment, the enemy could drop an 82mm on your head from on high, and there was really not a damned thing you could do about it. You just had to sit there and pray that the war gods were with you, that the shells would land somewhere else today. But when airborne, Mizell had much more control over his fate. He formulated a plan of egress. There was no way he wanted to leave by the same route that he'd come in on. Why give enemy gunners who'd missed you the first time another crack at it? So instead of going back north, he'd head east. The idea was to effect a maximum performance takeoff—a low angle liftoff at the greatest allowable rpms that sacrificed altitude for speed. He just needed enough elevation to clear the low wooden buildings that littered Plei Me's compound. Both pilots would keep their hands on the controls in the event either became incapacitated. Still, it was a dangerous gambit in such tight quarters. Clip one of the buildings with a landing skid, and he and everyone aboard would likely meet a fiery end. But in a battle this hot, there wasn't really much choice.[65]

Meanwhile, Hunter and the crew threw off the supply bundles as fast as they could, while men from the camp scrambled to on-load the wounded. Far more were queued up than the medevac could carry. The chopper's three litters were quickly taken, so casualties were simply stretched out on the floor. Hunter had been to Plei Me before and caught sight of two familiar faces helping to load the wounded. Spc. 4 Dan Shea, twenty-four, a team medic, and Sgt. 1st Class Joe Bailey, twenty-seven, a heavy weapons and intelligence specialist. Both were with Detachment A-217. He did not know Bailey well but had become close with the young medic. The bantam-weight Boston native had graduated from Boston College with an accounting degree in 1963 but decided to fulfill his military obligation before settling into the quotidian of professional life. The appearances of both men, exhausted and bedraggled, told the tale of the night's siege. When the wounded were finally aboard, the three men bent low and ran for the cover of a nearby trench. Fully loaded, Mizell pulled pitch and strained eastward at full power, skimming the rooftops until his speed had exceeded one hundred miles per hour. Only then did he push for altitude. As he cleared the camp, Mizell felt himself reflexively crouch down in his seat, as if that would somehow make him a smaller target. It was a silly notion, he would later write, especially when flying in something as big as a helicopter. But by the time they'd reached the tree line to the east, the danger had largely passed. Mizell banked his ship north and headed for Pleiku. It was just about 0900 hours.[66]

Back on the ground, Hunter, Shea, and Bailey crouched in their trench while enemy sniper fire cracked above their heads. Here and there, tendrils of black smoke rose from the camp, testaments to the battle of the previous night. And the steady *tack tack tack* of automatic weapons fire signaled that the battle was not yet over. Hunter surveyed his trench mates. Like the camp itself, it was clear that the SF troopers had had a tough go of it. Just then, Hunter caught Bailey eyeing the slender tree that served as the camp's makeshift flagpole. A South Vietnamese flag of yellow and red snapped in the morning breeze. Like all Special Forces camps at the time, Plei Me was ostensibly under the command of the host nation. This was, of course, a facile pretense. But appearances had to be maintained—just not today. "If we're going to get zapped," Bailey spat, "at least let's get zapped under our own flag." With that, the Lebanon, Tennessee, native scrambled from the trench and into the nearby team house. The staff sergeant reappeared a few moments later carrying a small souvenir American flag, perhaps four by six inches. He pulled down the South Vietnamese flag and ran up Old Glory in its place. Above, the tiny flag fluttered with the wind. But Bailey's movements had caught the eye of enemy gunners. He hustled back to the trench, as the shots kicked up clods of dirt around him. Now in full daylight, it was becoming clear that the VC were not ready to quit the battlefield as they'd done so many times in the past.[67]

A short while later, Moore, the twenty-four-year-old camp commander, appeared at the edge of the trench. He nodded to the thick line of black smoke that marked the Hog's crash site. The gunship that had run escort for Hunter's medevac had gone down just off the camp's dirt airstrip to the south. "There may be survivors," he said to the men assembled. "We need to go out." A quick plan was formulated. Moore would lead Bailey and a squad of about ten Montagnard strikers through the outer perimeter wire, and Shea would come along in case anyone on the chopper needed medical attention. With three Americans going out on the rescue mission, this left Plei Me with only seven SF troopers plus Hunter to hold the Montagnards together. The C2 surgeon and a couple of the troopers would stay behind with the 'Yards in this section and provide covering fire for the rescue team. The remaining A-217 team members were either interspersed to bolster the Montagnards's courage on the other defensive walls, or in the commo shack maintaining radio contact with tac-air and resupply assets. Heavy weapons specialist Staff Sgt. Robert T. Sloan continued to man the 4.2-inch mortar in the pit.[68]

But getting outside the camp wasn't as easy as simply opening a gate. The outer line of active defense was ringed with concertina wire. Beyond, the troopers had razed every bush and tree to create clear fields of fire all the way to the scrub forest and elephant grass that ringed the camp. The resulting "no-man's-land" was transformed into a maze of tangle-foot wire, Claymore mines, and trip flares. Moore's team would first have to pick its way through that before trying to reach the chopper. After finally negotiating the obstacle field, the team reached the edge of the dirt airstrip. Farther out, they could see the burning hulk of the downed chopper and began to edge toward it. The three Americans, Montagnards in tow, advanced on a line, Shea in the middle with Moore to his left and Bailey on the right. The men knew it was dangerous to try to reach the chopper crew. But, as Bailey had told Shea moments before, "They came in to try to help us. It's the least we can do to go out and see if we can help them." Just then, the tree line beyond exploded in a cascade of enemy small-arms and machine gun fire. They'd walked right up on a hornets' nest of carefully concealed bunkers and machine gun emplacements. Bailey was hit immediately. Everyone else dropped to the dirt and clawed for what cover they could find, as the barrage of enemy fire tore at the air and earth around them. Shea moved toward Bailey to render aid. The SF trooper had already struggled to one knee and shouldered his rifle. But before Shea could get to him, Bailey was hit a second time. *Someone's got a very good bead on him,* thought Shea. The medic surveyed the trooper. He'd taken a hit to the abdomen and had a sucking chest wound as well. Shea began artificial respiration. Enemy rounds continued to pluck at the earth while the medic worked. A few of the strikers, not bothering with an ordered retreat, bolted one-by-one back the way they'd come, taking casualties along the way.[69]

Back at the perimeter, Hunter and the others poured on covering fire, trying to suppress the enemy fusillade coming from the brush and around the chopper. Above the din, Moore yelled for Shea to get Bailey, alive but utterly incapacitated, back to the compound. The captain called for white phosphorus mortars to screen the retreat, but none were available. Moore then sent two of the remaining Montagnards to help Shea carry the stricken trooper. But before the three could lift Bailey off the ground, he was hit a third time. Moments later, Shea was bowled over as a 7.62mm rifle round obliterated the underside of his right forearm. Nevertheless, the young medic calmly struggled to his feet and pressed on, even as enemy rounds cracked around him. Meanwhile, Moore worked to cover the retreat, popping 5.56mm rounds toward the enemy muzzle flashes. Slowly and steadily, Shea dragged his wounded buddy by inches until the two had reached the relative safety of the perimeter wire. Hunter and the others met the wounded men at the concertina and pulled them through.[70]

The physician took one look at Shea and surmised that his wound was not life-threatening. It was Bailey that had him most concerned. Shea tried to apply pressure, but the SF trooper was bleeding profusely from three entrance wounds to his chest, blood pooling in his mouth. The NCO was already fading in and out of consciousness. Hunter rolled him over and knew instantly that it was over. Massive exit wounds. Bubbling lung tissue. Exposed ribs. Shards of bone fragments. "There's no way I can stop this bleeding," he thought. "It's just disastrous." All he could do now was try to comfort him. Hunter locked eyes with the dying man, took his hand, and moved in close. "It's going to be okay. I'm here." Bailey took a final, gurgling breath, shuddered, and then was gone. The Kentucky native, who would've turned twenty-eight in December, left behind a wife and young daughter. Hunter held his hand for a moment more, then went to release it so he could shift his attention to Shea. But he couldn't let go. Terror suddenly welled up within the physician. For one horrifying moment he believed that he'd somehow become linked to the dead man, that he himself would be dragged along with Bailey over the threshold to that undiscovered country known as death. For all the wounded and dying that he'd already treated in Vietnam, Hunter had never experienced such a moment. And it shook him deeply. But then he saw that it was only Bailey's congealing blood, fibrous and clotted, that had bound their hands. He pulled free and turned to the wounded medic.[71]

Hunter examined Shea's blasted right forearm. As he suspected, the wound was not life-threatening but had done grievous damage nonetheless. The muscle, nerves, and tendons on the bottom half of Shea's forearm had been blown away. But the bullet had missed the large bones of the lower arm. And that was fortunate, for it would help the surgeon stop the bleeding and lessen the likelihood of infection. Hunter cleaned and bandaged the wound, administered a tetanus shot, and handed the wounded trooper a few pain pills. He also gave him a handful of antibiotics with instructions to take them over the next few days. And that was it. Shea was on his own. Normally, a wounded American could expect to be medevaced. But not here, and not now. It was simply too dangerous to risk another flight in. The burning chopper south of camp served as grim testament to that fact. Until the security situation improved, Hunter resolved that there would be no more medevacs into Plei Me. And after all, weren't such judgment calls a large part of the rationale for why he'd been flown in the first place?[72]

"You know, Dan," Hunter told his friend. "I'm not going to medevac you."

"That's okay," replied Shea. "I'm safer here."[73]

"But we both kind of knew that that wasn't true either," Hunter would later say. "At that point, people were beginning to realize that we were in danger of being overrun."[74]

As if to further drive home the point, Moore had finally crept his way back into the compound, and he had come bearing souvenirs from the battlefield. With full daylight and tac-air prowling the skies above Plei Me, Moore took the opportunity to call his troopers into the team house to show them what he'd found. In the center of the room sat a simple wooden mess table draped in a plastic oilcloth printed with brightly colored fruit. It reminded Hunter of his grandma's kitchen back on the farm in Kansas. Moore plopped down what he'd found. A few kit bags. Some gear webbing. A leather pistol holster. For the big finish, he produced a brass belt buckle with a large red star at its center. Moore swept his hand across the array as if to say, "And there's a lot more where this came from." He looked at the men assembled. "There's VC, and then there's *VC*," he said wryly. "And we've got the *VC*. This is the NVA."[75]

"That's when we began to realize the perilousness of our situation," Hunter later recalled. "That's when we knew that, for Plei Me, the 'Black Pajama War' was over."[76]

1st Lt. Robert Berry

A few hours earlier and about twenty-five kilometers to the northeast, 1st Lt. Robert H. Berry stood watching near the junction of Highway 14 and Provincial Route 5 as one helicopter after another thundered overhead toward the southwest. The chopper pilots were using the road as a visual reference as they flew in the direction of Plei Me. *That's a lot of activity,* he thought. The A-217 executive officer, who had turned twenty-two just a month before, was three days into a recon sweep north and east of camp. On 17 October, he and Sgt. 1st Class Jimmie Beech, the team's intelligence sergeant, had taken a company of about eighty-five CIDG fighters on a patrol mission to investigate several recent intelligence reports that the Viet Cong were moving in strength to the north and that Plei Me may be the target. But so far, "Operation Chuong Duong 40" had been a bust. It had been the same story since June: reports would flood in about heavy enemy activity in the area, the camp would send out sweeps to see what's what, and then . . . nothing. The patrol had been out of contact with the camp since nearly the beginning of the sweep. The PRC-10 FM radio they'd been issued just didn't have the range. Even with the AT-271/PRC "long antenna" attached, maximum range was only about nineteen kilometers under optimal conditions. Not that anyone relished using the long antenna, anyway. Damned thing was a magnet for sniper fire. The time had come to head back, so the troopers had pulled the CIDG into a tight perimeter the night before and camped atop the hill overlooking the road junction. They moved out at about 0630 hours, but Berry called a halt when he saw all the helicopter activity. If something big was in the works, the last thing he wanted was to have his patrol chewed up by friendly fire as he moved down the road.[77]

Such was the life of a Special Forces trooper on the edge of nowhere. The military was in his blood; that much was true. The San Diego native had spent his young life following his father from one duty station to another. The elder Berry began as a Marine but later switched to the Air Force so he could work on jet engines. But Berry hadn't chosen *this* life. The Army had chosen it for him. Indeed, he'd begun his military career as an enlisted intelligence specialist. And after graduating Officer Candidate School in 1963, had asked to return to that career branch. But the Army needed bodies for its unconventional operations, so here he was. *At least it was Airborne*, he'd thought at the time. Berry deployed to Vietnam as part of 5th Special Forces Group in April, arriving at Plei Me a month later. This was actually his second tour in-country. He'd done an abbreviated stint of just under three months the year before. But Berry also knew that a Special Forces assignment wasn't exactly "career enhancing." In a time of Cold War, with thousands of Soviet tanks poised to overrun Western Europe, commanding a regular Army infantry company, artillery battery, or armored squadron offered a young officer a much better chance to make his mark. But it was simply in his nature to put maximum effort into whatever assignment he was given. Whether that meant standing athwart the communists at the Fulda Gap or patrolling the wastes of the Central Highlands, he'd give his all to the job.[78]

Berry raised one of the choppers overhead. He was asked to authenticate several times, which in his experience was unusual. *Definitely something big going on,* he thought. The XO thumbed through his codebook, and when the chopper pilot was finally convinced of Berry's identity, he confirmed it: the camp had been hit, and it didn't look like the VC were going away anytime soon. "We're going to be going south down this road," Berry radioed back. "Make sure no one targets us. Out." He'd made up his mind. It sounded like the camp could use all the help it could get. And he had eighty-five able-bodied fighters at his disposal. Beech concurred, and the patrol once again set off down Route 5. "Provincial Route 5" was a somewhat grandiose appellation for what essentially was a single-lane dirt track. The road was bracketed on both sides with choking vegetation that looked thick enough to conceal an entire battalion. Ideally, an infantry commander would have deployed screening units off the road, but the jungle was simply too thick. Indeed, one could barely *see* a few feet into the overgrowth, much less move through it. As it stood, they might walk into an ambush at any moment. Berry sent a squad of CIDG forward a short distance to act as a point element. At the very least, it might give the rest of the column a few moments to react. It was the best they could expect given the terrain.[79]

The next several hours passed without incident. Tac-air fighter-bombers were now roaring overhead, having obviously joined the fray at Plei Me. In the distance, the heavy *thumps* of ordnance grew more distinct. Eventually, the road began to rise, and Berry knew they were coming to the hill just north of camp. The column was only about five hundred meters out now. An old French fort, long abandoned, crouched near the top of the hill. Berry was about a hundred meters north of the fort when he suddenly heard the *tack tack tack* of rifle fire erupt forward of the column. It sounded like the point element had run into something. He sprinted forward to see what had happened, but by the time he'd arrived, it was already over. A few enemy casualties were splayed out here and there. To the side, but not off the road itself, Berry spied a makeshift bunker emplacement. It appeared that the ambushers hadn't bothered with the dense foliage to the sides. And it had cost them dearly. His squad of Montagnards had blown right through a very poorly executed ambush, suffering no casualties in the process. Berry let his eyes roam over the dead. They were helmet-less and wore no uniforms save for the dark shirts and trousers common to the peasant guerillas of the Highlands. *Whoever they were,* he thought, *they weren't very well trained.* Berry radioed the camp and told them he was coming in. The patrol walked through the main gate on the camp's east side at about 2130 hours. Incredibly, they had met no further resistance after the attempted ambush near the abandoned fort. Unknown to the Americans at the time, the NVA had been forced to more widely disperse their forces in an attempt to mitigate the punishing close air support strikes. This likely contributed to the ease with which Berry's patrol was able to close into camp.[80]

Maj. Charles A. Beckwith

Back at 5th Group headquarters in Nha Trang, Col. William A. "Bulldog" McKean, head of all US Special Forces in Vietnam, had been working options for getting some help into Plei Me with his counterpart, Maj. Gen. Doan Van Quang, commander of South Vietnamese Special Forces. Detachment A-217's Moore, and the LLDB commander at Plei Me, Capt. Trần Văn Nhân, had actually gotten the ball rolling when the two had sent urgent calls for reinforcements up their respective command chains earlier that morning. The requests were received at II Corps Tactical Zone head-quarters in Pleiku by 0518 hours, but reserve forces were scarce at the moment. The only available ARVN units in the area had been assigned a reserve mission, and II Corps commander Maj. Gen. Nguyen Phouc Vinh Loc was initially reluctant to strip Pleiku's defenses to reinforce Plei Me. Besides, any overland relief force would likely take days to get into the fight. No, at least in the short run, the burden of bolstering the camp would fall on 5th Group. McKean and Quang decided that Project DELTA would be their best bet to quickly reinforce the camp. Begun the previous year, DELTA was a joint venture between US and South Vietnamese Special Forces and specialized in long-range reconnaissance and other missions throughout South Vietnam's uncontrolled, jungle territory. Under the aggressive and mercurial Maj. Charles A. "Chargin' Charlie" Beckwith, thirty-six, DELTA's hallmarks had become mobility and stealth—two essential capabilities if Plei Me were to be quickly and successfully reinforced.[81]

DELTA, along with two companies of the 91st Airborne Ranger Battalion, was at the moment running a recon operation near the coastal hamlet of Phu Cat in support of Operation Than Phong 6, the latest in a series of largescale II Corps missions to root out continuing enemy activity in northern Binh Dinh Province. DELTA's mission was to take place in three phases, with four-man recon teams operating in the rural backcountry to detect and observe Viet Cong activity, locate supply points and storage areas, and call in air strikes and artillery fires when warranted. The two Ranger companies had been recently tasked exclusively as a rapid reaction force for DELTA operations. The plan was to insert the Airborne Rangers by helicopter to exploit any discovered targets or to support the recon teams should they come under attack. From Beckwith's perspective, the mission was especially important because it marked the first time the new arrangement would be tested in the field. He and his senior officers had parked themselves in nearby Qui Nhon to closely monitor the ongoing operations. By morning on 19 October, DELTA and the Rangers had completed Phase I and were standing by to initiate the next phases. But Beckwith and his team would soon discover that there were bigger fish to fry.[82]

Indeed, at 1330 hours on 20 October, Beckwith received the warning order to pull all units back to Qui Nhon in preparation for a move to Pleiku. Two hours later, Beckwith and fourteen hand-picked DELTA troopers, along with the 91st's two companies, had assembled on the Qui Nhon Airfield tarmac and were preparing to board two transports that command had rustled up for the move. The American contingent included Maj. Charles "Tommy" Thompson, Beckwith's executive officer (XO). Thompson was all set to rotate stateside in two weeks. His replacement, Maj. A. J. "Bo" Baker, a hulking but good-natured former University of Arkansas football player, had been in-country only two days and had come along to get his "whistle wet." Beckwith also had along his top enlisted man, Sgt. Maj. Bill DeSoto, a grizzled paratroop veteran of World War II and Korea. Beckwith regarded DeSoto as a man to whom he could trust his very life. The 5th Group sergeant major, John Pioletti, had lobbied to come along, too. Beckwith described Pioletti as a "first-class guy" but worried that there would be hell to pay if anything happened to his CO's "right arm" on his watch. Other senior leadership included Capt. Thomas Pusser, senior adviser to the Airborne Rangers. The team featured several highly experienced NCOs as well. Among them were men like Sgt. Terrence Morrone, another Ranger adviser; Sgt. 1st Class Marion "Mike" Holloway, a recon trooper and heavy weapons specialist; combat medic Spc. 5 Richard P. Loughlin; and Sgt. Ronald "Robbie" Robertson, a communications specialist.[83]

Beckwith took one look at the C-123 and C-130 and nearly balked. Maximum airlift capacity for the Provider was just sixty-seven fully armed troops and ninety-two for the Hercules. Surely, there was no way they could get all 175 men and their equipment aboard and still get safely off the ground. Nevertheless, they packed the bellies of the transports with men "standing on top of each other" and somehow struggled airborne. By 1700 hours, they had landed at New Pleiku Airbase. The question now became how best to get DELTA and the Rangers into the fight. While the unit was offloading its equipment, Beckwith headed off to receive his briefing about what came next. For him, the mission to relieve Plei Me would prove his first true baptism by fire. And it was a test thirteen years in the making.[84]

He'd always seemed destined for martial pursuits. Born in Atlanta in 1929, Beckwith came from a working-class family that owned three trucks and made ends meet by delivering gasoline for the Pure Oil Company. Beckwith's mother raised him alone after his father died when he was just eleven. Standing six feet, two inches tall and two hundred pounds, Beckwith was a broad-shouldered, solidly built man, with a prominent brow and intense, deep-set eyes. He played guard on a football scholarship to the University of Georgia before being offered a tryout with the Green Bay Packers. Apparently, the physical struggle offered by a life in football wasn't enough for Beckwith, who'd also been a Reserve Officer Training Corps (ROTC) cadet at Georgia. He turned down the offer and instead opted for a career in Army combat arms. At twenty-two, he was commissioned a 2nd Lieutenant in 1952 and commanded a rifle company in the waning days of the Korean War before moving on to spend three years with the 82nd Airborne Division. In all, he spent six years in the regular Army before landing with Special Forces at Fort Bragg, North Carolina. His relationship with the 7th Group (Airborne) began as a marriage of convenience: the still-new Special Forces simply needed officers to fill its ranks, while Beckwith wanted a new challenge. He thought he might get it when in 1960 he deployed to Laos as part of Operation White Star (code-named Project Hotfoot), a counterinsurgency effort begun in 1957 to help counter the communist Pathet Lao insurrection. Now a captain, Beckwith's job was to work with other SF troopers to train the Royal Laotian Army, along with fighters from the Hmong and Yao tribes, to conduct guerilla operations against the Pathet Lao, as well as North Vietnamese elements infiltrating south along the Ho Chi Minh Trail. While he managed to get shot at a time or two, Beckwith would later declare that he was still "hungry" for something to really sink his teeth into.[85]

That opportunity came two years later when Beckwith landed an assignment that would not only deeply impact his life but that of US special operations as well. Beckwith was selected for a one-year stint as the exchange officer with the British 22nd Special Air Service (SAS) Regiment, an elite special operations unit founded in 1941. Beckwith was given command of the regiment's 3 Troop, A Squadron. One thing that had always irked Beckwith about the US Special Forces was that its troopers were not assessed and selected in the way he thought was proper. Indeed, reasoned Beckwith, even though he'd been through the same Jump and Special Warfare schools as every other trooper, he still believed that he'd been "handed" his Green Beret simply by virtue of having been assigned to SF. He hadn't, in his eyes, "earned" it. "Now I knew that wasn't right," he would later write. "Men ought to earn the right to wear a distinctive badge." This was the ethos of the SAS, he believed. Beckwith watched as the regiment ran grueling fifteen-week selection courses, comprised of some of the most brutal physical, mental, and emotional challenges possible, and still not admit a *single* candidate. And SAS aspirants typically came from some of the hardest-charging units in the British Army. American Special Forces could use a healthy dose of that, he concluded.[86]

He soon got the chance to see the SAS in action. Beckwith accompanied the regiment to Malaya for counterinsurgency operations against remnants of the communist Malayan National Liberation Army along the Thai-Malay border. Begun in 1948, the Malayan Emergency had officially ended by 1960, but a few stragglers still held on in the backcountry. The British had quickly learned during the Emergency that in a jungle country like Malaya, large, conventional military formations weren't the answer, so 22 SAS had been tapped to lead the way. Regimental operators were completely at home working in small teams and lived in the jungle like the insurgents. Moving freely and living off the land, SAS teams gathered intelligence and stalked the enemy as they saw fit. Twelve years later, Beckwith was getting a taste of what those operators had had to deal with, as the regiment bushwhacked its way through choking, leech-infested jungle that put to shame anything he'd experienced in Laos. The old SAS hands, many of whom had fought here during the height of the Emergency, showed him the tricks of the trade for navigating such terrain. But it was the SAS's Immediate Action Drills that he found especially inspiring. The Brits had devised drills for nearly every possibly combat contingency—and ran them with live ammunition. "I'd never done this in the States," Beckwith later wrote. "It was great!"[87]

Still, the Special Forces captain wasn't impressed with every bit of advice he got from the SAS operators. After several tough days of slogging through the thickest jungle imaginable, Beckwith emerged covered in lacerations, filth, and a days-old beard. As he repaired to a nearby muddy river for a wash and shave, he was warned against it. The key, said the SAS operator, was to build up a thick layer of dirt on one's body to protect against the swarming mosquitos infesting the forest. Beckwith would have none of it, silently questioning the Brits' commitment to hygiene. He dove into the river, washed, shaved, even went for a swim. He felt better than he had in days. But by a week later, he had come down with one of the worst cases of leptospirosis his British doctor had ever seen. A potentially life-threatening bacterial disease, leptospirosis is usually transmitted through contact with contaminated water—just like that muddy river in which he'd chosen to swim. Unable to walk, Beckwith had to be medevac'd from the operation. Another valuable lesson learned.[88]

During his hospital recovery, Beckwith immersed himself in a loaned copy of 1956's *Defeat into Victory*, British Field Marshal William Slim's classic memoir of the Allied recapture of Burma during World War II. But it was Slim's section on the usefulness of small, special tactics units that particularly caught Beckwith's attention. The message he gleaned was this: In certain irregular conflicts, it was absolutely invaluable to have units with the capability of operating deep in hostile territory to disrupt an adversary, gather intelligence, cooperate with indigenous elements, conduct sabotage, and even assassinate enemy leadership. For Beckwith, it was as if a light had been switched on. This ability seemed apparent with 22 SAS. He'd found the Brits to be especially well-trained, tough, resourceful, and willing to undergo the most severe privations in order to accomplish the mission. It was a capability he fervently hoped US Army Special Forces could develop. Not that the SAS was perfect. From his observation, Beckwith believed that the British were often too hurried in their actions and lacked the superior planning capabilities of the US military. The special unit he had in mind would be a hybrid of sorts, combining the tough audaciousness of the SAS with the organizational ability of the Americans. In short, a direct-action special operations unit that was "not only a force of teachers, but a force of doers."[89]

Beckwith returned to Fort Bragg inspired. He'd seen the future of American Special Forces, and it worked. But getting anyone to listen to his ideas was another matter. No one back at 7th Group much cared for what the young captain had to say. Beckwith had crafted a detailed report calling for the development of an SAS-styled unit for Special Forces. He pushed his paper on anyone who might listen, but it went nowhere. He even tried to circumvent Army bureaucracy by sending the report directly to his Georgia senator. That too proved a dead end. Finally, at the end of his rope and seriously considering quitting altogether, Beckwith got a lifeline from one of the few superior officers sympathetic to his idea, Lt. Col. Buzz Miley, commander of 7th Group's B Company. Miley brought Beckwith aboard as his operations officer, where he thrived. When Miley got an appointment to MACV in Vietnam in January 1964, Beckwith was—to his utter shock—offered the job of operations officer for all of 7th Group. Was it some sort of trap, or perhaps a buy-off so he'd finally shut up about his new special operations unit? He didn't know. But as a newly minted major and the ops officer for the entire Group, he now exercised a great deal of influence over training methods.[90]

After getting approval from his superiors, Beckwith set about implementing far more stringent training procedures. First, he emphasized a focus on the fundamentals of infantry tactics, an area he saw as lacking in SF training because many officers had never even commanded conventional units. "To break the rules you need to know what the rules are," he later wrote. "You can't be unconventional until you're conventional first." Beckwith ran squad, platoon, and company-sized exercises, from attacks and retreats to delaying actions and blocking maneuvers. And, harkening back to his SAS experience, Beckwith had the units run the drills using live ammunition. After three months of conventional infantry training, he shifted the men back to irregular warfare. The grueling training regimen culminated in an evade-and-escape exercise in the mountains near Pisgah, North Carolina. Broken down into four-man teams, the troopers were required to hump footlockers full of sandbags up one mountain and down the next, all while being pursued by a rifle company from the 82nd Airborne.

Beckwith was roundly criticized for an exercise both his superiors and many of the men saw as unnecessarily harsh. But to Beckwith, it was a grand stress test for the troopers. How would they handle the adversity? How would it affect team unity? Would they have the fortitude to press through, even when they'd hit the limits of their endurance? These were the questions that aspiring elite operators would need right answers to. Later, while at the US Army's Command and General Staff College at Fort Levenworth, Kansas, Beckwith began to receive letters from some of the men who'd been through the course. Their experiences in the burgeoning war in Vietnam had changed their perspective. "All the time up there we thought you were crazy," wrote one NCO. "I cussed you at the time, but now I realize what we trained for."[91]

Beckwith figured he too would soon get the chance to put that training to the test. But when he volunteered for Vietnam in early 1965, it seemed he would once again be stymied. To his chagrin, Personnel Assignment had slated him as a sector adviser with MACV. What were these people thinking, he wondered. Placing someone with his extensive special operations experience in an advisory role was like using a sports car to haul freight. Incensed, he wrote a letter to friend Irwin Jacobs, the adjutant for 5th Group, the Nha Trang–based Special Forces command in South Vietnam. What could be done to put him with the Group? Long weeks passed. Finally, Jacobs came back with good news. Beckwith was going Special Forces after all. Itching to get into the fight, Beckwith arrived at Nha Trang on a late-June Friday. There, he met up with his new commander, who'd just taken over the Group the previous week. Thanks to Jacobs' intervention, not only would Beckwith be operating with Special Forces, McKean told him, but he was also being given command of a new unit called Project DELTA. Begun in May 1964 under the code name Leaping Lena, A-detachments began training select Vietnamese Special Forces and CIDG personnel for long-range reconnaissance missions deep in hostile territory. Renamed Project DELTA in October 1964, the program had morphed into a joint US-Vietnamese Special Forces command responsible to MACV and the South Vietnamese General Staff. Aside from training and running recon teams, DELTA also provided advisers to South Vietnamese Special Forces. Operational Detachment B-52, a new command and control B-team to coordinate such efforts, had just been created earlier in the month, and as its CO, Beckwith was tasked with shepherding the program through its early stages. And that was just fine by him. At long last, he'd finally gotten his hands on a unit where he could put his special operations ideas to work.[92]

But less than forty-eight hours in, and Beckwith already didn't like what he saw. Not one of B-52's thirty team members was anywhere to be found at the 5th Group compound just outside town. He soon discovered that most of the men were shacked up with local women in shabby hotels and enjoying other diversions in downtown Nha Trang. He didn't waste any time getting control over the situation. His message was clear: get with the program or get out. Most opted to get out. By Monday afternoon, Project DELTA was down to seven troopers. Fine by Beckwith. The idea was to find and kill the enemy, not lie on a beach and sip booze. He wrote up a "help wanted" flyer and stuffed a handful into each mail bag going out to about ninety A-Teams 5th Group had scattered throughout the country: "WANTED: Volunteers for Project DELTA. Will guarantee you a medal, a body bag, or both." Beckwith laid out the qualifications he was looking for. A recruit had to be a volunteer; he had to have been in South Vietnam at least six months; he had to have earned the Combat Infantryman's Badge; and he had to be at least a sergeant. No one else would be considered. The response was overwhelming; Beckwith soon had more candidates than he knew what to do with. But just like the SAS, he aimed to ruthlessly assess and select the applicants. Only the fittest would be allowed through.[93]

The next step was figuring out what to do with those who qualified. Initially, Beckwith decided to pursue the reconnaissance portion of DELTA's mission using four-man patrols he called "recon teams." Usually, each team was a mix of LLDB and US Special Forces personnel. Teams were inserted by helicopter deep into the backcountry, where they'd spend up to a week stealthily patrolling and gathering intelligence. If substantial enemy activity or troop concentrations were discovered, the teams would radio their findings and let MACV decide how to proceed. DELTA's recon mission soon expanded to include a host of operational options, which included everything from directing airstrikes, conducting bomb damage assessments, and rescuing downed aircrews to hunter-killer assassination missions, psychological operations, and many more. In addition, DELTA ostensibly had access to its own rapid reaction force, the 91st Airborne Ranger Battalion, a well-equipped and trained airmobile light infantry unit commanded by Beckwith's counterpart, Maj. Phạm Duy Tat. But the battalion operated under the direction of South Vietnamese Special Forces, to whom DELTA also provided advisers. Prying loose more than one company at a time from the LLDB's Maj. Gen. Quang was an eternal headache. While Beckwith understood the value of stealthy recon operations, he also knew that a four-man recon team alone in Indian Country was especially vulnerable. He had to be able to count on a dedicated rapid reaction force not just to exploit intelligence opportunities but to safeguard his recon teams. After a fair amount of politicking—and manipulation—Beckwith eventually managed to wrest from Quang two dedicated companies for DELTA missions. Now those men, along with their American partners, were about to face their first true test at Plei Me.[94]

While Beckwith had had some success recruiting from A-detachments in-country, his ruthless selection process still left him shorthanded. In order to fill DELTA's ranks with those he deemed worthy, he was eventually forced to cast a wider net in the applicant pools outside Vietnam. The 1st Special Forces Group in Okinawa, Japan, represented one such reservoir. From there, Beckwith landed 1st Lt. Euell T. White, thirty-one, and the rest of his twelve-man A-team. White's team had just spent months studying the habits and history of a specific Montagnard tribe in anticipation of taking over a backcountry CIDG camp. But when they arrived in Nha Trang in August, they were told that DELTA would be their new assignment. Part of the detachment would be assigned to the recon teams. The other, which included White, was to provide advisers to the 91st Airborne Rangers. He was assigned as the executive officer for the 91st's senior American adviser, Capt. Thomas Pusser. He was slated to take over for Pusser when he DEROSed in December. White and the rest of team leadership got Beckwith's "medal, body bag, or both" speech. Then, in an expletive-laced tirade, the DELTA commander laid down the law forbidding women from the DELTA compound. The message was clear: his men were here to fight, not fornicate.

"I'm a puritan, myself," he concluded. Unable to help himself, White laughed out loud.

"Lieutenant," Beckwith growled, "what do you think is so funny?"

White gathered himself. "Sir, your language would never give you away as being a puritan."[95]

Although Beckwith laughed off his cheeky new lieutenant, it was a risky move for White. Beckwith had a habit of making snap judgments about those he encountered. And once he'd formed an opinion of a man, it was set in stone. According to White, there were two kinds of men in Beckwith's world: "piss cutters" and "dip shits." The former meant he regarded you as a good man and soldier—high praise, indeed, from Beckwith. But if he deemed you the latter, you'd better find someplace else to go. Beckwith seemed to have filed White in the piss-cutter column right off the bat, though at first glance, White didn't meet some of Beckwith's stated requirements. He'd never served in Vietnam and had not earned the Combat Infantryman's Badge. But to the DELTA commander, the first lieutenant from Florence, Alabama, had other qualities to recommend him. White's military résumé might have contained two especially appealing nuggets for Beckwith: he'd worked his way up through the enlisted ranks before being commissioned, and he had ample experience in conventional arms, an area Beckwith had deemed lacking in Special Forces when he'd taken over as operations officer for 7th Group. An added bonus might have been White's age. At thirty-one, he was older than the average lieutenant and had been around the block a time or two. Indeed, White's Army career had been long and winding. He enlisted at seventeen in 1951 and specifically requested airborne. He got his wish, as his first assignment was the 82nd Airborne Division at Fort Bragg, but because the division had been held in strategic reserve during the early Cold War—and thus not deployed to Korea—White had not fought in the war.[96]

By the time he'd gotten his commission in 1962, White had nearly eleven years in the Army, first with the 82nd and later with the 25th Infantry Division. Even though he'd never made it past the eighth grade, White was nevertheless deemed valuable enough for a direct commission. This meant that the usual requirement that officers complete a four-year college degree and ROTC program had been waived. White set off for the Basic Officer Leader Course at Fort Benning as a twenty-eight-year-old noncommissioned officer. Other than a few other fellow former NCOs, he found himself surrounded by college graduates who were years younger. During one particularly grueling drill under the relentless Georgia sun, White got a taste of the age-and-experience gap that separated him from some of the other candidates. White was tasked with distributing water to the dehydrated candidates but was warned not to give more than half a canteen cup. Too much water too fast would make the men sick. When a young second lieutenant demanded more, White told him no. The man proceeded to make a spectacle of himself. "He had a tantrum like a kid," White recalled. White bore the tirade without comment, but when he'd finished his job, he pulled the young man aside for a bit of one-on-one mentoring. "I said, 'You're going to be a platoon leader, and you're going to have men you're responsible for. You've got to learn to control yourself better than that.'" But rather than take offense and double-down on his attitude, the man instead "latched on" to White for the remainder of the course, asking questions and learning everything he could from the veteran NCO. It was a surprising and gratifying moment for White.[97]

As a newly minted second lieutenant, White's first assignment was with the 1st Infantry Division at Fort Riley, Kansas. There, he commanded a platoon as a second lieutenant, and, as a first lieutenant, was granted the rare opportunity as a company commander. But as a senior parachutist, airborne was still in his blood. He and his buddy, 1st Lt. Caesar "Smitty" Smith, another senior parachutist, had a friendly competition going as to who would be the first to land an airborne assignment. One day, White got a phone call alerting him that he'd been assigned to 1st Special Forces Group in Okinawa. Trouble was, he'd never volunteered for the job. In fact, White knew next to nothing about Special Forces. Even from his days at Fort Bragg with the 82nd, all he and his fellow paratroopers knew about SF was that they were just "those weirdos over on Smoke Bomb Hill."

But White knew one other thing about Special Forces: it was an airborne billet. And that was good enough for him. He called his buddy at home to crow about his new assignment. The next morning, Smith was having coffee with some other junior officers and mentioned White's new assignment in passing. "Hey," a 1st Lt. Jim White chimed in. "That sounds like *my* assignment. I've got a buddy up in the Pentagon who's setting that up for me." It turned out that when Division had called down to have Personnel pull Jim White's file for the transfer, they'd grabbed Euell White's by mistake. But by that time, says White, the Army didn't want to admit its error. "I got called down to Personnel, and they asked me whether I'd volunteer," he says with a chuckle. "I didn't even volunteer until they told me that I was already going. I got assigned to Special Forces to save face for the bureaucracy."[98]

But once he'd joined his new A-team in Okinawa as its new executive officer, White started to wish the assignment *had* gone to Jim White after all. According to White, the team captain was a "crook" engaged in skimming funds and shunting them into his own pocket. Most of the other team members, says White, were in on it too. When White arrived, the captain had wasted no time feeling out his new XO, who also happened to be the team's funds officer. If the scam were to continue, White would have to be onboard. Once the team arrived in Vietnam, he was told, it would be tasked with building a Special Forces camp near Khe Sanh. All those construction costs would bring ample opportunities for graft, and they'd all make out nicely. White, who by that time had been in the Army thirteen years, was neither interested nor intimidated. He let them know in no uncertain terms that he would administer funds only according to regulations. After several refusals to play ball, White says he became *persona non grata* with the team.[99]

The situation came to a head just as the team was preparing to deploy to Vietnam. "I was dreading it, I tell you," he says. "I had a knot in my stomach over going with that team." Then, a reprieve came in a most unexpected form. A few days before they were scheduled to leave, White was summoned to the C-team commander's office. The lieutenant colonel said he was pulling White off the A-team because he wasn't qualified. Although White wanted out, he was nevertheless flabbergasted. He'd come from the 1st Infantry with copious command experience and nearly perfect proficiency reports. How, asked White, was he "not qualified"? The colonel, who White described as a "good guy," listed various complaints logged by the team captain. White easily rebutted them all. Finally, the colonel admitted the truth: he couldn't in good conscience keep White on an A-team when its captain didn't want him. He'd read between the lines and knew the captain's complaints had no merit. But he had to do what he thought best for the mission. Though humiliated, White was also deeply relieved. He was reassigned as the executive officer for Capt. James Walker's A-team and began intensive training on the Montagnard tribe they'd soon work with. After a few months of real-warfare exercises in Korea and Taiwan, White and his new team were off to Vietnam. Of course, they'd soon discover that it was DELTA, not a Special Forces camp that awaited.[100]

When DELTA and the Rangers moved to the Phu Cat-Qui Nhon area to support Than Phong 6 in mid-October, White, who'd been promoted to captain in September, had stayed behind in Nha Trang. Beckwith had tasked him with coordinating the 91st's transition into the ARVN supply chain. In the past, the Airborne Rangers had been equipped and provisioned through Project DELTA. This meant that the battalion could generally get almost anything it needed and with little delay. Moving to their own army's supply system would likely mean just the opposite. The Rangers were not happy with the change, and the move was meeting resistance all along the 91st's command chain. It was, in short, a miserable assignment. Then White got a call on the secure radio from Beckwith on the afternoon of 20 October. His CO was in Qui Nhon but was preparing to move DELTA and the Rangers to Pleiku as a first step toward reinforcing Plei Me. White, along with everyone else at Nha Trang, had been transfixed all day by the radio chatter about the siege. The attack on Plei Me had become the hottest news in Vietnam. Beckwith gave his new captain a choice: if he were to make progress with the supply chain changeover, he was to stay in Nha Trang and see it through. If not, White should get himself to Pleiku and link up with the team.[101]

In a way, it would have been much easier had Beckwith simply *ordered* him to come. But by giving him the choice, White wondered if this was his

CO's way of testing him, of seeing if he was truly the "piss-cutter" Beckwith believed him to be. One of the NCOs who'd come over with White from Okinawa overheard the radio conversation. He took his teammate aside. "He'll get you killed if you go out there," the sergeant said gravely. But the truth was, White had already made up his mind. He was making no progress whatsoever on his "mission." Indeed, the Airborne Ranger staff wouldn't even speak to him about the changeover. But even if he were, White wasn't about to sit back in Nha Trang while his unit headed off to the biggest fight in Vietnam. He was certainly afraid; there was no denying it. But he knew that fear could be harnessed, could give him an edge in his coming travails. With that settled, White checked on transportation to Pleiku. Maj. Gen. Quang, the head of South Vietnamese Special Forces, was due to fly into Pleiku the next morning aboard one of DELTA's C-47s. It looked like he'd found his ride.[102]

THE ARMORED TASK FORCE

Meanwhile, II Corps senior adviser Col. Theodore Mataxis continued working to persuade II Corps commander Vinh Loc to dispatch an overland relief force for Plei Me. DELTA and the Airborne Rangers would help prevent the camp from being overrun in the short term, but Mataxis suspected Plei Me would need a more substantial force to fully secure its safety. Vinh Loc was understandably reluctant to strip Pleiku of its defenses. His current reserves amounted to just one armored cavalry squadron and two Ranger battalions. The remaining corps assets were engaged in separate operations and could not be immediately recalled. Marine Alpha Task Force, consisting of two South Vietnamese Marine battalions, was operating near Ban Ma Thuot to the south, while another two-battalion Airborne task force was participating in Operation Than Phong 6 near the coastal hamlet of Bong Son. Vinh Loc had been personally overseeing the Bong Son operation when he received word of Plei Me and returned to his II Corps headquarters at Pleiku by early afternoon on the 20th to assess the situation. Vinh Loc was acutely aware that the communists had long coveted Pleiku. Indeed, aside from its status as the provincial capital, it was also the main government stronghold in the Western Highlands. He naturally feared that Plei Me might simply be a diversion, with the capture of Pleiku the enemy's actual objective. If the communists were able to take the city—if only for a short time—the propaganda victory would be incalculable and would deal a terrible blow to the validity of Saigon's new government.[103]

Still, at the urging of his American advisers, Vinh Loc eventually relented and agreed to release nearly all his corps reserve on the afternoon of 20 October and tasked the 24th Special Tactical Zone headquarters with organizing Plei Me's relief. Under Brig. Gen. Cao Hao Hon, the 24th STZ, based in Kontum, had been established in March to assume responsibility for military operations throughout Pleiku, Kontum, and Phu Bon provinces. In that capacity, Hon had already overseen the successful relief of the besieged Special Forces camp Duc Co in August. Hon and his staff had flown to Pleiku that afternoon to establish a forward command post to more closely coordinate the relief effort. Plei Me's relief formation was dubbed an Armored Task Force and commanded by Lt. Col. Nguyen Trong Luat, who'd headed a similar unit as part of the Duc Co relief. The ATF consisted of the 3rd Armored Cavalry Squadron, which included its headquarters section, a company of fifteen M113 armored personnel carriers commanded by Capt. Du Ngoc Thanh, a company of sixteen M41 light tanks under Capt. Nguyen Manh Lam, along with a platoon from the 222th Artillery and a platoon of the 201st Engineers. The only infantry support slated for the relief force was the four-hundred-man 21st Ranger Battalion under Captain Nguyễn Văn Sách. This left the 22nd Ranger Battalion, with 420 men, as the only substantial unit available to defend Pleiku if attacked.[104]

But Hon and his senior adviser at 24th STZ, Lt. Col. Archie D. Hyle, worried that this would not be enough. They'd seen the communist tactic of the "lure and ambush" too many times. The idea was simple: the enemy would bring considerable pressure on an isolated Special Forces camp or other installation and then ambush the relief force that would inevitably be called in. That's exactly what had happened at Duc Co. While the communists' aim was certainly to overrun that camp—the last government outpost in Western Pleiku Province—they were also keen to destroy the expected reaction force sent to rescue it. But while Luat's ATF had indeed participated in the successful Duc Co relief effort, it was but one of several II Corps assets employed. As noted, those other forces were now committed elsewhere. Sending the ATF alone, even with the addition of the 21st Rangers, would likely doom both the relief force and the camp's defenders. If the mission were to have any chance of success, the Americans believed they'd have to wring more troops out of Vinh Loc. Hon agreed. For now, Luat would have to be kept on a short leash until more forces were forthcoming. He ordered the ATF commander to proceed down Highway 14 toward the Provincial Route 5 junction at Phu My, about nineteen kilometers south of Pleiku. At that point, Route 5 broke southwest toward Plei Me and would be the road an overland reaction force would have to take in order to relieve the camp. But once there, Luat was to go no farther and instead engage only in "aggressive patrolling" of the area. The hope was that the task force's movements might divert enemy attention away from Plei Me in the short run, while at the same time not moving too far away from Pleiku in the event the enemy attacked the city. The ATF departed at about 1630 on the 20th and had reached the Phu My vicinity some three hours later. Luat set up a bivouac to wait out the night and began his patrols on the morning of the 21st, keeping his sweep radius at no more than a few miles while his superiors looked for ways to augment his force.[105]

Back at Pleiku, Beckwith conferred with Lt. Col. John Bennett, 5th Group's second in command, along with Lt. Col. Bill Patch, the C2 commander in charge of all Special Forces activity in II Corps. Plei Me, explained the officers, was in serious trouble, had sustained numerous casualties, and was in danger of being overrun. It was imperative that the camp be reinforced as soon as possible until a more substantial relief force could be organized and dispatched from II Corps headquarters. DELTA and the Airborne Rangers were to be that initial relief force. The pressing question remained how best to get them into Plei Me as quickly as possible. Bennett, whom Beckwith viewed as a sometimes overly ambitious officer, suggested that the men parachute directly into the camp. Beckwith, one of the men who would be dangling from the end of those parachute cords as he drifted down through a hail of hostile fire, understandably balked at his superior officer's suggestion. Luckily, Col. Mataxis, senior adviser for II Corps, had just arrived and overheard Bennett's plan. Mataxis intervened, stating forcefully that there would be no parachute drops into Plei Me now or in the immediate future.[106]

Soon after, 5th Group commander Col. William McKean flew in from Nha Trang to join the discussion. A consensus soon developed that the quickest and safest way to get the DELTA-Ranger relief force into the camp was by air assault. The challenge was to find a suitable LZ far enough away from camp so as not to tip off the enemy, while still being close enough so the relief force wouldn't tire itself out trying to get there. A more immediate problem was the lack of sufficient helicopter assets to accomplish the lift. At the time, Beckwith "owned" four aging, H-34 helicopters and two World War II–vintage C-47s, all flown by Vietnamese pilots he'd recruited and paid for out of DELTA's coffers. But this modest collection was woefully inadequate for a move of this size. It was exactly the sort of problem he'd dreaded.

Like the SAS, Beckwith believed that DELTA, rather than relying on other units or services, should have direct command and control over all mission assets. DELTA operations required tight coordination between kinetic and transportation assets. Even a small delay could threaten mission success and even cost lives. In the future, Beckwith concluded, DELTA would need to own and control a much more robust fleet of dedicated aircraft.[107]

But as things now stood, Camp Holloway's 119th Aviation Company was the main transport unit for II Corps. But the unit was already involved in Operation Than Phong 6 near Bong Song. This was the same mission that Vinh Loc had been personally overseeing when he'd received news of Plei Me earlier that afternoon. McKean, whose men were at Plei Me, insisted that Mataxis cancel the operation and shift the 119th's choppers to the relief effort. Mataxis was reluctant at first. He was Vinh Loc's senior adviser, after all, and was probably at least somewhat invested in the Than Phong operation. But it was quickly becoming clear that Plei Me was evolving into the most important fight in South Vietnam. Mataxis would just have to find the helicopters somewhere. With the mission officially greenlit, Beckwith spent the rest of the night poring over area maps, anxious to find the best LZ candidates and routes of advance. He even spoke with some of the forward air controllers who'd been flying support. The enemy, he was told, had invested the Plei Me area in force, especially to the north, west, and south of camp. Getting anywhere near the camp would be a daunting proposition. Beckwith later wrote that he had a feeling this mission was going to be especially difficult and dangerous. People almost assuredly would die. But it was what he and his team had trained for. And tomorrow, that training would be put into action.[108]

6

THE LONGEST DAY
(21–22 OCTOBER)

To transport the DELTA-Ranger relief force, Mataxis had finally settled on Company A of the 1st Aviation Battalion (later the 155th Aviation Company) based at Ban Ma Thuot, about 180 kilometers south of Pleiku. Nicknamed "Stagecoach," the company had been en route the previous day for a ten-day mission to Phu Cat as it, too, was slated to participate in Than Phong 6. But bad weather had forced Company A to divert to Pleiku for the night. Once there, the crews were ordered to off-load all other gear and prepare for a possible air assault the following morning. Because of the 119th's commitment at Bong Son, Company A was about to be challenged like never before. Stagecoach would serve as the primary helicopter transport unit for the first five days of the siege. Meanwhile, Mataxis also managed to temporarily wrangle several lumbering H-34 choppers from the Marine Corps 363rd Medium Helicopter Squadron out of Qui Nhon, 160 kilometers to the east. With the "how" now solved, the next question was "where."[1]

By 0630 hours, Beckwith and McKean were already airborne in one of Company A's Hueys trying to answer just that. They eventually chose a clearing about five kilometers northeast of camp. On the trip back to Camp Holloway, Beckwith looked out the side door of his Huey and saw the UH-1B helicopter gunship running escort for the recon mission. The chopper was commanded by 1st Lt. Harold A. Preseindefer, twenty-five, and piloted by Joseph S. Huwyler, a twenty-three-year-old warrant officer from Watertown, New York. Also aboard were the crew chief, Spec. 5 William J. Johnson, thirty-five, and twenty-two-year-old PFC Michael E. Davis, the ship's door gunner. All at once, the chopper's main rotor spun free of the Huey's body in a violent flurry. At two thousand feet, the gunship simply dropped like a stone and exploded upon impact into the jungle. All aboard were killed. The crash would mark the first aircrew lost by Company A in Vietnam. To Beckwith, the loss of the escort crew seemed to portend bad things ahead. Nevertheless, the DELTA commander believed he'd found the right spot.[2]

At 0730, fighter-bombers and Huey gunships rumbled in to blister DELTA's LZ prior to the landing. Shortridge, orbiting the area in his 0-1 Bird Dog, called down further bomb strikes along DELTA's likely route of advance through the jungle. Meanwhile, DELTA and the Airborne Rangers climbed aboard their transports back at Holloway. The move would be accomplished in three lifts, with the first taking off from Holloway at about 0805. The Huey slicks and H-34s came in waves, each lift approaching the LZ like a swarm of angry locusts, the M-60 door gunners spraying the LZ and surrounding forest with abandon. In turn, each ship flared and then touched down just long enough to expel its six-trooper load before thrashing away to make way for the next. DELTA and the Airborne Rangers piled off the choppers and fanned out toward the tree line to secure the LZ. They encountered no resistance. The first lift complete, the transports sped off for Pleiku, where the second load of troopers waited expectantly on the tarmac.

By 1030 hours, all three lifts were complete. Beckwith conferred with his counterpart, Maj. Tat, commander of the two 91st Airborne Ranger companies. As the crow flies, the relief force was only about five kilometers from the camp, but the jungle was very dense and likely to contain Viet Cong patrols. The idea, said Beckwith, was to take it slow and stealthy. The last thing they wanted to do was give away their position before reaching the objective. Knowing that the enemy was most heavily concentrated to the west and south of camp, Beckwith thought it wise to first move east for a few kilometers before turning south toward Plei Me. Tat agreed. With the plan set, the relief force formed a column and moved out single file at about 1100 hours.[3]

The going was slow. Elephant grass, a local species that grew twelve feet tall and had razor-sharp blades, was especially thick. The men hacked their way with machetes with every step, sometimes even dropping to hands and knees to fight their way through the tangled mess. By noon, the men were already exhausted under the relentless sun, their skin a patchwork of stinging cuts and bites carved by grass, jungle brambles, and the voracious black ants that owned the forest. A short time later, the relief force came upon a small Vietnamese village that appeared to be empty. But signs were everywhere that it had been occupied just hours earlier, as thin wisps of smoke still trailed from numerous cook fires. Had the villagers received advance warning that the relief force was coming and bugged out? Or worse, had the Viet Cong come along in force and *taken* them away? Beckwith later recalled that Tat and his Rangers appeared unnerved by the discovery. As for himself, he claimed to have not given it much thought. Yet, stealth was the currency by which DELTA lived and operated. If the VC knew they were there, it represented a grave danger to the mission—and to their very lives.[4]

Soon after, Beckwith received a radio call from Lt. Col. Bennett, the 5th Group deputy commander. Bennett was circling the area in an 0-1 Bird Dog and was calling for a situation report. He also ordered Beckwith to mark his current position with smoke. Beckwith demurred. Whatever he thought about the suspicious Vietnamese village, the last thing he was going to do was signal his location with a smoke grenade. In response, Bennett lit into the DELTA commander, letting him know in no uncertain terms that he was not moving through the bush with sufficient urgency. While Beckwith managed to hold his tongue, he gave little credence to Bennett's criticisms. For it was he, not the colonel, who was on the ground in hostile territory, chopping his way through an impenetrable jungle.[5]

The thin line of troops continued to snake its way through the forest, a cacophony of birds and buzzing insects filling the air. Beckwith, who had placed himself about midway along the column, had come to appreciate such disquiet. For in his experience, it often seemed that when the jungle grew preternaturally quiet, it meant predators—including the human variety—might be lurking nearby. Just then, as if to give lie to his theory, shots suddenly rang out at the head of the column. Beckwith raced forward to see what had happened. When he arrived at the front, he learned that the point element had run across three communist soldiers and exchanged fire. One hostile had been shot and killed, but the other two had escaped into the thick foliage. Beckwith looked down at the dead enemy soldier. He had been carrying 57mm recoilless rifle ammunition, and the DELTA commander surmised that he had been involved with the siege and perhaps become lost. But more concerning was the way he was dressed. The dead man was clad in a khaki uniform and tan pith helmet. The uniform of the People's Army of Vietnam. Beckwith knew that intelligence had long suspected the NVA of operating in the South, but this was the first time he'd seen proof with his own eyes. As Maj. Tat searched the body, the Ranger officer became more and more agitated. While a dead NVA soldier was bad enough, Tat was probably more concerned about the two who'd gotten away. Wouldn't it only be a matter of time now before the NVA found them and attacked?[6]

Perhaps owing to the same concerns, Beckwith ordered the column to change route again and head even deeper into the jungle. If the relief force were caught out here, isolated and alone, they'd all be in very serious trouble. But just as before, the stifling heat and dense vegetation—along with a renewed urgency for stealth—slowed the column to a crawl. At about 1700 hours, Beckwith called a halt and established radio contact with Plei Me's commanding officer, Harold Moore. According to the coordinates Beckwith provided, Moore said that DELTA and the Rangers were only about thirty-five minutes from camp. But in reality, the task force was a good bit farther away. According to Shortridge, who'd been monitoring progress from his 0-1, DELTA was going the wrong way. He called for the relief force to mark its position with smoke. This time Beckwith complied. But when the FAC's plotted position contradicted Beckwith's own, Shortridge said the DELTA commander "violently disagreed." The FAC called in another Bird Dog to verify. When that pilot's plotting for the RF was within two hundred meters of Shortridge's, Beckwith was finally forced to agree that he'd drifted off course. Had DELTA continued on its errant course, Shortridge would later write that, "They would've ended up right in the middle of the VC."[7]

In the meantime, one of the Airborne Rangers was in immediate need of a medevac. Capt. Euell White, who had arrived in Pleiku after a sleepless night to find that DELTA was already in the field, had been beating the bushes all day for a ride out to Plei Me. No way, he was told. That airspace was closed to all helicopter transport. It was simply too hot to go in. Only if the camp called for an emergency medevac would he have a chance. It was then that White ran into Staff Sgt. Jimmie L. McBynum, a twenty-six-year-old 5th Group medic from Kinston, North Carolina. McBynum had heard that Plei Me was in trouble and was desperate to get into camp and augment its beleaguered medical staff. When White heard about Beckwith's medevac call, he found McBynum. This was their chance, he told the Special Forces trooper. They could link up with DELTA in the field and then walk the rest of the way to Plei Me. But McBynum balked. There was no telling how long that would take. The medic remained set on flying directly into camp.[8]

Now in the forest somewhere east of Plei Me, White jumped off the chopper just as the Airborne Ranger was being loaded. Beckwith's official after-action report lists the man as a "possible heat case," but White tells a different story. He says that the "heat case" was actually the Ranger who'd shot and killed the NVA soldier earlier that afternoon. According to White, the Ranger had never killed anyone before and had gone "berserk" over the shooting, apparently to such a disruptive degree that allowing him to continue with the column represented an unacceptable hazard to the mission and its personnel. Whatever the case, Beckwith clearly thought the situation serious enough to risk a medevac even at a time when stealth was of utmost importance.[9]

But no sooner had the DELTA commander gotten rid of one liability than he discovered he had a new problem on his hands. Tat had only grown more concerned in the hours since the shootout with the NVA stragglers. For him, it had been a game-changer. Believing it now folly to push on for Plei Me, the Ranger commander broke the news to Beckwith that he and his men would not continue and were instead turning back. Beckwith, in his own inimitable manner, reminded Tat of the mission to relieve the camp, and told the South Vietnamese commander that DELTA would push on with or without him. But Tat had made up his mind. With that, he and his Airborne Rangers disappeared into the jungle. Beckwith and his fifteen DELTA operators were now on their own.[10]

A few hours earlier, at about noon, Vinh Loc had met with his Vietnamese subordinates and American advisers at II Corps headquarters to hash out a plan for relieving Plei Me in force. At this point, the camp had been under attack for more than thirty hours. Intelligence estimates about communist intentions and capabilities continued to evolve. Initially, analysts believed that the attack was no more than battalion strength and that VC forces would quit the field when daylight came. The events of the previous twenty-four hours had proven the latter false. Intelligence analysts were starting to believe that the attack was at least a multibattalion affair, with perhaps one battalion directly engaged with the camp and another two or more lurking nearby to ambush any reaction force sent to relieve the camp. As with the previous day, Vinh Loc's American advisers pushed for more troops, including the 22nd Ranger Battalion, Pleiku's sole line of defense. Again, the II Corps commander balked at releasing his last corps reserve, and the situation devolved into a stalemate. Down at Phu My, Luat was ordered to move the ATF to a nearby bridge that local Viet Cong had blown the previous day so his platoon of engineers could effect repairs. But his previous orders stood: he was to move no closer to Plei Me.[11]

Despite now being a much smaller force, it was still another two to three hours before Beckwith and DELTA got close enough to camp to hear the shooting. At about 2000 hours, and now well after dark, Beckwith reestablished radio contact with Plei Me and requested a patrol be sent out to guide in his team. Sure, said the voice on the radio. "Come on in and join the party." The quip was almost certainly a case of the sardonic humor common to men in combat. Yet, Beckwith later claimed to have been particularly incensed by the remark—highly inappropriate, in his view, given the life-and-death circumstances at play. Nevertheless, the camp dispatched a patrol under cover of darkness to link up with Beckwith at the coordinates he'd provided.[12]

In the meantime, Beckwith wanted to get the lay of his surroundings. He and his top enlisted man, Sgt. Maj. Bill Desoto, slipped into the trees to survey the thin dirt road the team had been using as a reference point as it moved through the jungle. According to the map, the road should lead them directly into camp to the west. When they returned, Maj. A. J. "Bo" Baker, DELTA's new operations officer who'd joined the team just two days earlier, was waiting with news: Tat and his Airborne Rangers had returned. After a change of heart, the Rangers had turned around earlier that afternoon and had been following DELTA at some distance throughout the day. According to Beckwith, Tat intimated that his abandonment of DELTA and the mission would have caused him to "lose face." Beckwith, who'd certainly been perturbed that Tat had left earlier, was nevertheless glad to have him and his 175 Airborne Rangers back.[13]

Time passed, but the guide patrol never appeared. Beckwith and the team could hear a good bit of shooting in the distance. Had they been ambushed? Or was it just the sounds of the siege, now into its third night? At some point, he started to doubt the wisdom of trying to enter the camp under the chaos of night fighting. Indeed, if the NVA didn't get them, he was afraid some trigger-happy defender on the perimeter just might. And then there was the problem with what Beckwith viewed as the camp defenders' "flippant" attitude reflected in the "join the party" wisecrack. All of this convinced the DELTA commander to hold off on entering the camp until daylight. He radioed McKean back in Pleiku and informed his commander that the RF would stay in the jungle for the night.[14]

22 OCTOBER

Capt. Melvin C. Elliott

Capt. Mel Elliott was sipping a drink with a buddy in the officers' club at Bien Hoa Airbase outside Saigon when the call came in late Thursday on 21 October. The command post (CP) duty officer for Elliott's 1st Air Commando Squadron needed four fresh Skyraider pilots to go on alert. The current alert flight personnel, worn and frazzled, had just lifted off for their third and final mission of the day. Time for a break, so Elliott corralled three other A-1E pilots and headed for the CP to receive orders. He and wingman Robert Haines were to proceed to Plei Me, about twenty-five miles south of Pleiku, and fly cover for an Army C-7 Caribou making an emergency supply drop into the beleaguered Special Forces camp. An Air Force C-123 flare ship would light the way. The siege of Plei Me, now entering its third day, had become the hottest fight in South Vietnam.[15]

Originally from Glendale, Arizona, the thirty-six-year-old Elliott wasn't a Skyraider driver by trade. He'd instead come up through the Air Force ranks, first as an enlisted radio operator during the Korean War. But it was later, after completing the pilot training he'd begun in 1953 at Texas' Lackland Air Force Base, that Elliott found his true calling: jet fighter jock. Indeed, Elliott would go on to log more than 3,500 hours in the venerable F-100 Super Sabre during his twenty years in the cockpit. But the unique necessities of the burgeoning war in Vietnam—especially the need for a dominant and durable close air support platform—would require him and other fighter pilots to temporarily switch gears. "I took a fifteen-month 'break' to fly the Spad in Vietnam," he would later write.[16]

By 0030 hours on Friday, Elliott and Haines had set up orbit over Plei Me, awaiting the Caribou's arrival. Nearby, the C-123 intermittently sprinkled flares to earth, casting the camp and its environs in ghostly, flickering light. Below, the siege of Plei Me raged on, as tactical air support rained fire and steel onto NVA assault positions. This wasn't Elliott's first encounter with the camp. He'd been here two days earlier as leader of a four-plane flight of A-1Es out of Bien Hoa. Then, in those first frantic hours of the siege, Elliott had gotten a taste of just how hairy the situation on the ground was becoming. He'd first established radio contact with an orbiting C-123 flare ship commanded by Maj. Howard Pierson, with Forward Air Controller Capt. Richard "Dick" Shortridge in the right seat, and Special Forces Detachment A-217 commander Capt. Harold M. Moore on the ground. Moore, in a desperate attempt to staunch the relentless North Vietnamese assault, requested that Elliott's Skyraiders bring their napalm canisters right down on the camp's perimeter wire. Shortridge concurred, and directed the Spads in. So danger close were the strikes that even Plei Me's beleaguered defenders felt the heat blast, as 2,200 degrees of jellied gasoline scorched earthwork and enemy alike.[17] "At times, the igniters from the napalm cans were going over the wall into the trenches inside the compound," Elliott later recalled.[18] From that strike alone, camp defenders would later count the scorched bodies of twenty-three NVA soldiers hanging in the wire. Although Elliott's entire flight made it back to Bien Hoa that day, three of the four planes were peppered with bullet holes. It would stand as an ominous portent of what was to come.[19]

And now, two nights later, Elliott was back atop Plei Me, arcing his Skyraider in long, languid circles as he waited for something to do. An hour passed, but no sign of the Caribou. Fuel would soon become a problem, even for the Spad's prodigious tank. He'd need to lighten his load. "I advised the flare ship that we would be able to stay in the area longer if we expended the external ordnance we were carrying: napalm, CBU [cluster bombs], and rockets," he wrote.[20] Below, the camp marked a target with a mortar round, and the Skyraiders unloaded their ordnance in a fiery display, lighting the night. But then yet another hour ticked by, and still no C-7. At about 0215, Elliott called for a status update. The Caribou had been canceled. With his mission aborted and fuel running low, the pilot volunteered to strafe enemy positions before peeling off for Bien Hoa. Another mortar round marked a North Vietnamese position, and the Skyraiders rolled into their attack runs, engines roaring as 20mm autocannons ripped sky above and enemy below. But just as Elliott pulled out of his run, he noticed that the night sky seemed unnaturally aglow.[21]

"I looked at my left wing and it was ablaze! How it happened, I'll never know." [22] Elliott radioed Haines that he was on fire. Flames quickly ate through the wing, rendering control all but impossible. The pilot decided his best bet would be to make for the Plei Me compound and bail out. A tiny island of relative safety amid a sea of enemy troops. But as he neared position, the illumination flares chose just that moment to wink out, once again drawing the dark blanket of night over the ground below. Blind, he muscled the Spad into an orbit at about 800 feet, hoping another flare would light the way. It didn't. Just then, his controls failed. It was bail out now, into the darkness and whatever lurked below, or ride the burning wreckage to earth. As the crippled Skyraider began its final roll, Elliott heaved himself free of the canopy, pulled the D-ring on his chute, and drifted down into the gloom.[23]

Hunter

Some four hundred meters away, Hunter stood watch for his second straight night on the Plei Me line. The medical dispensary had been set ablaze in an earlier mortar attack, rendering it unusable for its intended purpose.

Its burned-out husk had been converted to a makeshift morgue for the Montagnard dead. And when there was no more room inside, the bodies were laid out upon a bare patch of ground outside. The first had been co-cooned in body bags. But when that supply had exhausted itself, the rest were simply wrapped in Army blankets and even the brightly colored blue, yellow, and red parachute silk left from supply drops. Rats, fat and brazen, scurried and fed among them, so the surgeon had moved his medical sup-plies away and into a bunker along the trench line. As a physician, Hunter's calling was to heal the sick and wounded. But, for now at least, he couldn't indulge in the luxury of being *only* a doctor—not with the enemy infesting the hills and ground all around. Indeed, for two days and three long nights, the NVA's small-arms and .30 and .51 caliber machine gun fire had swept the camp like a scythe, while 81mm and 82mm mortars showered death from above. Meanwhile, the enemy's B-40 rockets and 57mm and 75mm recoilless rifles had blasted away at the camp's own machine gun em-placements and sandbagged bunkers. No, since arriving under fire on the morning of the 20th, Hunter had been forced to wear two hats: that of the healer and that of the Special Forces trooper he'd trained to be. So alongside the bandages, antibiotics, IV poles, and albumin cans in his medical bunker, his M16 service rifle also stood ready.[24]

Capt. Moore, the detachment commander, had a strategy of forward defense. He'd ordered the troopers to move up from the dubious safety of the inner perimeter and out to the main trench line, partly to shore up the courage of the Montagnards manning the rifle pits and partly to make their own stand in the teeth of the assault. For if the NVA finally succeeded in breaching the perimeter, not a man in Plei Me would likely live to tell its tale. Three-man Montagnard fire teams were clustered along the trench line every ten or fifteen meters. The troopers and their LLDB counterparts, spread thin because they were so few in number, scattered themselves along all three legs of the camp. Each trooper was responsible for his sector. Bob Sloan and a team of Montagnards manned the 4.2-inch mortar at the center of camp. Someone monitored the side-band radio in the communications bunker at all times. Usually, it was Navarro, the communications sergeant. But it was always *someone*, for if Plei Me lost its only link with the outside world, all was truly lost. Within camp, everyone maintained contact using their short-range PRC-10 radios. In the event of the worst-case scenario—a complete overrun of an entire section of the line—the survivors would radio the alert and then rally back to the team house. From there, the only hope would be to escape and evade into the jungle. Everyone prayed it wouldn't come to that.[25]

And so it was that the physician-soldier now crouched in his perimeter bunker, alone and terrified, peering anxiously into the black void beyond the wire. Nighttime was by far the worst. It was the time when the NVA were most likely to attack—and the time when the troopers were least likely to see it coming. Illumination flares sprinkled down intermittently from a C-123 orbiting above, but they could only do so much. Each drifting parachute flare provided between ten and fifteen seconds of quivering, ghostly pale light by which Hunter could survey the ground to his front. And even then, there were deep and shifting shadows everywhere, shadows that might conceal something terrible. *Was that movement he'd seen? A belly-crawling sapper perhaps?* And then the flare would fizzle out and the oppressive pitch blackness returned. It was during these sightless interludes that he would pray for the next flare to fall. For Hunter was sure that unseen things were creeping ever closer, infiltrating his position each time the light winked out. The NVA were out there. That much was certain. There had been an attack on the wire just the night before. Only the defenders' massed fire and tac-air strikes had driven them off. And the night before he'd arrived, there had been full-on human wave attacks, replete with fixed bayonet charges and suicide satchel bombers. As if in testament, the enemy corpses still hung in the outer wire by the score, some hideously scorched by napalm, all bloated and putrefied after days under the merciless Vietnamese sun. How long would it be before they tried again?[26]

Sometimes, the night would fall nearly silent, the only sound that of the rats as they scrabbled through the trenches. Then, without warning, ear-shattering gunfire would split the night as Montagnards on either side of his little bunker would suddenly let loose with a wild volley. *Had they seen something? Were they under attack?* It was impossible to know, for they spoke no English and he no Jarai. Sometimes Montagnards from other sectors would rush over to see what had happened. Perhaps an American NCO would show up. Gunfire along the line seemed to have its own gravitational pull. Every man knew the dire consequences of a perimeter breach. But mostly he passed the long dark hours alone, the only SF trooper in his sector. No other American from whom he could draw strength or even commiserate. And on it went through the night. Light and dark. Sound and silence. Fear and isolation.[27]

Sometimes, when the flares were too long in coming and the suffocating darkness became unbearable, Hunter would rear back and lob a grenade from his M79 beyond the wire. He dubbed this tactic "preventive medicine." He hoped it would dissuade the enemy from infiltrating—or perhaps catch and kill him in the act if he tried. It was something he'd adopted during another siege of a Special Forces camp, this time at nearby Duc Co along the Cambodian border. As in Plei Me, Hunter had choppered in to tend the wounded but had quickly been pressed into the fight. Hunter and another trooper were given a section of the perimeter to man. The commanding officer eyed the green, young physician's M16 suspiciously. "Can you hit anything with that?" he had asked. Apparently, Hunter's response didn't inspire confidence. The officer instead handed him the far-more-forgiving M79 grenade launcher with instructions to blast anything that tried to get through. He didn't know whether it was an effective tactic, but it helped assuage his fear—a little. But it was also cause for worry. Was it a waste of precious ammo? Would he have enough when the final assault came?[28]

Indeed, everything was in short supply. Food, water, and medical supplies were hard enough to come by, but without ammunition to keep the beast at bay, the rest hardly mattered. The camp had been cut off by road since the siege began the night of 19 October. For now, aerial resupply was the only lifeline to the outside world. Directly south and just beyond the wire stretched a 1,500-foot airstrip large enough to accommodate a C-123 Provider cargo plane. But landing was a no-go. NVA gunners nested in the surrounding hills and poured heavy machine gun fire at any approaching aircraft. Instead, lumbering C-7s, 119s, and 123s, flanked by screeching A-1Es for cover, were forced to make harrowing, low-altitude supply drops into the teeth of NVA antiaircraft fire.[29]

Worse, Plei Me was not a large target to begin with. Seen from the air, the camp resembled an equilateral triangle, each side about 160 meters long. Two rows of barbed and concertina wire bounded the outer limits of the triangle. A second triangle of roughly half that size lay within and delimited the camp itself. This constituted Plei Me's "livable space." It was crowded with personnel and low, wooden buildings with corrugated metal roofs. This was where Army and Air Force supply pilots were forced to make their drops. A main fighting trench and another line of concertina delineated the camp's outer perimeter, with sandbagged bunkers spaced along its boundary. A heavily fortified .50 machine gun bunker occupied each of the triangle's three corners. Several interlocking communication trenches crisscrossed the camp, making it possible for defenders to move between positions without exposing themselves above ground. Between the inner and outer triangles was a cleared "no-man's-land" of staked, interlocking belts of tangle-foot wire, Claymore mines, and trip flares.[30]

But although aircraft came in as low as three hundred feet to improve accuracy, the drops were hit or miss. Even throttled back, resupply planes still roared in at seventy-five yards per second, with no room for drift and a scant half-second timing error at most. To facilitate accelerated descent—and thus, as little wind effect and drift as possible—Special Forces riggers working aboard the cargo planes prepped supply pallets to be much heavier than normal loads, so that the G-13 chutes would slow the parcels as little as possible.[31] Still, while some pallets landed inside the inner perimeter where eager defenders awaited, others went astray, coming down in the no-man's-land between inner and outer boundaries—perilous to retrieve because of friendly Claymore mines and enemy fire. Still others smashed down beyond the wire and into the waiting arms of the NVA. For these last, F-100s and 105s roared in like silver streaks to blast the supply-laden bundles, lest they fall into enemy hands. But even when the enormous, life-giving parcels managed to land on target, it was not always a blessing. Low-altitude drops compounded the higher rate of fall. At just three hundred feet, chutes rarely had enough altitude to fully deploy. Instead, the overladen bales came down like boulders, sometimes shattering structure and man alike. One drop bundle had torn a gaping hole in the team house roof. Another had flattened the latrine, releasing a miniflood of vile sewage into the area. Worse yet, two unlucky Montagnard Strikers were crushed as they huddled in their gun trench, 1,200 pounds of errant supply pallet crashing down.[32]

But at the moment, it wasn't resupply drops that had Hunter's attention. It was the thundering pyrotechnic display of close air support at work. Above, an AC-47 Spooky turned in lazy circles above the camp, dropping flares and raining hellfire all along the perimeter with its multibarreled Gatling guns, long red tracers snaking to earth like flaming ribbons. Also known as "Puff, the Magic Dragon," the AC-47 was essentially a flying weapon. Though a modified C-47 transport plane, Spooky carried with it carnage, not cargo. The aircraft boasted a complement of three M134 Miniguns, each a six-barrel rotary machine gun capable of spitting six thousand rounds per minute. Like the Skyraider, the AC-47 was ideally suited for close air support. Durable, heavily armed, and with abundant fuel capacity, Spooky could loiter over targets for hours, putting voluminous fire on enemy formations.[33]

Beyond, the rest of tac-air went about its deadly work. F-100s and 105s streaked overhead laying into NVA positions with cluster munitions and napalm. Twin-engine B-57 Canberras unloaded high explosive 500- and 750-pound bombs, sending shockwaves and shrapnel through Plei Me's defenders and besiegers alike. The concussive force could burst eardrums, blood flowing from ears and nose. Friendly shrapnel wounds—some superficial, some mortal—were also common as CAS brought its munitions in close. Hunter and the others had quickly learned to keep their heads down whenever a strike rolled in. And now, just as the latest of these percussive thunderclaps barreled past, Hunter managed to peek up from the trench works in time to spot a pair of Skyraiders pulling off their attack run. As it began to peel away, the trailing Skyraider appeared to be hit by ground fire. Somehow, above the din, Hunter could hear the engine cough and sputter as its propeller went dead and the plane went into a glide. "That's not right," Hunter thought. "He's hit." Moments later, the plane piled to earth some three hundred meters outside camp.[34]

Elliott

It was the trees that broke his fall. Elliott had come down in a wooded copse southeast of camp. Dangling about fifty feet above ground, his only hope was that the lines held long enough for him to swing to the nearest tree trunk and work himself free. A fall from this height meant a shattered leg or worse. Not an option with NVA patrols already scouring the area for the downed pilot. Once he'd shed his shoulder harness and was back on solid ground, Elliott evaluated what remained of his survival gear. What he found did not inspire confidence.[35]

"I had lost my hunting knife during the bailout, so I was forced to abandon the survival kit that was a part of the parachute," he wrote. "I had a .38 caliber revolver with five rounds of ammo, a pen-gun-flare, a strobe light, a two-way radio (which at times was a luxury to A-1 pilots), my Mae West [flotation device], and a brand new 'chit book' from the Bien Hoa Officers Club."[36]

That meant no food. No water. But the radio was a godsend. Elliott raised wingman Haines, who was orbiting the area trying to get a fix on his downed partner. Once the two had established Elliott's location, the pilot asked his wingman to fly in the direction of Plei Me so he'd know which way to walk toward safety. Meanwhile, Haines radioed the camp. "Can somebody go out and try to pick him up?" he called. First Lt. Robert Berry, the camp's twenty-two-year-old executive officer, volunteered to lead a small team to find the downed pilot. Berry gathered Sgt. Eugene Tafoya, a veteran NCO with twenty years in the Army, a squad of Montagnards, and staged near the south leg of the camp perimeter. While the NVA antiaircraft fire had been murderous in the area, it didn't appear that they were in strength near the camp's perimeter wire. Berry, Haines, camp commander Moore, and the flare ship switched to the same FM radio frequency, this last made possible by the Air Force's recent upgrade from Korean War–era PRC-10 radios in their C-123s to the more powerful and wider-ranged ARC-44s.[37] Berry and his team would slip out under cover of night, then key his radio when he was in position. Indeed, darkness had now become a friend. Moore called off the flare ship so the patrol could pick its way unseen through the wire and into the dark jungle beyond. Anxious minutes ticked by. Finally, Berry's handset clicked over the command post receiver. Once more, the C-123 began trickling glowing illumination flares to earth as the young XO began his perilous search.[38]

Haines, although low on fuel, radioed that he would buzz along Elliott's line of movement, hoping to help the Special Forces trooper find his buddy. But every time he flicked on his landing lights to show Berry the way, NVA gunners would open up with .51 caliber machine guns, shell cartridges the size of cigars. Bright green tracers clawed skyward, desperate to bag their second Spad of the night. Undaunted, Haines rolled around and roared in full throttle, taking the machine gun nest head-on. A bright red torrent of 20mm cannon fire blazed to earth, but the NVA gunner held fast, giving as good as he got. Fuel now critical, the pilot had no choice but to peel off for Pleiku.[39]

Meanwhile, Berry and his team struggled through the elephant grass that grew in dense, bamboo-like clumps. The edges of its leaves were razor sharp and made it nearly impenetrable. Torturously, the team pieced its way toward where they believed Elliott to be. Berry knew that Elliott was equipped with a strobe, so he radioed the C-123 circling overhead to hold flares in hopes of spotting Elliott's signal. Tafoya and the Montagnards set a small perimeter and settled in to wait. Finally, the last shimmering flare winked out. Berry waited for his eyes to adjust. No strobe from Elliott, but Berry could hear the NVA moving through the area, as eager as he to find the downed pilot. And they were coming closer to his patrol's position. It dawned on Berry that Elliott wasn't the only prize the NVA were hoping to bag in those predawn hours. Defeated, the young XO called off the search and painstakingly worked his way home. Ironically, it was while belly-crawling back through the wire and to safety that he experienced his biggest fright of the night. There, fading into view, the words "FRONT TOWARD ENEMY" materialized out of the gloom. He'd come face-to-face with one of his own Claymore mines. Packed with powerful C-4 explosive and containing seven hundred 1/8-inch steel balls that spray out like a shotgun blast, the Claymore is a deadly effective antipersonnel weapon. "The most harrowing thing I encountered," Berry said. "And I was like, 'This is not a good situation.'" Carefully, the Special Forces trooper picked his way past the Claymore's trip wires and back into camp. As for Elliott, quarry to a hundred prowling enemy soldiers, he would spend his night in the bush, hunted and alone.[40]

Capt. Dale Potter

Two hundred and fifteen miles to the south, at Bien Hoa Air Base just outside Saigon, Capt. Dale Potter, thirty-one, had heard rumblings of a big battle raging up north. Scuttlebutt had it that several aircraft had been shot down in support of a tiny Special Forces camp in the Central Highlands. Naturally, the Combat Search and Rescue pilot's attention pricked up. After all, downed aircraft meant downed pilots in need of rescue—if they were lucky enough to have survived, that is. And plucking aviators out of the thick of things was just the sort of mission the Air Force chopper pilot had trained for. Indeed, it was the 38th Air Rescue Squadron's very *raison d'être*.[41]

The squadron's Detachment 6 at Bien Hoa was equipped with the venerable Kaman HH-43 "Huskie," at the time a one-of-a-kind asset in South Vietnam. Developed to serve as both a rescue helicopter and an aerial fire fighter, the Huskie had several features that made it uniquely suited for combat search-and-rescue missions in Vietnam. The first was its distinctive intermeshing rotors that turned in opposite directions, negating the need for a tail rotor. Aside from attracting unwanted attention because of their loudness, helicopter tail rotors are especially vulnerable to enemy fire. The unique motion of the intermeshing rotors also created a powerful downwash—just the ticket for pushing aside or just plain flattening dense brush that might otherwise conceal a stricken pilot or serviceman. HH-43s were also equipped with a forest penetrator-hoist system. Akin to a heavy pendulum and cable connected to a winch, the system allowed Air Force CSAR crews to hover atop jungle canopies that sometimes towered hundreds of feet above the forest floor. Crew chiefs were then able to lower the heavy penetrator to earth despite the dense foliage. Once on the ground, the spring-loaded penetrator snapped open to deploy a three-pronged "seat" large enough to accommodate up to three passengers. A Stokes litter could also be used to haul up serious casualties from the jungle floor. This versatility rendered the Huskie the premier search-and-rescue platform at the time. Indeed, other rescue helicopters, including Bell's workhorse UH-1 Iroquois—the "Huey"—were handicapped early on by the need to find a clear landing zone before setting down. Not so for the HH-43. The HH-43's standard four-man crew consisted of a pilot and co-pilot up front with a crew chief-hoist operator and a pararescueman-medic in back.[42]

Pararescuemen, also known as "parajumpers," or PJs for short, are a hard-charging lot. Aggressive, highly trained, and motivated, they are often referred to as the Air Force's version of Green Berets or Navy Seals. Their job of rescuing downed air crews and other personnel often results in exposure to the most hazardous conditions and hostile fire. Of the nineteen Air Force enlisted during the Vietnam War to receive the Air Force Cross— second only to the Medal of Honor—ten were awarded to pararescuemen.[43]

As for Potter, he'd already logged hundreds of hours flying the Huskie by the time he'd arrived in Vietnam in September 1965. Born in 1934 in the ranch house of his Joseph, Oregon, family farm, Potter began his career as a young Naval ROTC student at Oregon State. "I wanted that white uniform. I thought it was classy," he would later say with a chuckle. But it wasn't long before that Navy white had lost its luster. Bitten by the flying bug, Potter discovered that Navy protocol required that he spend eighteen months with the fleet before applying for flight training. "The Air Force said, 'We don't have any of those silly rules. Come with us and you can go straight to pilot training.'" And that's just what he did. Commissioned an Air Force second lieutenant in 1956, Potter was flying B-25 bombers less than two years later. But it was in 1959, when he transitioned to helicopters—and air rescue— that he knew he'd found his calling. After a three-year stint flying choppers in Europe, Potter landed in Phoenix flying scores of Air Force rescue missions across Arizona. "People were always getting into trouble in the Grand Canyon," he recalls.[44]

Indeed, Potter was no stranger to challenging rescue operations. On one mission, he and his crew got the call that a baby on the Havasupai Indian Reservation deep in the Canyon was near death and in need of immediate extraction. Upon landing, Potter spied a group of Indians sitting in a circle around the infant. "It was like they were administering last rites for this little baby," he says. The crew stood by for hours as the flight surgeon struggled to administer an IV to bolster the severely dehydrated infant. Near dusk, black thunderheads began to swell ominously overhead. Getting caught at the bottom of the Canyon in such a storm would be treacherous and would likely doom the baby. And it didn't augur well for the crew, either. Instrument flight was especially hazardous for chopper pilots. Visual was always the best bet. At last, the surgeon deemed the infant stable enough for travel. Potter, wasting no time, pulled pitch and roared out of the Canyon, desperate to beat the approaching squall line. Above the rim, he could see a furious line of thunderstorms blocking the route back to Phoenix. The only choice was to swing west in hopes of finding refuge and care for the baby. Finally, the lights of a small town materialized out of the murk, as violent thunderclaps rocked the chopper and blue-white lightning flashed all around. "It was dark then, and we didn't know our way around this town," he recalls. "Then we spotted a football field at the center of town. We just landed right in the middle of it." As fate would have it, a hospital sat right next door. Potter and crew rushed the baby over, and she survived.[45]

And so it was that now, at first light on Friday, 22 October, Potter was right back in the thick of things. Command had put his ship on alert status. His CSAR crew, which included copilot Capt. L.C. Henry, crew chief Staff Sgt. Richard A. Connon, and pararescueman Staff Sgt. Lenny "Leon" Fullwood, was indeed bound for the fight at Plei Me. A close air support pilot had been shot down overnight and was alone in a sea of enemy troops. Potter's HH-43F—the Huskie's latest iteration featuring performance enhancements and an up-armored cockpit sheathed in titanium plates—would take the lead as Rescue One. Meanwhile, Capt. Raymond L. Murden would pilot Rescue Two, the backup helicopter that would stand ready to swoop in and rescue the rescuers in the event Potter's primary chopper was shot down.[46]

Murden and Potter had known each other for years. The two had gone through pilot training together at San Antonio's Lackland Air Force Base and helicopter school at Stead Air Force Base in Reno. Then, as luck would have it, the pilots landed assignments together in France. By the time Potter and Murden got back to the States in 1962, both the men and their families had become close friends. By 0700 hours, both crews had taken to the alert trailers, Spartan living quarters situated right on the flight line so aircrews could launch within minutes of getting the go order. And then the waiting began. Minutes became hours, and day turned to night. Still no go. "'Standby, standby, standby.' This went on all day, all day, all day," Potter recalls wryly. Something was preventing command from pulling the trigger on the rescue attempt. Back in the tall elephant grass of Plei Me, the NVA hot on his trail, no one knew this better than Mel Elliott.[47]

Elliott

After Berry's failed rescue attempt, Elliott had tried to move toward the camp on his own. Going was slow. It seemed that every time he'd made a bit of progress, fire would suddenly erupt in the jungle around him. Incoming and outgoing. Hit the deck, wait for the coast clear, then start moving again. Rinse and repeat. Finally, when it seemed futile to continue, the Spad pilot crept into the tall brush, covered himself with leaves and mud to camouflage his white skin, and waited out the night. Sleep was out of the question. The crump of mortars and staccato small-arms fire alternated with tac-air strike runs, while ferocious black ants wriggled and bit beneath the fetid leaf litter. Nevertheless, he had to bear up and remain still. To slap and thrash at the gnawing insects would invite decidedly unwanted attention.[48]

Finally, just after dawn, Elliott heard the telltale whine of an 0-1 Bird Dog circling the area. He snapped on his two-way radio and raised the pilot. In all the tumult, Elliott had forgotten his call sign and had to identify himself by name. When the pilot was satisfied Elliott was indeed who he said he was, the two worked out his rough location by identifying landmarks in the area. Now in broad daylight and with the heat of the day building, Elliott opted to remain in his hide. Hours ticked by. Thirst set in. If only he'd been able to free his survival kit from the chute! At last, as night came on, Elliott once again heard the O-1 buzzing overhead. "Sit tight," came the pilot's voice. "A Huey's on the way."[49]

Some minutes later, Elliott heard the distinctive *whump, whump, whump* of the Huey's rotor churning nearby. "Move to a place where we can pick you up," crackled the pilot's voice over the radio. Elliott crept to a small dirt track nearby and clicked on his strobe. Overhead, he could just make out the darkened shadow of the chopper as it made its first orbit, lights blacked out. On its third pass, the Huey flicked on its floodlight, scanning the foliage for the downed pilot. Just then, the roar of a .51 caliber machine gun split the night. No more than fifty yards from Elliott's position, streaks of green tracers clawed out of the gloom to down the Huey. The chopper again went black, peeling off and out of the area. Elliott was again alone. But not for long. Not ten minutes after the Huey had been chased away, an NVA patrol came sweeping down the same dirt track Elliott had just used, their flashlight beams crisscrossing and cutting the night. Elliott could hear the soldiers chattering amongst themselves as they searched for their quarry. Just twenty feet off the trail, the pilot flattened himself to earth, desperately trying to become one with the very soil itself. Two feet from where he lay, the beam of a flashlight swept the ground. He held his breath and waited. A long minute passed. Then, all at once, the soldiers turned and moved down the trail and out of earshot. Quietly, Elliott slinked some distance away and found a new hiding spot. It was now about 8 p.m. He'd been on the ground for nearly eighteen hours. It was clear that the NVA had no intention of making his escape easy. Higher command would have to find another way. In the meantime, there would again be no sleep. Overhead, tac-air fighter-bombers roared in and out delivering their payloads. Mortars *crumped* and *boomed*. Hungry and hunted, filthy and bedraggled, the pilot settled into his hide and steeled himself for another night alone in the jungle.[50]

⸎

By 0600 on Friday, DELTA and the Rangers were ready to move. The relief force had spent the previous fitful hours coiled into a tight defensive perimeter about a thousand meters north of Plei Me. Beckwith had provided Moore with the RF's grid coordinates and told the young Special Forces captain to bring in air strikes everywhere except his meager tract. He then put the relief force on "half-alert"— half the men awake, half asleep. Some, like DELTA troopers Capt. Euell White and Major A. J. "Bo" Baker, huddled together for warmth, shivering beneath a poncho in the cold, Highlands night. But there was very little sleep to be had. Tac-air spent the night blasting the jungle all around the RF's position.[51]

"The bombs were so close at times that the concussion would lift us off the ground," White recalls.[52] Four journalists, including Charles Burnett of KTLA-TV in Los Angeles, were also hunkered amid the relief force. Beckwith later claimed that Burnett had boarded one of the airlift choppers back at Pleiku without permission, apparently hoping to land the scoop of a lifetime.[53] It would prove a fateful decision. Nevertheless, the journalists were understandingly anxious about their situation, as a maelstrom of munitions rained down around them. At least one demanded to know how Beckwith would provide for their safety. "Beckwith's reply is not appropriate for printing," says White, "but the essence of it was to lie down, be still, and be quiet."[54]

Now, as the first rays of sunshine peeked above the horizon, Delta Sgt. Maj. Bill DeSoto, a wizened veteran of both World War II and Korea, mustered the RF for its movement four hundred meters east to pick up the red clay dirt road that led into camp. The plan was for the relief force to parallel the road through the jungle and let the narrow track guide them in, but the going was painfully slow. Choking vegetation ground the RF's progress to a snail's pace. After nearly two hours, and still about eight hundred meters out, Beckwith's force finally crested a ridge above the camp. Below, the DELTA commander spied various NVA positions, including an ambush site that the communists had set to hit anyone trying to relieve the camp. Miraculously, the position was not manned.[55]

"I was damn glad," Beckwith wrote. "I told my guys and Maj. Thut [Tat] it would take us too long to reach the camp continuing through the jungle. 'My plan is to veer off to the east, hit the road just as it goes over the hill, then run like hell to the camp gates.'"[56] At about four hundred meters out, and now in broad daylight, the crowd of rambling RF troops finally caught the attention of NVA gunners. Beckwith gave the order to make a run for it, as the relief force began taking sporadic small-arms fire from nearby enemy positions. Earlier, the DELTA commander had radioed ahead that the RF was coming in. Plei Me's defenders held their fire and threw open the main gate as the mass of men careened over the last open ground toward safety, each no doubt praying that his luck would hold a few moments longer. But it was just then that NVA fire began to find its mark. A South Vietnamese Ranger lieutenant was shot dead, and at least two Americans and two ARVN Rangers were lightly wounded. Then Burnett fell, his long blond hair flailing as the Los Angeles newsman caught a bullet through the eye. Dragging in their dead and wounded, the RF dove for cover in the trench line as the sizzle of incoming rounds popped and snapped. Hunter, who had rushed to the area, scrambled to treat the still-breathing newsman, by far the most seriously injured. The surgeon quickly ran an albumin IV to offset the journalist's plummeting blood pressure. Beckwith later claimed that Desoto had repeatedly warned the newsman to keep his blond hair covered, presumably to lessen the likelihood of his being targeted. "My sergeant major kept telling him, 'If you don't keep your hat on, you're going to get to porked.' And, as fate would have it, he had his hat off and he was running down the road."[57]

It had been two and a half days since the communists had begun their siege. The five-kilometer trek from the insertion LZ, through thick, enemy-infested jungle, had alone taken Beckwith's RF a full day to negotiate. Nevertheless, an outside element had at last reinforced Plei Me.

Meanwhile, back at II Corps headquarters, an even more substantial relief element seemed finally to be in the offing. Indeed, the impasse between Vinh Loc and Mataxis had been broken that Friday with the intervention of I Field Force, Vietnam commander Maj. Gen. Stanley Larsen based in Nha Trang. Field Force was a recently created corps-level US command with responsibility for overseeing American military activities in II Corps. The command had at its disposal elements of the recently arrived 1st Cavalry Division (Airmobile), based about ninety kilometers east of Pleiku at An Khe. The 1st Cav was the first full US division to deploy to Vietnam. Its new airmobile signifier was the result of a reworking of Fort Benning, Georgia's, 11th Air Assault Division (Test), which had been experimenting with the use of helicopter transport to move and support large formations of combat infantry. With a much more active role in Vietnam looming for the United States, Army planners stepped up the creation of the new airmobile division in June 1965. Elements that supported the new unit's mission were retained from the 2nd Infantry Division already based at Fort Benning and combined with the 11th Division's air assault assets. The result was the first airmobile division in Army history. Maj. Gen. Harry W. O. Kinnard, who'd overseen the 11th Division's air mobility exercises, was placed in command. An ambitious go-getter, Kinnard was perhaps the perfect pick to get the fledgling airmobile concept off the ground. The 1939 West Point grad had made full colonel by twenty-nine, had parachuted into France with the 101st Airborne Division during the Normandy Landings and won the Distinguished Service Cross for extreme gallantry during Operation Market Garden. Kinnard had also served as Gen. Tony McAuliffe's operations officer at Bastogne during the Battle of the Bulge. Kinnard is credited with urging McAuliffe's iconic "Nuts!" retort to the German demand for Bastogne's surrender. The general knew that Vietnam was to be the proving ground for the Army's new air assault concept, and he was eager to show what the 1st Cav could do.[58]

Interestingly, Larsen, not Mataxis, was technically Vinh Loc's senior II Corps adviser. Loc was, among other things, a man highly sensitive to military formalities. He believed that, as a major general, his senior corps adviser should be of an equivalent rank. To facilitate military cooperation between MACV and Saigon, Gen. William Westmoreland, overall commander of MACV, had recently appointed Larsen to the post. In practice, however, that role continued to be filled by Mataxis, who in the shakeup had recently been named Larsen's deputy. At any rate, Larsen flew to Pleiku on 22 October to add his voice to the growing chorus encouraging Loc to release more troops for Plei Me's relief. Adding to the urgency was the fact that 1st Cav intelligence analysts were now estimating that there were likely at least two *regiment*-sized enemy units operating between Pleiku and Plei Me. If at full strength, this meant that the enemy could have more than four thousand troops in the area. Such a force made it possible for the communists to simultaneously besiege Plei Me and to severely threaten any ARVN units sent to its rescue. Pleiku's relief force had to be strong enough to push through a powerful ambush. Over the ensuing discussions, Larsen eventually pledged to move in elements of the 1st Cav to assume responsibility for Pleiku's security if Loc would agree to release to Hon II Corps' remaining battalion, the 22nd Rangers. Loc consented—and went one step further, giving Hon the go-ahead to pull an additional unit, the 1st Battalion, 42nd Infantry Regiment, from the 24th Special Tactical Zone at Kontum and have it meet up with Luat's ATF, still milling about in the Phu My area. The newly released 22nd Ranger Battalion, under the command of Capt. Phạm Văn Phúc, would then be airlifted into a position to the ambushers' rear. This brought the combined strength of the Plei Me reaction force up to nearly 1,200 troops. Whether it would be enough to defeat the anticipated ambush and relieve the beleaguered Special Forces camp remained to be seen.[59]

It now remained for 24th STZ planners to choose the best avenue of approach. There were three options: Route 5 from Phu My to Plei Me, a road to the east of Route 5, and a cross-country approach. The road to the east of Route 5 was quickly ruled out, as five bridges necessary for its traverse had been knocked out by local force Viet Cong. Planners also determined that, while the cross-country route would greatly reduce the risk of ambush, its broken ground and dense vegetation would likely take at least four days to negotiate. That left Route 5 as the only reasonable approach. Intelligence identified the most likely ambush site, and an airstrike was preplanned to prep the area before the ATF rolled through. In addition, the 22nd Ranger Battalion would air assault to an LZ just west of the likely ambush site. Its mission would be to sweep east toward Route 5, eliminating any enemy forces encountered, and finally to establish a blocking position so that ambushers would be caught between it and the ATF.[60]

For his part, Larsen ordered Kinnard to move a 1st Cav force to Camp Holloway to secure Pleiku and the II Corps headquarters. The initial task force, dubbed "Task Force INGRAM" after its commander, Lt. Col. Earl Ingram, consisted of the 2nd Battalion, 12th Cavalry, a battery of 105mm howitzers from the 2nd Battalion, 17th Artillery, an aerial gun section of the 1st Squadron, 9th Cavalry, two airlift platoons from the 229th Assault Helicopter Battalion, and other supporting units. Ingram commenced the airlift of his task force from An Khe at 0800 hours on Saturday, 23 October, completing the move to Holloway by about 1300 hours. Meanwhile, Kinnard, sensing that the 1st Cav's role in the relief effort was bound to grow in coming days, secured permission from Larsen to send the division's entire 1st Brigade to Pleiku. The brigade, which had operational responsibility for Pleiku Province, was at the moment engaged in Operation Scrimmage east of An Khe along Highway 19 near Binh Khe. The brigade, under deputy commander Lt. Col. Harlow Clark, who'd assumed temporary command after his boss, Col. Elvy Roberts, suffered a leg injury, was extracted from the Vinh Thanh Valley by 1500 hours on the 23rd and had completed its move to Holloway by midnight. There, 1st Brigade assumed operational control of Task Force INGRAM. Aside from providing security for Pleiku, Clark's brigade had two other missions: to provide artillery support for Operation Dan Thang 21—the mission to relieve Plei Me—and to act as a reaction force in case things went from bad to worse at the camp. Kinnard had ordered the establishment of a division Tactical Operations Center at Pleiku under Brig. Gen. Richard T. Knowles for just such a contingency. And it was he who assumed overall command of the American task force.[61]

Back at Plei Me, Beckwith wasted no time taking charge. And from the moment he was safely inside the wire, the DELTA commander hadn't liked what he saw. After three nights under siege, the camp was in general disarray. With the hundred or so Montagnard family members who'd sought shelter inside the camp on the siege's first night, Plei Me was certainly overcrowded. A thick red dust covered everything. Worse, about sixty bodies by Beckwith's count were stacked inside what was left of the medical dispensary, while others were laid out on the ground outside. Some of the dead were in body bags, others wrapped in Army blankets. When the supply of both had run out, defenders took to bundling the corpses in the brightly colored parachute silk left over from supply drops. Beckwith also spotted what he took to be more Montagnard dead—along with numerous body parts—hanging in the perimeter wire. He was almost certainly mistaken about this last, however. Due to the CIDG's defensive posture in the gun trenches, it was highly unlikely that any of them would have become entangled in their own protective barriers. At the same time, the repeated assaults on the wire by NVA sappers and infantry made it much more likely that what Beckwith was seeing were actually the bodies of communist soldiers. Regardless of their identity, the stench of decomposing flesh was overwhelming and hung like an oppressive cloud. Consequently, Beckwith was convinced that there was a serious lack of discipline in the camp.[62]

As the senior officer in camp, Beckwith now assumed command. He got with Moore and berated the young SF captain for the camp's condition. With things in such turmoil, how were they supposed to mount a coherent defense, he bellowed. Beckwith declared that he was the "new mayor of Plei Me" and told Moore that he and his troopers would fall in line. Hunter, the C2 surgeon who'd arrived about forty-eight hours earlier, witnessed the exchange and later wrote that he believed Beckwith had behaved "boorishly" in the encounter. Looking back, Hunter says he understands why Beckwith needed to assert his authority but disagrees with how he went about it. According to Hunter, Moore had done a commendable job during the siege. The surgeon described him as a thoughtful planner and "a quiet, steady presence" whom Hunter credited as at least part of the reason he was still alive. As for Beckwith, Hunter wondered, what did he expect? Did "good" leadership and discipline mean risking the lives of medevac pilots to carry out the dead under a hail of antiaircraft fire? Should camp defenders, exhausted, short of water, and under nearly continuous attack, have spent their energy burying corpses rather than manning the gun trenches?[63]

Still, Hunter readily admits that he was relieved when Beckwith and DELTA arrived. These were the professionals, the hard-chargers who were a breed apart even from Special Forces troopers like himself. In their wizened faces, shadowed by age and experience, he saw sharp-edged fighters tempered in the fires of World War II and Korea. "I don't know if there was a guy in DELTA younger than twenty-five," he recalls. "Charlie Beckwith had gray whiskers, and everybody just looked tough. Bill DeSoto looked as if he could eat snakes. I felt better." While their ordeal was by no means over, that even a handful of such men had come to stand on Plei Me's ramparts bolstered the physician's courage. Now, they would finally be able to sally forth and clear those NVA positions and trenches, so close and threatening, on the camp's north side. *Now,* he thought, *we're going to start taking back territory. We're going to start to break the siege.*[64]

Capt. Myron Burr

Meanwhile, the deadly duel between American airpower and NVA gunners continued unabated. Daytime was both a blessing and a curse for pilots and aircrews. For tac-air, enemy positions were far easier to see and hit by the light of day, but what was good for one was also good for the other. By night, fighter-bombers were nothing more than disembodied engine sounds under the cover of darkness. But during the day, they stood out in stark relief against bright blue skies and were perfect targets for enemy gunners. The same went for supply aircraft. Big C-7 Caribous and C-123 Providers made fat targets as they lumbered in in broad daylight to make their drops, but at least the crews had a better chance of hitting their mark. The men of the 310th Air Commando Squadron knew all about it. The Air Force squadron, along with the Army's 92nd Aviation Company, had assumed the lion's share of resupply missions for Plei Me. Today was no different. At 0830 hours, a C-123 from the 310th lifted off from Nha Trang for what would already be the squadron's third sortie of the day. The supply plane, commanded by Capt. Leonard Dasbach and piloted by Capt. Edward Beck, was bound for Plei Me with ten thousand pounds of badly needed ammunition. When the Provider arrived at about 0915, flights of B-57 and A1-E fighter-bombers were working over NVA positions near camp. Dasbach radioed to coordinate with the two FACs controlling the airspace and was told to set up an orbit until tac-air had cleared. Lt. Col. John A. Martin, a forward air controller with the 21st Tactical Air Support Squadron, then coordinated with Dasbach while the other controlled the fighter-bombers. The idea was for pilot Beck to time the start of his approach just as tac-air pulled off their runs. Hopefully, the enemy would still have their heads down when they made their pass.[65]

Once the CAS strike had cleared, Beck began his approach on a northwest-southeast vector. He dropped the Provider to three hundred feet and came in at about 170 miles per hour. Surface winds were negligible, so there was less chance of drift. As long as the release went off without a hitch, the pallets had a better-than-average shot at landing on target. Provided, of course, the massive C-123 wasn't shot down before it could make its drop. As if on cue, the surrounding hills lit up with NVA antiaircraft fire, as the heavy slugs laced upward to meet the aircraft. The aircrew could hear the heavy machine gun rounds crackling near, but none hit home. They were lucky. Those aboard knew that several Providers from their own squadron, as well as Caribous with the 92nd, had already been hit, some so badly that they might never return to service. Air crew members had been wounded as well. So far, none had been killed, but all aboard knew that every supply drop over the camp was a dance with death. At any moment, a string of those fat .51 caliber projectiles could find its mark and tear you from the sky. There was no such thing as a free run over Plei Me.[66]

Suddenly, the big craft was over the drop zone. Moments before, loadmaster Staff Sgt. George McCluskey had disengaged the safety lanyard to "trigger" the load for release. Now given the verbal greenlight, McCluskey pulled the release pin. Load weight and momentum did the rest, as gravity propelled the supply pallets violently rearward. Just 1.5 seconds later, the heavy bales had pulled loose from the plane, their bright yellow and blue parachute silks billowing as five thousand pounds of bundled ammo careened to earth. The supply drop was right on target. Beck pulled the aircraft into its return orbit. The loadmaster and Special Forces kickers in the cargo hold would have to hustle. They'd have just about four minutes to stage the second half of the load before they were once again over the DZ. Just then, Dasbach's radio crackled to life. Another flight of fighter-bombers was inbound, Martin said. Can you extend your approach until they've made their run? Dasbach agreed, and the C-123 initiated a wider orbit to give tac-air enough time to clear. But at about two and a half kilometers southeast of camp, the second half of the load—five thousand pounds of ammunition—suddenly tumbled to earth. As before, the loadmaster and kickers had staged the load and removed the safety lanyard. But this time, the release pin holding the load in place broke free. Dasbach radioed Martin. "We've got a problem," said the aircraft commander. "Our mechanical gate release failed. If there's a chance the VC will get it, it needs to be hit." Martin and Dasbach agreed that the C-123 would set up and orbit around the supply bundles until the FAC could arrive and pinpoint their location.[67]

Martin called in a flight of Skyraiders to hit the downed bundles. All around the camp, huge divots left by CAS bombs had been gouged from the earth, as if by some giant ice cream scooper. Skyraider pilot Capt. Myron W. Burr, thirty-one, came up on the radio. The Air Force pilot had spent his career flying piston-engine supply planes like the C-123, but the growing need for Spad pilots in the CAS role had pressed him into new service. This was his maiden combat flight. Martin radioed that he'd mark the target with white phosphorus. The FAC then rolled his 0-1 and dove on the target, firing 2.75-inch rockets into the heart of the errant supply bundles. Now it was the Skyraiders' turn to finish the job. Burr scored a direct hit on the first pass. But as he was pulling out of his run, he immediately noticed a dramatic power loss, engine coughing and sputtering. Burr applied more throttle but quickly realized that he soon wouldn't have enough power to stay aloft. In its wake, the Spad trailed an inky black line of smoke. Must've been hit by ground fire, he thought. Word had by now gotten out among the pilots who flew over Plei Me: if you had to punch out, don't do it south of camp. Of course, that's exactly where Burr now found himself. Per standard operating procedure, the pilot jettisoned his remaining bomb ordnance and banked toward Plei Me, desperate to make the relative safety northeast of camp. But the Skyraider was dropping like a stone. Burr muscled the canopy open but there was no time to bail out. All he could do was ride the ship to earth and pray for the best. Moments later, the Skyraider smacked into the jungle below, snapping into pieces like dry kindling. Fire and smoke poured from the wreckage. It was just after 1000 hours.[68]

The plane had flipped over. Burr, still in the cockpit and hanging by his shoulder harness, wasn't sure at first where he was. Then, the sound of crackling snapped him to attention. *Fire. The plane is on fire. Have to get out. Now.* Burr hit the release on his seat belt and tumbled to earth. And then he just ran, no looking back, a single-minded imperative to escape the plane before it exploded. He reached the relative safety of a tangle of elephant grass about twenty-five meters away. In the distance, gunfire snapped and popped. Burr checked himself over. Other than a few scrapes and a gash on his left leg, the pilot was miraculously unhurt. Whether he stayed that way would depend on how soon friendlies could arrive and pick him up.

He knew there were FACs in the area. Luckily, he'd been equipped with an emergency radio. But when he took it out to raise help, he realized that he'd completely forgotten his call sign. For security, downed pilots were trained to authenticate using their unique identifiers when calling for help. After all, the enemy would like nothing better than to lure in a rescue craft with a false distress call. It finally came to him: "Toll 92." Burr raised a FAC circling the area and the two devised a rescue plan. Burr was to remain hidden until the air controller could bring in choppers to effect pickup.[69]

A short time later, the FAC had rustled up a Vietnamese Air Force (VNAF) CH-34 Choctaw transport helicopter and four UH-1B escort gunships from the 155th Aviation Company. The choppers' presence, however, soon attracted enemy ground fire. The VNAF pilot refused to make the pickup under such conditions, and the rescue mission was in danger of being aborted. At that moment, gunship pilot 1st Lt. Edward T. Pledger took matters into his own hands. He would rescue the downed pilot. Already overladen with armaments, Pledger first had to fire off his rockets to make room for the additional weight. He blasted a suspected NVA position, then swooped in. Burr, who'd been in radio contact with both the FAC and Pledger, was ready and waiting. He broke from cover and made a mad dash for Pledger's Hog as it settled onto its skids fifteen meters away. Burr jumped aboard headfirst, Pledger pulling redlines as the Huey clawed skyward. Burr, who had a wife and four daughters back home, had promised his family that he would make it home. When doctors checked the pilot over more thoroughly back in Saigon, they discovered that the crash had fractured several of his spinal vertebrae. Burr made good on his promise when he was sent home to the United States to recover. He would retire a full colonel after twenty-nine years in the Air Force, his last assignment as the associate dean of the Air War College at Maxwell Air Force Base, Alabama. In retirement, Burr went on to become a competitive sprinter with the U.S.A. Track and Field Association, winning gold and silver medals both at the state and national levels. He died in the summer of 2018 at the age of eighty-four. He left behind a wife, three sons, two daughters, and nine grandchildren. His remains rest in Arlington National Cemetery.[70]

After receiving Moore's situation report, Beckwith conferred with Tat about their next move. A discrepancy would later arise between Beckwith's official after-action report filed 15 November 1965 and his memoir published in 1983. What was not in doubt at that moment, however, was the enemy's disposition upon the high ground about four hundred meters north of camp. Plei Me had received continuous fire from the ridge throughout the siege, including from likely heavy machine gun positions, and its elevation allowed NVA snipers to put fire down into the camp. What was in doubt, however, was what, if anything, Beckwith wanted to do about the enemy presence there. Beckwith later wrote in his after-action report that he and Tat determined that the "area immediately surrounding the camp must be cleared." But in his memoir, Beckwith claims that he wanted instead to merely solidify the camp's defenses and determine enemy strength and capabilities before taking any further action. Under this version of events, Beckwith says he radioed Pleiku and recommended this plan to McKean. Again, according to Beckwith's memoir, McKean did not agree and instead ordered the DELTA commander to "get outside the camp, rummage around, and clear the enemy out of there." Beckwith contends he argued against this course of action but was overruled by McKean. For his part, Capt. White said that when he and his team came over from Okinawa, Beckwith had told them that he would take any mission if he thought it could be accomplished, regardless of cost. "In other words," White recalls, "you're expendable."[71]

Regardless of who gave the order, a three-company assault force was organized to clear the northern slope. The force consisted of one CIDG company commanded by a Detachment A-217 NCO and the two Airborne Ranger companies. Before the sortie, Beckwith conferred with Capt. Thomas W. Pusser, a twenty-six-year-old West Point grad from Chesterfield, South Carolina, and the senior adviser to the 91st Airborne Rangers. The two agreed that the Vietnamese leadership of one company was stronger than the other. Pusser argued that he should stay with the weaker company to help shore it up. After all, he'd amassed a lot of experience with the Airborne Rangers and believed he could better motivate them. On the other hand, Pusser's new executive officer, Capt. Euell White, thirty-one, had never met his counterpart before today. It would be better for White to take the stronger company, Pusser concluded. Technically, the Americans were only "advisers," with command decisions still resting with their Vietnamese counterparts. But mission success often depended on more than just American advice. For one thing, the DELTA advisers controlled CAS strikes and could coordinate with FACs overhead to call in support. But beyond that, the Americans' presence could act as a steadying influence on the Vietnamese, especially when trouble arose.[72]

Pusser held a final briefing with the other advisers and Special Forces NCOs who would go out. The assault force was to first sweep up the hill, eliminate any enemy positions, conduct a body count, and gather intelligence materials and weapons from the field. The companies would then wheel around and backtrack toward camp, covering any territory they might have missed. Pusser's company would maneuver to remain on White's right flank throughout the movement. When the briefing concluded, Pusser told White to find the news reporters and invite them to come along and cover the operation. White found them huddled in the team house. "If you want to see the action, this is where it is," he said. All three declined the invitation. The DELTA trooper shrugged and returned to make his final preparations.[73]

At about noon, White heard the heavy *whump whump whump* of one of DELTA's H-34s as it settled onto its skids in an open space between the buildings. Plei Me's airspace was technically closed to helicopter transport because of antiaircraft fire, and this was an unauthorized flight. But Beckwith's three South Vietnamese pilots—whom he would later praise as the finest he'd ever worked with—were willing to run the gauntlet for their commander. It's unclear why—or even if—Beckwith had called in the chopper. He had made it clear, both at the time and later in his memoir, that he believed the unburied corpses stacked around camp were bad for morale. When his requests to have them flown out were denied, he might have tasked his own people with coming in. Or, perhaps his loyal Vietnamese pilots had taken it upon themselves. At any rate, White ran into someone from the chopper a short time later. The H-34 had taken some antiaircraft fire on its way in, and Jimmie McBynum, the 5th Group medic White had met the day before, had been hit and killed. The news was a gut-punch. If only, White thought, he had been able to convince McBynum to come with him on the medevac, he might still be alive. The DELTA trooper learned later that when McBynum heard that a helicopter would be flying directly into Plei Me that afternoon, he jumped at the chance. And yet, from the moment he'd gotten the okay to fly in on the H-34, the Special Forces trooper reportedly knew he wouldn't live to see another day. The medic had even sought out a chaplain to make his peace before boarding. When a friend urged him not to go, McBynum had reportedly said that he simply had to. It was his duty. In yet another of war's grim ironies, he would never make it off the chopper. The medic had been in-country for just ten days and was leaving behind a wife and six-week-old daughter in his native North Carolina. McBynum would be posthumously awarded the Silver Star and Purple Heart for his service.[74]

Sometime between 1300 and 1400 hours, the three companies moved out the front gate on the camp's east side and turned left toward the north ridge. The two Airborne Ranger companies advanced abreast in a skirmish line, with the CIDG company to the rear. The Rangers passed the now-abandoned Montagnard family longhouses on the right but encountered no resistance—indeed, saw not a single living soul—as they swept up the hill. Had the NVA pulled out? The companies worked their way along the ridge, then made ready to turn back down the hill. Pusser's radio had quit working, so he took the opportunity to tell White. He found his XO searching the body of what they believed to be a Chinese officer. American intelligence had for some time suspected the Chinese of embedding officers with North Vietnamese units. If true, this would be a very valuable piece of intelligence, to be sure. North Vietnamese prisoners captured in the vicinity a few weeks later testified that each NVA regiment infiltrated into the South had a Communist Chinese adviser. "My radio's out," he told White. "Call the camp and tell them that if they want to get me, they'll have to do it through my counterpart." The adviser then moved off to rejoin his company.[75]

White's Rangers were just beginning their turn when heavy fire suddenly tore into their flank and rear. Those who weren't immediately hit dropped and clawed for cover. For a split second, White believed Pusser's Rangers had inadvertently opened fire on their sister company. Then he saw it: a well-concealed series of enemy machine gun positions, no more than one hundred meters from the camp's outer wire. They had been there the whole time, but the assault force had walked right past them. Also well concealed along the ridge was a battalion of the NVA's 33rd Regiment. The communists had waited for the last of the CIDG company to clear the positions before opening fire. All three companies were now completely exposed. White and his South Vietnamese counterpart managed to turn their men into position, but rather than direct his troops to lay down suppressive fire and then maneuver to knock out the positions, the Airborne Ranger commander instead ordered a frontal assault. In the French colonial style, the company commander, swagger stick in hand, urged his men onward. His Rangers rose from cover and charged headlong into the maw—where they were met by a murderous wall of automatic weapons fire. White watched as the heavy rounds sawed through the onrushing Rangers like saplings. A few feet away, a Ranger platoon leader was shot through the crotch and died before he hit the ground. Everywhere, men were falling dead and wounded. The northern slope soon transformed into a charnel house.[76]

Just then, White's radio crackled to life. A forward air controller circling above had napalm available. The FAC asked if he could bring it in without hitting any friendlies. White turned to get the opinion of his counterpart. After all, White was the adviser, not the commander. But while the Vietnamese captain had not been timid during the fight, the thought of a napalm strike near his position seemed to break something in him. It was a phenomenon White had noted among the Vietnamese before. To White, they seemed to have had an inordinate fear of the fiery weapon. "When I mentioned napalm, he became a different person," White says. "He was just ready to get out of there." Ignoring his adviser's question, the captain instead screamed for his men to retreat. In order to effect an orderly withdrawal, the South Vietnamese would need to pull back by sections, each providing covering fire for the other until the company reached a predetermined rally point to the rear. None of that occurred. Instead, the Rangers simply turned and ran. The withdrawal quickly degenerated into a headlong rout.[77]

Finding himself suddenly alone, White turned to follow the Rangers. Just then, a 7.62 mm rifle round punched through his back like a red-hot poker. The bullet exited through his right side and crashed into his right forearm. White crumpled and scrambled for cover, bullets churning the earth around him as NVA gunners tried to finish the job. The DELTA captain knew he was in a bad way. He certainly couldn't depend on the Rangers for help. They were long gone by now. And neither of his American NCOs seemed to know that he'd been wounded. White keyed his radio. If ever there were a time for napalm, now was it. He'd find out soon enough whether he was far enough away. Moments later, a flight of F-105 Thuds rocketed overhead, napalm canisters tumbling to earth and erupting in a molten deluge. Incredibly, the moment the jets passed and the flames died away, NVA fire resumed unabated. White later learned that the communists had constructed a series of deep and sturdy tunnels throughout the area. Small spider holes were connected at each end, as were the .30 and .51 caliber machine gun emplacements. Gunners would duck inside the openings when they spotted a strike inbound and then pop back out and resume fire once the danger had passed.[78]

The gunners once more turned their attention to White, who had holed up in a shallow depression. The napalm strikes ineffective, White radioed the camp and told them he'd been wounded. "There's nothing we can do for you right now," came the reply. He set about bandaging his arm as best he could, while enemy incoming kicked at the dirt all around him. The outlook appeared bleak. The pain came on in sharp waves, and White could feel himself slipping into shock. But he knew that if he fainted, this would be his last day on earth. He'd never felt so exposed, so utterly alone. He began to wonder how long it would be before the North Vietnamese crept up on his position and either killed him outright or dragged him away as a prisoner of war. His thoughts soon drifted to his wife, Euna, and daughter, Sherry Lynn, back on Okinawa. The thought of their having to go on without him was gut wrenching. Some time passed. Suddenly, White looked up and saw that one of his DELTA NCOs, Sgt. 1st Class Marion "Mike" Holloway, had come back for him. The two had met for the first time only hours before. The sergeant belly-crawled his way to White's little depression and pulled the captain to a safer spot in a nearby fighting hole. Holloway, a heavy weapons specialist, looked at White's five foot eleven inch, 185-pound frame. "I'm going to call in a smoke screen. When I get the screen out, we're going to have to go. And you're going to have to go on your own feet because you're too big to carry." The sound of Holloway's calm, reassuring voice helped snap the DELTA captain out of his shocked state. White nodded, and Holloway fed the coordinates into the radio. Moments later a mortar crashed down nearby, blanketing the area in a thick cloud of smoke. It was go time. Holloway pulled White to his feet and the men lurched toward camp. But the screen didn't last long. Soon, NVA gunners began to zero in, so the men dropped prone and crawled until they'd made it over a rise that offered some protection. From there, the duo staggered the rest of the way into camp.[79]

Because of hostile fire, the main gate wasn't an option. White and Holloway went back through a hole in the wire that had been made for a previous sortie. On the way in, White spied another DELTA NCO. He would later write that he was seized with a dreadful premonition. "Tom Pusser's dead, isn't he?" he asked the sergeant. "Yes," came the reply. White had not known Pusser long but had been immediately impressed with what he saw as a tremendously dedicated soldier. Right before the Plei Me operation, White had accompanied Pusser to Saigon for a short R&R. The young captain was not married and had no children, but he was especially close to his thirteen-year-old sister, Betsy. White, who had a young daughter, helped Pusser shop for gifts at the Cholon PX for his little sister. The DELTA captain's tour would have been up in December, and he was to have been home by Christmas. Pusser would receive the Silver Star and Purple Heart posthumously.[80]

The sortie had also cost the Airborne Rangers and CIDG eleven dead and another twenty-six wounded. A Vietnamese Special Forces lieutenant was also killed in the attack. Due to the chaos and heavy fire, and with significant elements of the assault force pinned down for hours, the companies were not able to get everyone back into camp until about 1840 hours. For their part, the Rangers had managed to carry in the bodies of several of their dead but had left Pusser's behind. As the Central Highlands night fell across camp, the young captain's body remained exactly where he had fallen.[81]

As for White, the bullet had narrowly missed his spine and kidney. A hit to either probably would've killed him outright or at least made it impossible for him to escape with Holloway—which would have ultimately led to the same result. But the bullet had still done egregious damage to his insides and right arm. The DELTA captain was carried down into a bunker that served as a makeshift medical dispensary. White drifted in and out of consciousness. He was aware that someone was hovering over him, cleaning and dressing his wounds, but doesn't recall speaking to the man. But he caught glimpses of the doctor's smudged name tag by the bunker's dim light: HUNTER. It was a name he'd try his best to remember. The pain ebbed and flowed like a tidal surge, building and then receding. That he couldn't empty his bladder only made matters worse. His urethral sphincter—the muscle that controls such things—had seized, "shocked" by the bullet's impact. At times he was aware that some of his DELTA teammates had come to look in on him. There was Maj. Bo Baker, the new operations officer White had huddled with for warmth the night before. Later, Sgt. Maj. Bill DeSoto's face materialized out of the gloom. The rawboned old paratrooper repeatedly checked on White through those long hours. But if Beckwith came to the bunker that night, White has no memory of it.[82]

Meanwhile, the DELTA commander had seen what the disastrous attempt to clear the north ridge had wrought and later wrote that he was lucky to have gotten any of the Rangers back alive. He asserts in his memoir that he once again radioed McKean and reiterated his desire to first fortify the camp before launching any further operations. The camp's water supply was critical, so Beckwith requested a resupply drop of several hundred five-gallon cans of water, along with additional ammunition. Beckwith hadn't yet done a full assessment of just how much ammo they had, but he was sure the camp would be hit that night. The last thing he wanted was to run out of ammo in the middle of an assault on the wire. Beckwith then went a step further and requested a box of cigars and a case of whiskey for his men. McKean nearly balked, but Beckwith was already starting to believe that the siege was far from over. In fact, the DELTA commander had met with Thompson, DeSoto, Baker, and Pioletti after the ill-fated attack, and they'd all agreed they'd be lucky to get out of this alive. He thought having whiskey and cigars to look forward to would make the coming trials just a little easier to endure. McKean finally relented, and a supply drop was laid on. The drop came in three bundles, with the first landing outside the wire. The next two, however, were on target and included water, extra ammo . . . and the whiskey and cigars.[83]

But supply drops weren't the only incoming air traffic that afternoon. A few miles away, United Press International reporter Joe Galloway sat holding on for dear life as the Huey transport he was riding in thundered toward Plei Me. The camp was still officially closed to such aircraft, but that didn't matter much to the chopper's pilot, Capt. Ray Burns. The 119th Aviation Company slick pilot had run into his buddy Galloway the day before, and his fellow Texan was upset, to say the least. The newsman had caught wind that Beckwith and his team were airlifting out of Holloway to reinforce the Plei Me camp. Galloway had pulled out every stop getting to Pleiku, but by the time he'd arrived on the tarmac the morning of the 21st, Beckwith and company were long gone. Galloway was fit to be tied, storming up and down the flight line and "cussing like a sailor." Plei Me, he knew, was closed. Beckwith had been his only real chance of getting there—and getting the story.[84]

Just twenty-three, Galloway was already making a name for himself as an intrepid young reporter willing to go wherever the fight was. He'd just spent months slogging through the rice paddies of I Corps with the US Marines. In August, Galloway had caught the tail end of the siege at Duc Co. He'd gone out with the newly arrived 173rd Airborne Brigade to link up with then Maj. Norman Schwarzkopf, senior adviser to elements of the Vietnamese Airborne Division trying to break the siege. In early fall, the Refugio, Texas, native transferred to MACV headquarters in Pleiku to cover the much-heralded introduction of the 1st Cavalry Division into the Central Highlands. Galloway soon made fast friends with fellow Texan 1st Lt. Charles "Chuck" Oualline, a Huey slick pilot and section leader with the 119th Aviation Company based at nearby Camp Holloway.

Oualline hailed from tiny Aransas Pass on the Texas Gulf Coast and had been bitten by the flying bug when he was just ten years old. His uncle owned a piece of property that he used as a landing strip for his tiny Piper Cub. One day, the Navy was running an exercise nearby and had to make an unexpected helicopter landing at his uncle's makeshift airfield. The pilots invited young Oualline into the cockpit and showed him how everything worked. They even let him sit in the pilot's seat. "After that, I was hooked," he says with a chuckle. Since joining the 119th in July, Oualline had flown the usual "ash and trash" runs out to various Special Forces camps. Loads usually consisted of C-rations, fuel, ammo, bags of rice—even live chickens and pigs. On one flight, one of the chickens got loose, screeching and squawking as it buffeted about the Huey's interior. Luckily, one of the rice bags had spilled over, and grains had piled up in the chopper's Plexiglas chin bubble. Next thing he knew, the Oualline looked down between his feet to find the chicken calmly pecking away at his impromptu snack. There was no choice but to leave it to its lunch. But once on the ground, Oualline chased it out the side hatch. The bird disappeared in a flurry of feathers and was gone. Just another day in the Central Highlands.[85]

Oualline took the young reporter under his wing and introduced him around. Galloway soon discovered that several of the 119th's pilots also hailed from the Lone Star State. It wasn't long before the newsman was whiling away the nights playing poker and drinking "copious amounts of Jim Beam" with his fellow Aggies. Galloway was especially close to Burns, a "homeboy" who'd grown up in Ganado, just an hour or so up the road from Refugio. So when Burns saw that his buddy needed a hand, he was right there to offer it.[86]

The next day, Burns found Galloway. Yes, Plei Me was closed, the pilot confirmed. Several planes and at least one helicopter had already been shot down. But then he grinned. "You know, come to think of it, I'd love to have a look myself. I'll give you a ride." And so it was that Galloway now found himself strapped into the back of Burns's Huey late on the afternoon of the 22nd. As the chopper neared Plei Me, Burns suddenly banked the Huey hard, nearly laying it on its side as he cork-screwed the craft down to an open area below. For a few brief moments, the triangle of Plei Me was perfectly framed through the open side door, as Galloway watched white puffs of smoke erupt here and there throughout the camp. They were under mortar attack. All at once, Burns pulled back on the stick violently and flared for landing. The Huey had barely settled onto its skids before Galloway had leapt out to the red dirt below. Nearby troopers piled a few Montagnard casualties aboard to take his place. It might have been an unauthorized flight, but there was no sense wasting a chance to get out some of the wounded. With incoming mortars, Burns wasn't wasting time, either. After scrambling away, Galloway had just enough time to catch a glimpse of his friend through the Plexiglas. Grinning broadly, Burns threw him the "single-finger" salute, pulled pitch, and thundered away into the darkening sky.[87]

Moments later, a senior NCO Green Beret came running up.

"I don't know who you are, but Major Beckwith wants to see you right away," said the sergeant.

"And who would that be?" Galloway asked.

The sergeant pointed. "It's that big guy over there jumping up and down on his hat."

The young reporter shuffled over to where Beckwith stood glowering.

"Who are you?" Beckwith snarled. "A reporter," came Galloway's reply.

Beckwith's face darkened like a storm cloud about to burst. "You know, son. I need everything in the goddamned world. I need resupply, ammo, medevacs, everything. And what has the Army in its wisdom sent me? A goddamned reporter. Well, I have no vacancy here for a reporter, but I'm in desperate need of a corner machine gunner . . . and you're it."[88]

Beckwith walked the young newsman over to the east side of camp, left of the main gate. There, squatting at the rim of a slit trench and behind a parapet of sandbags, sat the dark form of an air-cooled, M1919 Browning .30 caliber machine gun. A few meters forward of the position was the main perimeter trench manned by Montagnards. The DELTA commander gave Galloway the two-minute tour, showing the reporter how to load, aim, clear, and fire the weapon. Once he was at least reasonably sure of the reporter's competence, Beckwith issued his final instructions. "You may shoot the little brown men outside the barbed wire," he said. "They are the enemy. You may not shoot the little brown men inside the barbed wire. They belong to me." And with that, Beckwith stalked away to other concerns. Galloway would man the weapon for the next three sleepless nights. His position was never probed, but mortar, machine gun, and sniper fire were constant companions. Sleep, when it came at all, was snatched in snippets during daytime lulls in action.[89]

Meanwhile, Hunter and Dan Shea were deluged with wounded. The medical men spent the next several hours triaging and treating what seemed like an endless flow of pulverized flesh. Both men had themselves been wounded by that point. Shea had been shot through the arm on the morning of the 20th during the failed rescue attempt of the downed gunship crew and had been working wounded ever since. For his part, Hunter had taken shrapnel fragments during an earlier attack and had stitched his own lacerations. Both were exhausted and nearing their breaking point. Hunter had so far resisted calling in medevacs. The antiaircraft fire was just too intense. Indeed, treating the wounded onsite, and thus sparing the medevac crews, was part of the reason he was here in the first place. But now he had several wounded Americans, two of whom were critical. He'd stabilized White but knew that the DELTA trooper would not live without open surgery to repair his insides. And then there was the television news reporter, Charles Burnett, who'd been shot in the head on the run into the camp that morning. His prognosis was not good, but he was still holding on and might be saved with proper care. Several others, like Shea and heavy weapons specialist Bob Sloan, had been working and fighting through their wounds for days. It was time to get them out.[90]

Hunter relayed his request for a medevac to C2 back at Pleiku. It was a dangerous mission, to be sure. Plei Me's airspace had been officially closed to helicopter transports since the shoot-down of the 119th's escort gunship Wednesday morning. Medevac pilots could not be ordered to go in, so the call was put out for volunteers. Soon, several medevacs came in low and fast and made for the makeshift landing pad nestled between several buildings at the camp's center. White and the other wounded Americans were loaded aboard, along with a few of the more critically injured Rangers and Montagnards. Then, the heavily laden choppers struggled upward and then forward, skimming low to build airspeed before grasping for altitude. One by one, they finally broke to the east and disappeared into the night. Just then, a flight of Thunderchiefs screeched overhead to deliver a tac-air strike nearby. It was a close call. A few seconds later and it would have been a disaster.[91]

C2 had kept the troopers apprised of the efforts to relieve the camp. By now, word had filtered through the ranks that Luat and the ATF were still stalled south of Pleiku. Exasperated, Plei Me's weary defenders steeled themselves for a fourth night under siege. They now had a few more men to help them, but they were still isolated and alone in Indian Country. The bloody assault that afternoon to clear the northern slope had done nothing but fill more body bags. The NVA were still there in force, and they were close—as the machine gun positions they'd discovered just one hundred meters from the wire could attest to. The communists could sweep down the hill whenever they liked. Flare ships circled above, sprinkling artificial illumination to dissuade them from trying. Beyond the wire, tac-air did its part, rocking the surrounding hills with thunderous concussions and fiery blasts. As before, the SF troopers, now with DELTA's help, roamed the battered ramparts to shore up the Montagnards and newly arrived Airborne Rangers. The communists continued to pummel the garrison with heavy recoilless rifle and mortar fire throughout the night. Despite Beckwith's concerns, the NVA did not launch a ground attack against the camp that night.[92]

Aerial view of Plei Me Special Forces Camp. *Courtesy of Terri Owen and projectdelta.net*

Left to right: Major A. J. "Bo" Baker, Major Charles "Tommy" Thompson, and Major Charlie Beckwith of Detachment B-52 (Project Delta). *Courtesy of Terri Owen and projectdelta.net*

Major Charlie Beckwith prepares to fire an M-79 grenade launcher. *Courtesy of Terri Owen and projectdelta.net*

Major Charlie Beckwith (left) looks on as Major Charles "Tommy" Thompson (right) calls in a close air support strike on enemy positions just beyond the wire. *Courtesy of Terri Owen and projectdelta.net*

Plei Me Special Forces camp, immediately after siege ended. 25–26 October 1965. *Standing, left to right*: Maj. A.J. "Bo" Baker (DELTA), 1st Lt. Robert Berry (executive officer, Detachment A-217), Capt. (and Dr.) R. Lanny Hunter (C2 surgeon), Sgt. Terrence Morrone (DELTA), two unidentified DELTA troopers. *Kneeling, left to right*: Spec. 5 Richard P. Loughlin (DELTA), Sgt. 1st Class Marion "Mike" Holloway (DELTA), Maj. Charles "Chargin' Charlie" Beckwith (DELTA commander), Maj. Charles "Tommy" Thompson (DELTA deputy commander). *Courtesy of Lt. Col. Robert Berry (Ret.)*

South Vietnamese soldiers near one of Plei Me's communication trenches. *Courtesy of Terri Owen and projectdelta.net*

Weary American Special Forces troopers gather around their team house table during a lull in the siege. *Courtesy of Terri Owen and projectdelta.net*

Maj. Charlie Beckwith talks to Detachment A-217 commander Capt. Harold Moore at Plei Me Camp, Oct. 1965. *Courtesy of Joe Galloway*

Parachuting supplies into Plei Me Camp, Oct. 1965. *Courtesy of Joe Galloway*

Sgt. 1st Class Joseph Bailey, 27, Detachment A-217, 5th Special Forces Group. Bailey and a small rescue team went outside the wire on 20 October in an attempt to reach the crew of a helicopter gunship that had been shot down just off the dirt airstrip south of camp. He and his team ran into a wall of NVA automatic weapons fire. Bailey was hit three times and died moments after being dragged back inside the perimeter wire. *Photo credit: https://www.vvmf.org*

Capt. Thomas W. Pusser, 26, Detachment B-52 (DELTA), was cut down in a hail of machine gun fire on 22 October as he led a company of Vietnamese Airborne Rangers in an attempt to clear the north ridge outside of Plei Me. Pusser had been due to DEROS in December. *Photo credit: https://www.vvmf.org*

Staff Sgt. Jimmie L. McBynum, 26, medic with 5th Special Forces Group. Despite the danger, McBynum had been desperate to get to Plei Me as soon as possible to help his fellow troopers. He'd turned down a chopper ride into the field on 21 October because he thought it would delay his arrival in Plei Me. Instead, he hitched a ride on an unauthorized chopper flight into camp around midday on 22 October but was killed by antiaircraft fire before he could get off the helicopter. *Photo credit: https://www.vvmf.org*

WO1 Don Glenn Knowlton, 24, 119th Aviation Company. Knowlton was the co-pilot for Croc 8 and was killed when the helicopter gunship was shot down south of camp on 20 October, just two weeks before his 25th birthday. *Photo credit: https://www.vvmf.org*

Spec. 5 Franklin D. Racine, 23, 119th Aviation Company. Crew chief aboard Croc 8. Also killed along with other crew of Croc 8 on 20 October. Racine's wife was expecting a baby boy any day. Racine, who was haunted with the feeling that he wouldn't survive Vietnam, had often told friends that his only hope was to live long enough to see his son born. Racine's son, Mark Allen, would be born five days after his father was killed in the skies over Plei Me. *Photo credit: https:// www.vvmf.org*

WO1 Ronald W. Macklin, 27, 119th Aviation Company. Aircraft commander for Croc 8. Like Racine, Macklin was often plagued with thoughts that he wouldn't live through his tour. Macklin was killed along with his crew on 20 October. *Photo credit: https://www.vvmf.org*

Spec. 5 Wesley McDonial, 30, the Croc 8 door gunner on temporary duty status from the 25th Infantry Division, was killed when his helicopter gunship was shot down just south of camp on 20 October. *Photo credit: https://www.vvmf.org*

An American Special Forces trooper positions a mortar tube while his Montagnard mortar team look on. *Courtesy of Terri Owen and project delta.net*

1st Lt. Charles "Chuck" Oualline in the cockpit of a 119th UH-1B in 1966, refueling "hot" at Buon Brieng SF camp. *Courtesy of Charles Oualline*

1st Lt. Jerry Riches (right) and Chuck Oualline (left), who were both in the 119th at same time, on standby for a mission. Door gunner in background is unidentified. Rice bags can be seen. Such "ash and trash" missions out to Special Forces camps were common for slick (transport) helicopter pilots. *Courtesy of Charles Oualline*

Dale Potter and his crew with rescued pilot Mel Elliott in front of Potter's rescue chopper HH-43 "Huskie" at Bien Hoa Airbase in Saigon on October 24, the day after the successful rescue. *Left to right*: Tech Sergeant Rick Connon, USAF (hoist operator); Capt. Mel Elliott (rescued Skyraider pilot); Capt. Dale Potter (seated in chopper); Capt. Dave Henry (Potter's copilot); Tech Sergeant Lenny Fullwood (pararescue jumper). *Courtesy of Dale Potter*

A recoilless rifle sits momentarily idle outside a sandbagged trench, while smoke drifts across Plei Me's wrecked landscape. *Courtesy of Terri Owen and project delta.net*

Four body bags from the crash site recovery mission, most likely on 28 October 1965. Riches participated in recovery. Ron Macklin, Don Knowlton, Frank Racine, and Wesley McDonial were flying a helicopter gunship mission in support of Plei Me on the morning of 20 October when they were shot down over the camp. All aboard were killed. It took more than a week before things died down enough to risk the recovery mission. *Courtesy of Jerry Riches*

Jerry Riches, 23, 1st Lieutenant, 119th Air Mobile Light Company, Vietnam, earlier in 1965 (prior to Plei Me). Note flak vest rolled up in front of the pilot's seat. The guys would lay them in the chin bubble of their choppers to provide some protection from ground fire. *Courtesy of Jerry Riches*

A South Vietnamese soldier scrambles for cover. *Courtesy of Terri Owen and project delta.net*

Drinking Numpai (a potent rice wine important in Central Highlands Montagnard culture). At unknown Special Forces camp. Can see the sandbag fortifications in background. Capt. Richard "Dick" Shortridge, is second from left in white tee shirt. 1965–1966. *Courtesy of Richard Shortridge*

Shortridge stands in front of his 0-1 Bird Dog observation plane. 1965–1966. *Courtesy of Richard Shortridge*

Montagnard women (they look like children, but Montagnards are a small people) carry bundles of wood outside an unidentified Special Forces camp. 1965–1966. *Courtesy of Richard Shortridge*

Unidentified Montagnard village. 1965–1966. *Courtesy of Richard Shortridge*

Montagnard men, women, and children. 1965–1966. *Courtesy of Richard Shortridge*

Badly needed aerial resupply pallets drift to earth while Montagnard Strikers look on. Were it not for the tireless efforts of Air Force and Army aerial resupply crews, the camp likely would have been overrun and Plei Me's defenders would not have survived. *Photo credit: Terri Owen and projectdelta.net*

Euell White was awarded the Bronze Star Medal for valor for actions at Plei Me by the Commanding General of the Ryukyu Islands, Okinawa 1966. *Courtesy of Euell White*

7

SPRINGING THE TRAP
(23 OCTOBER)

POTTER

Back at Bien Hoa, Potter and company were at last cleared for takeoff at 0100 hours on Saturday. Capt. Mel Elliott, the downed Skyraider pilot, was still out there and needed help. The plan was to fly to New Pleiku Airbase and get the latest on the Plei Me situation, but to do that, Potter's flight would first have to stop for a refuel at a small airfield outside Ban Ma Thuot, about 145 kilometers south of Pleiku. "The weather should be good," came the official word. But twenty minutes out of Bien Hoa and Potter's flight was already in the "soup," dense cloud cover that on this night rose to more than seven thousand feet, effectively blinding the pilots. Naturally, pilots preferred to fly by sight, known formally as Visual Flight Rules. Under VFR, a pilot could keep his ship straight and level simply by maintaining some sort of fixed visual reference point such as the horizon. But flying blind was deadly serious. Extreme disorientation and vertigo could quickly set in, and with no sense of up or down, a pilot risked unwittingly inverting his aircraft and flying straight into the ground. Even absent cloud cover, night flying was hazardous. A largely agrarian country, South Vietnam was an exceptionally dark place at night, offering little in the way of artificial light from civilian infrastructure. Helicopter pilots in 1965 didn't have the night vision goggles of today, after all. Instead, they relied on ambient light from the moon and stars to guide them. But this was far from a given—especially at the tail-end of the Central Highland's monsoon season, when dense cloud cover could roll in at any minute, blotting out what little natural light there was.[1]

That left Instrument Flight Rules (IFR), which allowed pilots to fly blind by relying solely on instrument data. Although Potter was instrument rated, it certainly didn't mean that he was proficient flying blind. And he was one of the lucky ones. Indeed, most helicopter pilots in Vietnam's early days weren't IFR-qualified. Instead, they were usually given just enough instrument training to remain upright if they happened to fly into a cloud, not that flying choppers by IFR was optimal. Part of it has to do with the nature of the helicopter itself. It is an inherently unstable aircraft. Unlike airplanes, which can remain level and fly by themselves for short periods, helicopters require pilots to actively fly them at all times in order to maintain control. IFR only exacerbated the labor-intensive nature of helicopter flight. Pilots needed to constantly monitor—and trust their lives to—instruments like artificial horizon, airspeed indicators, turn and bank indicators, altimeter, vertical speed indicators, radio magnetic indicators, and so on. In a way, instrument-only flight at the time was as much a leap of faith as it was advanced training. None of that faith, however, would prevent them from slamming into the side of mountain. Instrument flight could tell a pilot whether he was level, but it couldn't warn him that he was about to plow nosefirst into a five-thousand-foot peak hiding in the murk. Such a grim fate had recently befallen an Air Force C-130 crew near Camp Holloway. The pilots had attempted to descend through the clouds to make a visual landing at the camp when they slammed headfirst into "Titty Mountain" south of Pleiku, killing all aboard. Flying blind into these so-called rocks in the clouds was an ever-present danger in the Central Highlands.[2]

No, Potter and company preferred to actually *see* where they were going. Standard operating procedures required pilots to have at least seven thousand feet of altitude for terrain clearance in the Central Highlands. Fly under that in the soup, and you'd likely die in a fiery crash. Fly over it, and there'd be no way of telling when you were over your landing target. For Potter, it wasn't even close. Better to miss the camp, he thought, than to hit a mountain. He climbed to ten thousand feet and clear night skies. Rescue Two and Murden popped up out of the clouds moments later. Still, at this altitude and with a thick blanket of clouds below, they might as well have been on the dark side of the moon. Sure, Ban Ma Thuot could broadcast an FM signal over its tactical radio, and Potter had the ability to home in on it. But that wouldn't get him safely onto the ground. Indeed, instrument approaches were few and far between at the time and required the presence of at least two elements: the destination had to have specialized radio and radar equipment to guide the pilot in, and the helicopter needed to have particular equipment aboard that could receive that guidance. Neither Ban Ma Thuot nor Potter had anything of the kind.[3]

By about 0230, they had to be getting close. Suddenly, the clouds parted and a hole appeared. Pilots referred to these as "sucker holes," so named because they could sometimes trick a pilot into thinking he could duck down through the hole and safely descend. Once in the hole, however, there was no guarantee that the clouds were open enough to see the ground. Pilots could be "trapped" in the hole and become dangerously disoriented. Of course, the danger only worsened at night. With a mission to accomplish, Potter made the call. Heart thrumming in his chest, he dipped down into the hole, hoping he wouldn't be the sucker this time. Anxious moments passed. Then he saw it. There, flickering orange in the darkness below, were two rows of burning "smudge pots," oil drums used as makeshift runway lights for Ban Ma Thuot's three-thousand-foot grass airstrip. One leg of the dangerous journey was complete.[4]

After a quick refuel at the Special Forces camp, Potter's flight headed north to New Pleiku Airbase to get the latest scoop on the rescue mission. "Not here," he was told at the tactical operations center. "Army's running that whole show." Back to the Huskie and a hop over to Camp Holloway on Route 19 just east of Pleiku. There, Potter was directed to the mission briefing, a massive tent packed with hundreds of Army aviation and other personnel. "I came up here from Bien Hoa to pick up the pilot," he said above the din. "No," came the reply. "We're going to pick him up." Potter, who'd now been on alert for twenty-four hours and had just undertaken a treacherous flight through darkness and dense clouds over the Central Highlands, was dumbfounded. "Well, I just risked my life getting up here," he said finally. "I'm at least going to go out and watch." Still in darkness, the gaggle of Army choppers lifted off from Holloway, Potter in tow.[5]

ELLIOTT

Dawn broke to the rumble of an AC-47 orbiting the area. Momentarily heartened, Elliott crept from his hideout to see if he could spot the lumbering aircraft. But hope became horror when he realized that Spooky had spotted him first—and seemed to mistake him for an NVA soldier. For some minutes, Elliott hid behind a tree, moving around it "like a treed squirrel who is being hunted" as the gunship circled his position, weapons trained. Suddenly, the AC-47 let loose a short, ripping burst. But just as suddenly, it veered off and left the area. Elliott would later learn, luckily for him, that the aircraft had developed engine trouble and needed to return to base.[6]

A few hours later, at about 0800 hours, Elliott again heard the buzz of an 0-1 Bird Dog orbiting nearby. He raised the pilot, and together they tried to establish Elliott's new location. "I'm going to throw smoke to better mark your position," the FAC's voice crackled over the radio. But wherever the Bird Dog pilot was tossing his smoke grenades, they were nowhere near Elliott. The downed pilot never saw a wisp. The FAC announced he was going for more smoke and left. A short time later, another took his place, this time with better news. "A chopper is on the way to pick you up," came the pilot's voice. "Get to a suitable area." Elliott moved to a swampy opening that was relatively clear of trees but still overgrown with six-foot grass. He waited, the day's heat once again building in the direct sunlight. Would this finally be his moment of deliverance? The radio crackled. "The chopper's been diverted to a higher priority mission," came the FAC's voice. His faith truly shaken for the first time since he'd been on the ground, Elliott shuffled back to his hiding spot. The pilot decided that if he was ever going to be rescued, he'd need to put some distance between himself and the camp. He moved out.[7]

Along the way, Elliott found a small measure of comfort. Nearby, the trickling of a small stream. Although parched from nearly thirty hours with no water, the pilot knew better than to drink. But that didn't stop him from scooping the cool water over his face and neck. Even so small a thing can hearten. He pressed on. Finally, after he'd put about a mile between himself and Plei Me, Elliott came to a clearing with a bamboo thicket at its center. *That looks like a good spot*, he thought. But as he approached his new hiding place, the clump of bamboo suddenly erupted in a thrashing squeal, a dark object bursting from the brush. Had he stumbled into an NVA ambush? Heart pounding, body electrified with adrenaline, it took a beat or two for Elliott's fatigue-addled brain to process what he was seeing. *A wild pig*, came the realization. *It's just a pig.*[8]

Composing himself, the pilot nestled into his new hideout. In the distance, now farther away, he could hear the *crack* and *boom* as close air support worked to break the NVA's vise grip around Plei Me. A while later, he raised another Bird Dog circling nearby. The news was both good and bad. "I'm going to get some food and water to you," said the voice of FAC Capt. Bill Wittenberg. "I don't know how long it'll be before we can pick you up." The Kansas City native had just come on station and knew of the downed pilot's predicament. Wittenberg made several passes attempting to drop the food parcel over Elliott's position before being driven off by antiaircraft fire.

The Spad pilot's thirst and hunger would have to wait. A short while later, Elliott raised yet another nearby FAC. "Sit tight," crackled the voice of Lt. Jimmy D. Holmes, 21st Tactical Air Support Squadron. "Come back on the air in fifteen minutes." A quarter of an hour later, Elliott dutifully checked in. "An Air Force rescue chopper is about five minutes out," Holmes said. The FAC explained that Skyraiders would be dumping napalm all along a tree line just one hundred meters from Elliott's position. "Move into the middle of the clearing as soon as the A1-Es fly over." Did he dare let himself hope that this was finally it?[9]

POTTER

Earlier that morning, the sun was already up by the time Potter and the Army helicopters had arrived on station over Plei Me. But it quickly became clear to all that there'd be no rescue for the moment. "We got out there and the war was really, really cooking," Potter recalls. "It was action heavy." Capt. Dick Shortridge, the FAC who'd taken the lead when the siege of Plei Me began on 19 October, had close air support stacked up at one-thousand-foot intervals to nearly forty thousand feet. The FAC called in sortie after sortie: A1-Es, Canberras, F-100s and 105s, helicopter gunships, each two-craft flight sitting atop its perch like birds of prey, ready to swoop down and pound NVA positions all around the camp. But the communists gave as good as they got. Their trench works and the surrounding jungle and hills would flare to life with .30 and .51 caliber machine gun fire with every CAS run. "Nobody could get close to that fort," Potter recalls. "There was so much enemy action. You're sitting up there at seven thousand feet, and you just see this stuff spitting from the jungle."[10]

After a while, the Army helicopters tasked with Elliott's rescue were called off on another mission, and Potter flew back to New Pleiku Airbase. For the rest of the morning, Potter and company sat in the tactical operations center (TOC) listening in on the chatter from the battle. Finally, near noon, Air Force FAC Holmes called in.

"Okay, we think we've got all this beaten down. I think we can probably pick Elliott up or make a go of it."

Elated, Potter contacted Army aviation at Holloway to arrange escort. There was no way the two HH-43s would make it in and out alone. The Army agreed to give him command of a heavy fire control team supplied by A Company, 1st Aviation Battalion based at Ban Ma Thuot. Standard Army aviation fire control teams consisted of two armed Hueys equipped with M-60 machine guns at both doors and a pair of side-mounted 2.75-inch rocket pods. But a heavy team doubled the number to four, including one chopper outfitted with nothing but rockets for extra firepower. Potter and Murden rendezvoused with the gunships near Plei Me about an hour later. Potter radioed Holmes to make final preparations. High above, Shortridge was listening in to the radio chatter as he was directing air strikes and aerial resupply for the camp. Something about the HH-43 pilot's voice caught the FAC's attention.[11]

"That boy sounds familiar," he thought, but it wouldn't be until later, and quieter moments, that he was able to connect the dots.[12]

As for Potter and company, they soon discovered that the NVA weren't quite as "beaten down" as they'd hoped. In fact, a Quad-50 multibarreled antiaircraft machine gun was spitting fire from a tree line about one hundred meters from Elliott's suspected position. It would be suicide to attempt a chopper rescue with such a weapon that close.[13]

Undaunted, Holmes marked the target with a white phosphorous rocket and called in two A1-Es, each loaded with napalm, four canisters to a wing. The Skyraiders dove like raptors on the hunt, wingtip to wingtip as they jettisoned in unison all sixteen canisters over the target. The tree line erupted in a white-orange wall of flame, burning and boiling everything near. "No more Quad-50," Potter recalls. "And one hell of a fire." With the big NVA gun silenced, Holmes rolled in and fired off another rocket of Willie Pete to help zero in on Elliott's location.

"Okay, I think Elliott's between my smoke and the big fire," came Holmes's voice over the radio.

There was about a half-mile tract between the two.

"Okay, let's go in," Potter called to his fire control team.

Meanwhile, Ray Murden, per SOP for the Rescue Two backup, loitered up and away from the action. Potter keyed his mike.

"Raymond, you're so damned high up, it'd take you all day to get down here if we had a problem!"

A bit of good-natured ribbing even at this moment of peril. Then, he simply rolled in, Army gunships flanking. The terrain here was a patchwork of tree thickets and the ubiquitous elephant grass, looming ten to twelve feet high and hiding God knew what. Potter brought his ship into a hover near where Elliott was supposed to be. The intermeshing rotors, not unlike a giant egg-beater, did their work. The powerful downwash pushed the tall grass aside.

"There he is," someone called out.

There, standing amongst the wavering elephant grass, was the bedraggled visage of Mel Elliott.[14]

"You want to use the hoist?" asked Connon, the crew chief and hoist operator.

"Hell no," Potter replied. "I'm just gonna chop this elephant grass down with the rotors. I don't want to take time to unlimber the hoist and go through all that."[15]

To reinforce the point, Potter heard the snap and pop of incoming small arms fire even above the din of his chopper engine. Suddenly, the earth around him erupted in great geysers of mud, trees, and grass as his Army escort choppers laid down a 360-degree ring of fire and death.

"If these guys don't get me," Potter thought wryly, "I'll probably get out of here all right."

He brought the chopper down to just a few feet off the ground. The downed Skyraider pilot dropped to all fours and scrabbled his way toward salvation across the carpet-like wave of flattened grass. Pararescue Jumper Leon "Lenny" Fullwood hung out of the open door and watched as Elliott clambered up out of the muck, vines tangled about his neck and shoulders. Elliott scrambled his way up, planting his foot for purchase on what he thought was a landing skid. Fullwood reached down and took a firm hold.

"I've got him!" he bellowed.

Potter immediately pulled pitch and clawed skyward. But Elliott hadn't stepped on a landing skid at all—he'd stepped on a wheel. As soon as the chopper lifted off, the wheel rotated, spinning the Skyraider pilot off into the ether. The PJ's grip was his only lifeline. Dangling in midair, Elliott looked up into Fullwood's eyes.

"I'm not going back down there alone," he yelled, the rolling green terrain rushing past in a blur.

Fullwood heaved with all his strength and pulled him to safety. Bruised and battered, dehydrated and exhausted, Elliott had survived his thirty-five-hour ordeal.

Up front, Potter radioed his fire control team leader.

"We're ready to come out," he called.

"Come out on a 0-9-0 magnetic heading," came the reply.

Because rescue choppers coming off a pickup present an especially inviting target for enemy gunners, this was a moment of maximum danger. Potter strained for both speed and altitude as the escort choppers fell in below and behind, rocketing and machine-gunning the terrain with wild abandon. Above, Holmes called in a postrescue sortie for good measure.

At six thousand feet, the danger began to subside. The flight set course for Pleiku. Sometime later, one of the escort ships fell in alongside Potter's HH-43, its strange intermeshing rotors conjuring images of a giant, mechanized dragonfly.[16]

"Jesus Christ," the Huey pilot radioed. "How the hell do you fly that thing? It's making me sick just watching you."[17]

Elliott hitched a ride a few hours later with another Skyraider pilot who'd been diverted to take him back to Bien Hoa. After an intelligence debriefing and medical examination, his thoughts turned to his wife back home in Phoenix. Had the Air Force notified her about his shoot-down? No one he asked seemed to know for sure. By the time Elliott got a message home, it was just after 0500 hours Phoenix time. His wife hadn't heard a word about any of it. He briefly told her the story, assured her he was okay, and hung up. It was fortunate Elliott reached his wife when he did. Later that morning, she picked up a copy of the local newspaper. There, on the front page, was the story of her husband's ordeal. Following his ordeal at Plei Me, Elliott would return to his calling as an F-100 fighter jock, completing tours in the US, England, and South Korea before ultimately retiring as a lieutenant colonel in 1974.[18]

Meanwhile, back at Pleiku, Shortridge came calling. Command had put Potter and the rest of his rescue flight up for the night. They would return to Bien Hoa in the morning. After checking around, Shortridge discovered that the familiar voice he'd overheard on the radio that day belonged to none other than his old buddy, Dale Potter. The two had gone to high school together in Joseph, Oregon, population nine hundred, but the men had taken different paths to Vietnam. Now here they were, six thousand miles from home, unknowingly teamed up to rescue Elliott. That night, they caught up over an entire bottle of Jim Beam. "It didn't even faze me," recalls Potter with a chuckle. "I wanted to relax, but my blood was probably 50 percent adrenaline. Maybe a hundred percent."[19]

Then something strange happened later that night. Potter and company had been given their own room, with four sets of bunk beds, two men to a set. At about 0200, Potter got up to use the latrine. There were no mosquito bars over the bunks, so his body was covered in red welts.[20]

Jesus Christ, he thought. *I'll be glad when daylight comes so I can get back to Bien Hoa.* About ten minutes after he'd returned to his bunk, the door to the room burst open and the lights flicked on. Standing in the doorway, staggering drunk and wild-eyed, was an enlisted Army infantryman wielding a preposterously large knife.[21]

"I'm going to cut your fucking guts out," the soldier said to no one in particular. Potter, in the top bunk, reached over to where his holstered .38 caliber revolver hung by the bedside.[22]

I've just gone through hell, he thought. *This guy's not going to cut me up.* Just then, Potter heard the bolt of an M-16 slap home. It was Ray Murden's PJ, William "Pits" Pitsenbarger, in the bunk below. Potter knew that Pits, if it came to it, wouldn't hesitate to cut the would-be assailant in half. Suddenly, two more soldiers appeared in the doorway, corralled the drunken knife-wielder, and hustled him out of the room, apologizing the whole way.[23]

"You'd better get him out of here," Potter called after them. "He almost just died." Indeed, even in the fraternity of hard-charging pararescuemen, Pitsenbarger stood out. From Piqua, Ohio, the twenty-one-year-old had originally wanted to become an Army Special Forces Green Beret. But when he tried to sign up as a high school junior, his parents refused. Pitsenbarger switched gears after graduating and decided to become a parajumper. He and Potter would become close over the ensuing months. The two had arrived at Bien Hoa at the same time in September. Both were avid handball players and often spent nonflying days in friendly competition or just hanging out. To Potter, Pitsenbarger embodied what he'd come to see as the pararescue esprit de corps.[24]

"PJs are a breed of their own," he says. "They think they can whip the whole world. Which is what you want in a war."

On April 11, 1966, Pitsenbarger would exemplify that ethos. He had been dispatched from Bien Hoa as part of a Detachment 6 rescue flight to bring out wounded from a besieged, understrength US infantry company. The unit was cut off and being badly mauled by a superior Viet Cong force near Cam My, about fifty-six kilometers east of Saigon. In order to tend the wounded and expedite evacuation, he volunteered to be lowered to the ground through more than one hundred feet of dense jungle and a hail of small-arms fire. Charlie Company, 2nd Battalion, 16th Infantry had moved into the field as part of Operation Abilene with just 134 soldiers out of its usual complement of 291. By the time Pitsenbarger volunteered to join them, C Company was completely encircled by a veteran and aggressive Viet Cong battalion three times its size. As casualties mounted within the rapidly shrinking American perimeter, Pitsenbarger continued to stabilize and evacuate wounded. He managed to get nine men to safety before one of the rescue choppers was hit by voluminous small-arms fire and had to pull out for an emergency landing away from the action. Above, crew chief Sgt. Gerald Hammond motioned for Pitsenbarger to climb into the Stokes litter and evacuate before the chopper had to pull out. He refused, waving off his own extraction so he could remain on the ground with the handful of Americans who had not yet been killed or wounded.[25]

For the next several hours, Pitsenbarger tended wounded, gathered ammunition, and helped fight off Viet Cong assaults. He was wounded at least three times. Toward the end, for want of ammunition, the infantrymen were reduced to hurling smoke and tear gas canisters to staunch the enemy assault. Finally, when all seemed lost, Pitsenbarger pulled the corpses of the dead over a wounded American infantryman to keep him from being discovered. As darkness descended, the Viet Cong sent their women into the ragged US perimeter to strip the bodies of the dead and execute the wounded. Thanks to Pitsenbarger's gambit, the infantryman was spared. But the PJ, now unconscious from his wounds, groaned when the Viet Cong women came calling. They shot him between the eyes with his own .38 caliber revolver. Only a massive, danger-close artillery barrage saved the few Americans left alive. In the end, 106 of Charlie Company's 134 men had been killed or wounded at Cam My.[26]

Pitsenbarger was originally awarded the Air Force Cross for his actions during the battle. But in 1998, Potter, who had served as Pitsenbarger's Summary Courts Officer following his death, joined forces with the Air Force Sergeants Association, Pitsenbarger's father, and others to change that. The group put together an evidence package and petitioned Congress to upgrade the airman's award to the Medal of Honor. Congress agreed, and on December 8, 2000, Pitsenbarger's wife, Alice, along with his father, William F. Pitsenbarger, were presented with the airman's posthumous Medal of Honor in front of a crowd of thousands at Wright-Patterson Air Force Base near his hometown of Piqua, Ohio.[27]

Back in Joseph, Oregon, Beverly Shortridge was cleaning up the kitchen after the evening meal when the phone rang. While her husband, Richard, was away at war, she and her three children had moved in with her mother on the small family farm just outside town. It was a neighbor calling, and he had news that worried Beverly. It seemed that his brother had called from down Portland-way and said that he'd seen Dick's name in the local papers. Apparently, there'd been a big battle in Vietnam, and Dick was somehow involved. But that was all he knew. Fear washed over her in a sick wave. There was nothing she could do, and there was no one to call. And she certainly couldn't call Dick. Indeed, there was no such thing as international calls for servicemen in those days. The best the military could offer was an ad hoc patch system that worked with local ham radio operators to relay calls overseas. In rural Oregon, that was simply not an option. Shortridge and Beverly had not spoken since he'd arrived in Vietnam that summer. And they would neither see nor speak to each other at all during Shortridge's yearlong tour. All they had were their nearly daily letters to one another.[28]

Now, standing in her mother's kitchen, Beverly was utterly helpless. Whether her husband was alive or dead, unscratched or maimed, she didn't know. All she could do was pass the long hours until morning, drive to town, and devour whatever the newspapers could tell her. Beverly huddled with her mother over that long night, putting on her best face so as not to frighten the children. When dawn finally broke, she made her way into Joseph and found a paper. Yes, there had been a big battle—bigger than anything Dick had so far encountered. He was doing his duty, doing what he'd been trained to do. All she knew, though, was that he was still alive when the story had broken. What had happened in the meantime, seven thousand miles and fifteen time zones away, was anybody's guess. All she could do was wait anxiously for more news to arrive. She hoped it would be a letter from Dick telling her everything was over, and he was all right. Until then, all she could was wait.[29]

After being medically evacuated from Plei Me, DELTA Capt. Euell White had been flown to Camp Holloway on Saturday for further evaluation. While he was resting in the dispensary, he got a visit from one of the medevac pilots who'd volunteered to fly into Plei Me the day before. "Do you know who I am?" the pilot asked. White, still fuzzy from his ordeal, peered up into the man's face. He *was* familiar. Then it dawned on him. "I sure do," he croaked. It was the young second lieutenant who'd thrown a tantrum when White had refused his demand for more water back at Fort Benning's Basic Officer Leader Course. The same young man White had taken under his wing and mentored about leadership. And now here he was, one of the few medevac pilots who volunteered to fly into a hail of anti-aircraft fire to help save White and the others. The DELTA captain swelled with pride. The pilot stayed only a short time, and the two never saw each other again. But for White, it was a deeply gratifying moment. "It really made me feel good to see that he turned out so well."[30]

Later that day, White was flown to the 8th Field Hospital at Nha Trang for surgery. To his surprise, Col. McKean visited several times during his recovery. If there was anything he needed, McKean had said, just ask. The DELTA captain was astonished that the 5th Group commander had made the time. "I was a small pebble in this big brook," he says. And McKean wasn't his only unexpected visitor. On Sunday, 24 October, Gen. William Westmoreland stopped in to personally bestow the Purple Heart. The general made it a Sunday habit to visit wounded troops whenever his travels took him near a field hospital. About a week later, White was cleared to fly back to Okinawa, where he would spend most of the next two months on convalescent leave.[31]

When he first arrived, however, White was met by startling news. His wife and daughter had come very close to being told he'd been killed. First Group had a boat called the "Green Beret" that was used for SCUBA training and the like. Some teams deployed to Vietnam had taken along ham radios and soon developed a system for contacting their wives back in Okinawa. The teams would first radio the boat, and then whoever was manning the receiver would have the call patched into the phone system on the island. When news broke that DELTA Capt. Tom Pusser and White had become casualties at Plei Me, one of the teams had gotten the story backward and radioed back to the Green Beret that it was White who had been killed. The team had even held a wake in his honor. The duty officer aboard the Green Beret returned to shore that evening and steeled himself to visit White's wife and tell her the sad news. Luckily, the officer averted a lot of unnecessary anguish when he first double-checked with Group command before knocking on Euna White's door.[32]

By December, White was fully discharged from the hospital and even cleared by the surgeon to begin parachute jumps again, provided he made water jumps to soften the impact. He was honored at the 1st Group's Christmas banquet later that month, where he learned that McKean had recommended him for the Silver Star. He ended up earning the Bronze Star for Valor for his fight on the north ridge. White returned to Vietnam in 1968 to serve as a MACV adviser to the 5th ARVN Division. He would go on to earn his second Bronze Star—and Purple Heart—after being wounded by a rocket-propelled grenade during the 1968 Tet Offensive. In 1971, he returned for a third and final time, serving as the executive officer for the 101st Airborne Division.[33]

⌐◯⌐

By 0900 hours Saturday, Beckwith had ordered a sortie to knock out the two machine gun positions that had wreaked such chaos on the Rangers the day before. The DELTA commander surmised that the enemy had simply dug in too close for comfort and had to be pushed out. He knew that they'd already made a concerted effort to overrun the camp's northeast heavy machine gun bunker at least once and might be tempted to try again. He assembled a smaller assault force for the job, just one platoon of CIDG and one platoon of Airborne Rangers. But this time, supporting fires from camp, including mortars and machine guns, would coordinate with the assault. Still, the sortie would constitute yet another attack in broad daylight against an entrenched adversary who would know they were coming. Detachment A-217's 1st Lt. Robert Berry who had led the unsuccessful mission to rescue Mel Elliott in the predawn hours of 22 October, would take the CIDG platoon while an LLDB lieutenant would lead the Rangers. Sgt. Maj. Bill DeSoto would also accompany the assault force. The CIDG-Ranger contingent moved out under covering machine gun fire from the camp. At first, the units maneuvered well, laying down a base of fire while moving into position to knock out the emplacements. Suddenly, the LLDB lieutenant—the mission's ostensible commander—fell dead to Berry's left, a bullet penetrating his steel helmet and killing him instantly. Nearby, a lone NVA soldier wielding a grenade suddenly leapt screaming from a well-concealed fighting hole and charged the assault force. At about the same time, the platoons were enveloped with heavy small-arms and machine gun fire from nearby positions. DeSoto, the hardnosed paratrooper who'd come through World War II and Korea without a scratch, was hit in the shoulder by a .51 caliber slug during the fusillade, nearly ripping his arm off. The rapid succession of these events seemed to throw the assault force into a panic, and the situation threatened to become the second rout in two days. Luckily, supporting fires from the camp poured in, shooting the NVA soldier dead and putting up a wall of covering fire. Berry rallied the assault force and made an orderly withdrawal back inside the wire.[34]

Hunter went to work to stabilize DeSoto. The catastrophic nature of the trooper's wound immediately convinced the physician that another medevac was imperative. The dust-off came in a short time later, and DeSoto, along with some of the more seriously wounded Rangers, was loaded aboard. So was Moore. A few hours earlier, the detachment commander had taken a friendly fire shrapnel wound. He, Berry, and some of the other troopers had been gathered around the table in the team house when a particularly close tac-air strike had sent bomb fragments careening through the hole in the roof. Moore was hit right where the neck and shoulder join. It was not a life-threatening injury, but it was disabling none-theless. The young commander had shepherded his men through the siege's first days, but now his battle was over. As Hunter watched the Huey lift off into the late-morning sky, the surgeon assessed the larger situation. The medevac had not taken any antiaircraft fire on the way in. And the camp had received only the occasional mortar round over the last few hours. Scores of wounded Rangers and Montagnards remained in camp. He decided the time had come to get out as many as possible.[35]

The physician roamed the camp, making a note of the most seriously wounded. Those slated for immediate evacuation were tagged with a red medevac placard. Meanwhile, Thompson coordinated by radio with C2 and forward air controllers working the area to bring in the medevacs and their tac-air escorts. The dust-offs stacked up off to the east, while CAS laid fiery ordnance throughout the surrounding hills. The medevacs rolled in one by one right on the heels of the strike aircraft. The process was orderly at first, as Hunter and Sgt. Jimmy Beech established a system for getting aboard the seriously wounded. But the situation soon devolved into a shameful circus. Rangers—some wounded, some not—began to swarm each medevac as it settled onto its skids. Invariably, some unwounded Rangers made it aboard and escaped. Maj. Louis Mizell, who'd piloted the first medevac into Plei Me on the morning of 20 October, was one of the chopper pilots tasked with evacuating the wounded that day. He remem-bered a scene of absolute chaos.[36]

"I landed near the flagpole near the center of the camp," Mizell re-called in a letter about the incident. "I couldn't get off the ground as we had a lot people trying to get on board and hanging on to the skids. We were able to get a lot of them off. We were full on the inside, and I'm certain they were not all wounded."[37]

One Ranger, who hadn't been able to fight his way aboard, was one of those clinging to the landing skids of a Huey as it lifted off. Hunter watched as the medevac cleared the camp and gained altitude. The Ranger gradually lost his grip and finally plunged to his death in the surrounding hills. But despite some of the Rangers' reprehensible conduct, Hunter's medevac train had been a success. He had gotten out most of the wounded without losing a single chopper.[38]

Back in the team house, Beckwith and the troopers gathered to strate-gize ways of dealing with the stubborn NVA machine gun positions nearby. It was clear after two unsuccessful sorties that the communists had dug fairly extensive trench systems in the area. Bombing them hadn't worked, nor had assaulting them head-on. Beckwith and the troopers eventually settled on the idea of burning the enemy out of his trenches using flamethrowers. After all, the weapon had been used extensively in previous wars to do just that. But who knew how to use them? Berry, who'd just fought his way back inside the wire hours earlier, raised his hand. It turned out that the young lieutenant had trained on the weapon just before deploying from Fort Bragg. Then Sgt. Eugene Tafoya chimed in. The A-217 NCO had worked with flamethrowers, too. That settled it. Beckwith radioed McKean and requested the weapons be included in the next supply drop.[39]

Beckwith also took the opportunity to call in a more immediate resupply of ammo by slick choppers. The bulk of the 119th Aviation Company had been on its way to Bong Son on the morning of the 20th when news broke that Plei Me had come under attack. The company had lost four of its own that morning when one of its Hog gunships had been shot down running escort for the first medevac into camp. The 119th had camped overnight at its normal bivouac near Bong Son but was recalled to Holloway the next morning. Than Phong 6 would have to wait. Plei Me now took precedence. The first few days had simply been too hot, but now that the NVA's death grip seemed to be loosening, however slightly, the company was ready to get back into the resupply business.[40]

Still, 1st Lt. Chuck Oualline wasn't taking any chances. The loss of the Hog crew had anxieties running high. If he were going to fly into the camp, he would come in as low and fast as his Huey would allow. The harder he made it on NVA gunners, the better. Oualline had with him his hooch mate, 1st Lt. Joel Glenn, a newer pilot still in training. A few miles outside camp, Oualline dropped his Huey to the deck, skimming just a few feet above the earth at 115 miles per hour. It would've been thrilling had it not been so insanely dangerous. For while it made them a harder target for the NVA, an engine failure now would simply pile the chopper into the earth, smashing it to bits before the men knew what hit them. The ground below skittered past in a blur of greens and browns. With Oualline at the controls, Glenn had a few moments to look around. The young lieutenant could just make out a patchwork of enemy trenches on the approach to camp. Suddenly, Oualline pulled back on the cyclic stick and lowered the collective, coming up a bit and bleeding off airspeed. The last thing he wanted to do was overshoot and have to make another approach. The fewer opportunities for enemy gunners, the better.[41]

And then they were over Plei Me. The Huey settled lightly onto its skids, even as Oualline kept the gas turbine engine at full power. Dialing back the rpms, he knew, always resulted in a slight lag when trying to power back up for liftoff. Not an option on this day. If they had to leave in a hurry, he wanted to be ready. Behind was a blur of activity, as crew chief and door gunner kicked off crates of ammunition and C-rations, while troopers hustled aboard three or four wounded Montagnards. For Oualline, the waiting was the hardest part. The seconds crawled by. Silently, he prayed for the soldiers to *hurry . . . please hurry as fast as you can*. And they almost always did. But with each passing moment, the anxiety built like pressure in a steam pipe. He tried not to ponder the bullet that might at any moment crash through his Plexiglas windshield. Or the 82mm mortar shell that might even now be arcing toward him. Such thoughts, he knew, could paralyze him. It went against his every instinct to sit here, and yet he knew each time that he would. It was more than just his job. It was about his responsibility to the men on the ground. "They depended on us," he says. "We were their only lifelines. We knew it, and they knew it. All we pilots prided ourselves on completing the mission. We would do anything for them." Once the wounded were aboard, Oualline lifted the chopper off its skids, bound for Pleiku.[42]

Back at the provincial capital, the overland relief force was finally ready to move. At about 1000 hours, the 1/42nd, commanded by Capt. Mã Văn Nông, airlifted from Kontum to New Pleiku Airbase, arriving about one hour later. The battalion was then trucked down to Phu My to link up with Luat. The additional battalion brought the armored task force's (ATF) total strength up to nearly a thousand men. Luat, in his command M113 armored personnel carrier (APC) at the column's head, turned his reinforced task force southwest on Route 5 and moved out for Plei Me at 1400 hours, with the tanks and other APCs on point. Dismounted infantry from the 1/42nd patrolled the column's left flank, while two companies of the 21st Rangers screened to the right. About a mile to the rear, the 21st's other two Rangers companies, along with three M8 Greyhound light armored cars, provided security for two 105mm artillery guns and the assortment of transport vehicles that carried the ATF's fuel, food, and ammunition.[43] The going was slow. The provincial road was little more than a single-lane dirt strip, bracketed by a morass of choking vegetation that encroached to within a few feet of the roadbed sides. As the column meandered its way single file along this narrow track, it gradually stretched out to nearly two miles long. Progress was further slowed as the mechanized vehicles on point could move no faster than their supporting infantry could walk. Not that Luat was in a rush to hurtle his task force into the maw of a prepared ambush. Understandably wary of what lay around every bend, the ATF crept along at a snail's pace. Finally, at about 1700 hours, Luat ordered his armor to halt as it neared the edge of the anticipated ambush site. After preplanned air strikes had roared in to pound suspected NVA positions, Luat once again gave the go-ahead for the ATF to get rolling. But the supply train, about two thousand meters to the rear, didn't get the message. The contingent's commander apparently mistook the column's temporary halt as a sign that the day's march had ended. However, the troops manning the supply train seemed to make little effort to form up a defensive perimeter for the night. Some of the men even began to leisurely cook up their evening meals. Their actions would certainly have been much different had they known their night bivouac was already within the 32nd NVA Regiment's four-kilometer-long kill zone.[44]

AMBUSH ON ROUTE 5

The 32nd Regiment, under Lt. Col. Tô Định Khẩn, was a seasoned unit that had infiltrated down Hanoi's Group 559 strategic military transportation corridor—known colloquially as the "Ho Chi Minh Trail"—from its starting point in Na Nam Province, North Vietnam, during the second half of 1964. Because the Trail at that time could not yet accommodate regiment-sized units, the 32nd was forced to send its battalions south piecemeal. It was reportedly a grueling march, with hunger, sickness, and general privation the constant companions of the infiltrating units. Still, by late January 1965, all three of its battalions had completed their infiltration, terminating in northwest Kontum Province along the Laotian boarder. The regiment then spent the next nine months operating in Kontum and Pleiku provinces, racking up a lengthy campaign résumé, which included battles at Polei Kleng in March, Le Thanh in June, and most recently at Duc Co, where the regiment played an important role in the August siege of the Special Forces camp. The regiment had taken a terrible beating at Duc Co and had spent the previous two months recovering, resupplying, and receiving troop replacements infiltrated down the Trail. Still, it was likely because of its veteran status that Field Front Headquarters charged the 32nd with the more important task of the Plei Me siege: ambushing and destroying the ARVN relief column sent to rescue the camp. Likely drawing on its analysis of II Corps' response to the regiment's "lure and ambush" tactic employed at Duc Co, along with other intelligence assessments, Field Front command was able to predict with a fair degree of accuracy both the size and composition of Pleiku's relief force, and the route and mode of transport it would utilize to reach the camp. Communist leadership even anticipated that the United States would make available at least one, and possibly two, battalions to act as a reserve for the relief operation.[45]

The regiment consisted of three battalions: the 334th, the 635th, and the 966th, each augmented with an array of attached units. For the 334th, this meant the addition of a 75mm recoilless rifle platoon from the regimental company, a platoon from the regiment's machine gun company, and all of the regimental mortar company. As for the 635th, it too was bolstered by an attached machine gun platoon and had been given the remainder of the 32nd's recoilless rifle company as an attachment. The 966th Battalion, already short one of its four rifle companies, was to be held in reserve. In addition, the reserve battalion was to provide the 635th with two of its 57mm recoilless rifles and two 90mm B-40 rocket launchers. It was also ordered to hand over an additional B-40 rocket launcher to the 334th Battalion. The regimental 75mm recoilless rifle company was to participate in the ambush's early stages, then pull back and act as a reserve element to mop up any surviving ATF armor.

To deal either with American air support or any heliborne units entering the fray, Field Front headquarters also provided each battalion with its own antiaircraft company, outfitted with the highly lethal, Soviet-made 12.75mm DShK machine gun, its heavy rounds capable of reaching targets 2,500 meters away. Finally, the regimental engineer company was ordered to lay two controlled minefields to the column's rear, apparently to catch unawares any ARVN units trying to retreat north back to Phu My. The engineers were also to conduct "deception operations" near the ambush site, perhaps in an effort to mislead the ARVN and Americans as to the true disposition of NVA forces. All told, the 32nd and its assorted attachments stood at an estimated strength of approximately two thousand men.[46]

Field Front Headquarters knew that success depended on thorough preparedness. To that end, Khan had his regiment begin its preparations as early as 19 September. First, regimental reconnaissance teams conducted a detailed survey of both the ambush site and its environs. A sand-table replica of the site and surrounding area was then constructed, and units were tasked with running rehearsal exercises to hone their readiness. By 10 October, the regiment had departed for the ambush area, a four-kilometer stretch straddling Route 5, about thirty kilometers south of Pleiku and some ten kilometers north of Plei Me. Field Front command had issued the 32nd a very straightforward order: "Destroy the ARVN infantry and armor units moving on Provincial Route 21 (known as Route 5 in the South) from Phu My to Plei Me."[47]

But the monumental task of preparing such an expansive ambush still remained. First, regimental work crews needed to construct sturdy and well-camouflaged concealment fortifications at the preambush assembly area some distance from the road. Here, they would lie in wait unseen until the time came to spring the trap. Next, pathways from the assembly area to the actual ambush positions would need to be cleared and camouflaged to facilitate both ease of movement and concealment from aerial observation. Finally, the actual assault and firing positions themselves—some no more than twenty-five meters off the road—would have to be dug and outfitted. Khan fully understood that American airstrikes were inevitable, so these fighting positions would also require robust overhead cover. Meanwhile, the 17th Company, the regimental transportation unit, along with local force VC laborers, worked frenetically under the direction of the logistical Rear Services branch of the Central Highlands Front to prestage food, medicine, and ammunition for the coming operation. Making matters more complicated was that all these preparations needed to be made mostly at night to avoid premature detection. Furthering the preservation of operational security, Field Front's ambush order directed the men of the 32nd to "report by direct means" only. In other words, they were to maintain radio silence to avoid alerting the ARVN and Americans to their presence. To that end, information would have to be passed through field telephones and message runners only. Still, by 19 October, the 32nd was in place and ready to spring its trap.[48]

As noted, the 334th and 635th had primary responsibility for conducting the ambush. The 635th, with its additional recoilless rifles and 90mm rocket launchers, along with the remainder of the regimental 75mm recoilless rifle company, was tasked with attacking the head of the column, where Khan surmised the bulk of ARVN armor would be. The reinforced battalion, deployed on two hills overlooking Route 5, was to hit the lead elements from several different points in order to chop them up. The battalion would then canalize what was left into the valley between the two highpoints and destroy in detail any survivors. Meanwhile, the 334th, positioned on three small hills overlooking the road about two thousand meters north, was also ordered to conduct attacks from several different points in its sector in order to break the column into more-easily destroyable pockets. It was then to swing around to the column's rear, cutting off avenues of retreat and blocking any ARVN units that might try to reinforce the ATF from the north. As noted, the 966th was to be held in reserve about two thousand meters west of the primary ambush area, with orders to come to the aid of its sister battalions should the need arise. The battalion was also responsible for dealing with any air assault elements attempting to land in support of the ATF. Finally, the antiaircraft companies attached to each battalion were positioned to provide cover for their respective units. With the plan and units now in place, all that remained was whether the NVA could pull it off.[49]

At about the same time Luat's ATF had set off down Route 5, the 420 men of the 22nd Rangers, commanded by Capt. Phạm Văn Phúc, were standing by to be airlifted to a position west of Provincial Route 5 and about nine kilometers north of Plei Me. The 119th Aviation Company and other units of the 52nd Aviation Battalion would do the heavy lifting. The Rangers' destination was an LZ atop a low hill about two thousand meters off the road and about one kilometer north of the shallow mountain pass where 24th Special Tactical Zone planners suspected the communists would lie in wait for the column. After offloading from the 52nd's slicks, the battalion was to first sweep east toward the road, eliminating any enemy units it encountered, before turning south toward the pass. If all went well, the Rangers would already be waiting for the communists when they arrived. The 22nd was then to act as a blocking force to trap NVA ambush units between it and Luat's now-stronger ATF.[50]

CBS television journalist John Laurence and his crew, cameraman Jim Wilson and soundman P. B. Hoan, a Vietnamese national, had gotten wind of the battle at Plei Me and were desperate to cover the story. After getting themselves to Pleiku, the newsmen discovered they'd missed the ATF and would have to hitch a ride with the 22nd if they wanted to get into the action. But Laurence was still apprehensive. He, like other journalists in Vietnam, had heard his share of horror stories about South Vietnamese troops panicking under fire, throwing down their weapons, and fleeing. Going into combat with such soldiers could be a dangerous proposition, indeed. Still, Laurence and his crew had a job to do. After arriving in the large open field where the Rangers and their chopper transports sat waiting to depart, he stumbled upon 1st Lt. Edward Brady, an American adviser to the Rangers. Brady, an Annapolis grad who'd given up a promising career in the U.S. Navy so he could transfer to the Army and get to Vietnam, assured him his fears were unfounded. "I'd go anywhere with these little guys," he said. "They're great fighters." After some discussion, Laurence and his crew decided to roll the dice. They were joined by three other journalists: Charles Mohr of the *New York Times*; Vo Huynh, another Vietnamese and a stringer for NBC News; and Robin Mannock, an English writer with the Associated

Press. The men squeezed themselves aboard, and the slicks lifted off into the daylight skies.[51]

After a time, the choppers closed into what looked like an old corn-field atop a hill, the sun already sinking low on the horizon. Helicopter gunships had come in a short while earlier and raked the surrounding area with rockets and machine gun fire. But if there had been NVA in the area, they were gone now. The Rangers landed without opposition. Nearby, a Jarai village had taken some errant fire from the Hogs, and several villagers had been wounded. Brady and the senior American adviser, an Army captain, arranged with Camp Holloway to have the Montagnards medevacked for treatment. About two thousand meters down the hill, Laurence could see a thin red line of dirt road where it bisected the thick jungle below. This is where the column was supposed to pass. Beyond, rolling hills stretched to the horizon in a patchwork of greens and browns.[52]

Laurence and his cameraman rolled film on Brady as he explained what would happen next. Just then, the crackle of small-arms fire arose in the distance. The sound soon built to a crescendo, as recoilless rifle and machine gun fire merged with the concussive explosions as B-40 rockets and 82mm mortars found their mark. Rounds snapped and sizzled over the Rangers' heads, but the fire was not directed at them. The NVA had sprung its ambush earlier than expected. And it was here, not the mountain pass to the south, where it would happen. Indeed, Laurence and the 22nd had arrived just in time for a front-row seat. Some of the Rangers moved out and took up shooting positions; others began digging fighting holes. Still others simply stood transfixed as dusk came on and the intensifying battle raged below, glowing tracers of incoming and outgoing crisscrossing in orange and red in the gathering gloom. Laurence looked around and saw that the Rangers were making no effort to close with and attack the ambushers from behind. *Why aren't they attacking?* he wondered.[53]

Laurence turned to Vo Huynh, the Vietnamese journalist who had also ridden along with the Rangers. Huynh always seemed to have a superior grasp on military affairs, and Laurence had come to trust his colleague's tactical expertise. Huynh explained that Phuc, the 22nd's commander, might have had valid reasons for avoiding contact. The Rangers, a lightly armed battalion of only 420 men, were isolated and alone, after all. Phuc was likely afraid that his men would be outnumbered and outgunned should the enemy turn his heavy weapons on them. The battalion commander, explained Huynh, was also wary about exposing his troops to potential friendly fire from the column or even American CAS strikes raining from above. It's unclear whether Huynh's arguments had merit, but Laurence did later write that, after he'd gained more experience in Vietnam, he'd been "naïve" to believe Phuc's behavior was the result of cautiousness "to the point of cowardice."[54]

Some minutes earlier, at about 1750 hours, the main section of the ATF had opened up a five-kilometer gap between it and the now-stationary logistics train. The main body had now progressed to about thirty kilometers southwest of Pleiku and about ten kilometers outside Plei Me. The armor eventually rumbled to a series of sharp S-turns in the road, rolling hills and hardwood forest stretching into the distance on both sides of the track. As Luat's vehicles became bunched up in the road's snake-like undulations, recoilless rifle, machine gun fire, and Soviet-made 90mm B-40 rockets suddenly erupted from southeast and west of the narrow provincial route, while preset mortar shells crashed down all along the column's length. The NVA's 635th battalion had dug in on two small hills south of the curves. The vantage point offered gunners clear sightlines down the length of the column. The battalion's attached 75mm recoilless rifle company pounded away, as infantry squads charged forward to press the attack. But while the thick undergrowth on the shoulders no doubt provided camouflage for the assault waves, the road sat at a higher elevation than the brush, forcing the communist riflemen to attack uphill. Worse for the attackers, Luat and his men had been fully expecting the ambush. Indeed, there is little evidence that anyone panicked. Instead, the ATF's M41 Walker Bulldog tanks and M113 armored personnel carriers wheeled aggressively left and right and blasted the ambushers on both sides of the road with 76mm cannon and .50 caliber machine gun fire, while the supporting infantry let loose with everything they had. To top it off, CAS strikes were not long in coming. As night came on, F-100 Super Sabres and Huey gunships suddenly appeared over the battlefield like specters, ripping into NVA gunners with cannon fire and searing napalm. In the ATF's lead tank, Lt. Brady Anderson, a MACV armor adviser, was instrumental in calling in the deadly accurate strikes. Under this vicious pummeling, the communists were forced to break off the attack after just two hours, pulling back to secondary positions where remaining gunners could continue to deliver harassing fire.[55]

Five kilometers to the rear, however, the supply train and Rangers were taking a terrible beating. Responsible for this segment of the kill zone, the NVA's 334th battalion had opened up in conjunction with its sister battalion to the south. The ambushers poured fire into the hapless defenders from both the east and from their positions along three small hills west of the road. Unlike the ATF's main body, the logistics train was without the benefit of armor save for the three lightly armored Greyhounds. The Rangers took heavy casualties in the opening moments, as NVA gunners raked their positions. Many had been riding atop the vehicles rather than maintaining tactical deployment on both sides of the trains, thereby making it difficult for the Rangers to respond effectively when the attack came. Making matters worse, many of the soft-skinned supply trucks—some laden with the ATF's extra fuel and ammunition—were ripped apart by recoilless rifle fire and B-40 rockets, with secondary explosions sending white-orange fireballs and oily black smoke into the late-afternoon skies. Once the supply trains were pinned down, the NVA charged forward from the south with an estimated two- or three-company assault force. Only the timely arrival of tac-air strikes—and an American adviser—prevented the beleaguered supply train from being completely overrun. Earlier, thirty-two-year-old Capt. Paul Leckinger, the 21st Rangers' MACV advisor, was forward with the lead elements of the column and had become concerned about the lagging supply train. He had just come back to see what the holdup was when the 334th had sprung its trap. The Rochester, New York, native could see that the train element was quickly crumbling under murderous NVA fire and was in danger of being utterly routed. The adviser rallied the Rangers to his side and helped organize what was left of the supply train vehicles into a defensive perimeter. At some point in the chaos, however, Leckinger's radio became disabled, leaving him unable to communicate with either the ATF's command or to direct airstrikes on the surging enemy. Leckinger and the supply train were now totally cut off.[56]

Overhead, forward air controller Capt. Hank Lang had arrived in his 0-1 Bird Dog to call in airstrikes on NVA ambush positions. At some point Lang, who was Leckinger's roommate back at the MACV compound in Pleiku, got word that his friend had not only been with the supply train when it was ambushed but now wasn't responding to radio calls either. The FAC was determined to do whatever he could to save his buddy and the logistics train. As dusk came on, Lang was better able to see the muzzle flashes of friend and foe raging below. It didn't take long to figure out who was who. Desultory fire was emanating from what he quickly realized was the beleaguered defensive perimeter thrown up by the Rangers. Meanwhile, much heavier fire poured into it from all directions as a three-company assault force pressed the advantage. With no way to contact Leckinger, Lang had to improvise. The FAC wound his tiny Bird Dog through a hailstorm of antiaircraft over enemy positions, flickering

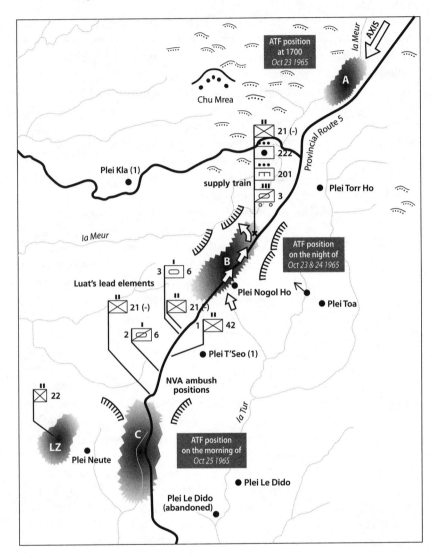

his landing lights like makeshift signal flares to mark targets for the F-100s prowling overhead. Over the next hour Lang pulled off a deadly balancing act, raining rockets and napalm hellfire on enemy positions while keeping the fighter-bombers and gunships clear of Leckingers' meager perimeter. As before, the NVA were eventually forced to break off the attack under the pounding. Leckinger reordered what was left of his force as best he could to wait out the night.

Losses had been substantial. Two M-8 Greyhounds had been totally destroyed, with another severely damaged. Two more 105 truck tractors and two gas tankers were also obliterated by rocket and recoilless rifle fire. Several other transport vehicles sustained heavy damage, as did the two 105mm howitzers. Leckinger, along with his fellow American advisers, survived unscathed, but the day's fight had cost the ARVN dearly. A total of fifty had been killed in action (KIA), another 102 wounded, and nineteen were missing in action. Not surprisingly, it was the supply train—lacking the firepower and armor of the main body—that had sustained the lion's share of these losses. NVA losses were put at fifty-one KIA by body count, with one soldier captured in action.[57]

As for Luat, his armor had held up exceptionally well, with no losses and only minor damage to a few vehicles. As NVA fire died away, the task force commander pulled the ATF's main body back north approximately one thousand meters, coiled his forces into a tight defensive position, and waited. Other than occasional harassing fire, the next several hours passed quietly. But Khẩn, the 32nd Regiment's commander, wasn't done. Determined to break the South Vietnamese armor, he ordered in his reserves. He'd held the 966th battalion about two thousand meters to the west to act as both a reserve element and a reaction force in the event ARVN troops were air assaulted to the rear of the regiment. Khan directed the battalion to divide into three, company-sized elements and move into ready positions on both sides of the road near the ATF's main body. At about 0315 hours, the newly arrived companies began their assault. And just as before, the attack was met by a fusillade of heavy armored vehicle fire and thundering CAS strikes. Under cover of night, the Air Force brought in its lumbering but deadly AC-47 gunship as well. Puff kept the field alight with illumination flares, even as the converted transport unleashed a torrent of 7.62mm minigun fire on the communists. Meanwhile, fighter-bombers doused the 966th in napalm while raking the battalion with everything from fragmentation and cluster munitions to 2.75-inch rockets and 20mm cannon fire. The fields along Route 5 became an abattoir. Once again, Luat's force took few casualties in the attack. The NVA weren't as lucky. After again suffering heavy losses, Khan was forced to concede that the ambush had failed. Leaving behind a small, rear-guard element to mask his retreat, the 32nd commander ordered a general withdrawal of his battered regiment west toward its base area in the Chu Pong Massif complex near the Cambodian border. By daybreak, all major of elements of the 32nd Regiment had withdrawn from the area. Now, all that remained for Luat's ATF was to finally make its way to Plei Me. That would soon prove easier said than done.[58]

8

THE GRIP LOOSENS
(24–28 OCTOBER)

As the sun rose on the morning of Sunday, 24 October, it seemed that the ATF had survived the heralded ambush, bloodied but largely intact. The ARVN had received in the last few hours only scattered harassing fire from the NVA's stay-behind elements. But the relief force had lost a great deal of its fuel and ammunition in the previous day's attack on the supply train. This, along with his uncertainty as to the disposition of NVA forces, led Luat to decide that he would advance no further without first receiving a resupply from Pleiku. Meanwhile, atop the hill overlooking the battle, the 22nd Rangers had still not moved. The battalion, whose orders had been to sweep east after insertion and destroy any NVA force it encountered, had instead remained at its LZ throughout the day and night. The Rangers had mortared elements of the NVA when they had come into range but had otherwise sat quietly atop the hill as the ambush raged below. Khan would almost certainly have been immediately aware that the 22nd Rangers had landed to his rear, but when the battalion made no effort to move forward and engage his troops, he decided to let them be. His principal order stood: destroy the ARVN column. So, rather than having his reserve element turn on the Rangers, he had instead ordered the 966th to prosecute the second, ill-fated attack on the ATF's armor.[1]

Journalists John Laurence and Charles Mohr, who'd both hitched rides with the Rangers the previous afternoon, later wrote that on the morning of 24 October, they watched from the hilltop as "groups of soldiers in mustard-brown uniforms" crossed the open fields below, in full view of the Rangers, before disappearing into the thick brush beyond. These were most certainly troops from the 32nd Regiment as they executed Khan's order to withdraw. As before, Laurence was incredulous that the Rangers, no more than five hundred meters from the retreating communists, would simply stand by without firing a shot and let them escape. By late morning, with the enemy long gone and the Rangers having finished their breakfast, the battalion finally moved down toward the road. The going was tough as the men pushed into the dense foliage at the base of the hill. Every yard, reported Laurence, had to be hacked open with machetes. After two hours of fighting their way through the oppressive heat and dense tangle of jungle, the troops and journalists came upon a quintet of dead enemy soldiers splayed out by a rushing stream. The bodies were clothed in the khaki of the NVA. As the group of Rangers, journalists, and American advisers looked on, Huynh shot film of the dead and then stood back. These men, Huynh told the onlookers, were soldiers of North Vietnam. While the NVA had operated at regimental strength at Duc Co in August, it was likely the first time any of those assembled had seen with their own eyes evidence that North Vietnam's regular army was here. Indeed, it was the NVA—not the black-pajama-clad Viet Cong—that had launched the siege of Plei Me, that had ambushed the column. The war had suddenly changed very much, indeed.[2]

It was early afternoon by the time the battalion had hacked its way through to the road. The jungle on both sides of the dirt track had been shredded and scorched from the previous day's action. Battalion commander Phuc announced that his men would go no further. He would simply wait there for the ATF to arrive. Frustrated, and surmising that the column couldn't be far off, Laurence and the small group of journalists that had come in with the Rangers the day before struck out on their own. Laurence later recalled that it wasn't long before he realized what a foolhardy decision that had been. Six journalists, alone, with enemy troops likely still in the area. No radio. No map. No protection, aside from the pistol carried by Wilson and another by Mohr. Cold comfort in a war zone of high-powered rifles and machine guns. Luckily, Laurence and company came upon the ATF's point element about five hundred meters up the road. With his goal of reaching Plei Me unchanged, Laurence was happy to hitch a ride with Luat, but he would have to wait a while longer. Lawrence would soon discover that the task force commander was in no hurry.[3]

Luat linked up with the Rangers later that afternoon. But instead of pushing on for Plei Me, he pulled the entire relief force back north to merge with the remnants of the supply train. There, Luat again formed a defensive perimeter in about the same spot as where the logistics train had spent the previous night and tended to his casualties, calling in medevacs for the most serious cases. As the day wore on, the armored commander's

American advisers once again urged him to press on for Plei Me. Luat again refused to move until he'd been properly resupplied. There are even some who claim that Luat and some of his junior officers wanted to abandon the Plei Me relief effort altogether and pull the task force back to Pleiku. According to one source, the armor commander was ultimately overruled by Vinh Loc himself.[4] At any rate, Luat did send a portion of the ATF—including some elements of the hard-hit 21st Rangers—back to Pleiku for ammo and fuel, while retaining his company of M41 Bulldogs, the 1/42nd infantry battalion, and the 22nd Rangers within his defensive laager. The ATF commander then added another wrinkle: if he were to push on for Plei Me, he would do so only under the steel umbrella of overwhelming American artillery support.[5]

Meanwhile, at II Corps headquarters, Mataxis relayed Luat's request up the chain. The news found an enthusiastic recipient in 1st Cavalry commander Maj. Gen. Kinnard, who was eager to get his new airmobile division into the fight. Larsen had issued a standing order that Knowles, the brigade task force commander, was to offer the ARVN assistance only if they explicitly asked for it. Additionally, Knowles would have to obtain permission from both Kinnard and Larsen before committing 1st Brigade men and materiel. Now that the ARVN were officially asking, Kinnard convinced Larsen to give the task force commander the latitude he needed. Larsen acceded, and Knowles ordered acting 1st Brigade commander Clark to get his artillery into position to support the ATF's movement. First, Company B of 2/12 Cav was air assaulted into a clearing about nine kilometers north of the ATF's perimeter. With the LZ at Objective FIELD GOAL secured without opposition, the rest of 2nd Battalion followed, along with a battery of 105mm howitzers from the 2nd Battalion, 17th Artillery. From here, Clark's big guns could deliver lethal arty support several kilometers down Route 5. Finally, Knowles arranged for an artillery liaison officer to be inserted with Luat's command to goose the armored commander into once again getting his column rolling. Capt. John B. Avera, with the 1st Battalion, 77th Artillery, went in with a medevac lift on the afternoon of the 24th. But even with American assurances of artillery support and the presence of Avera, it quickly became clear that Luat had no intention of going anywhere. The ATF would be spending yet another night on Route 5. No matter. The 1st Cav, much to its commanding general's satisfaction, was finally in position to get into the war.[6]

Back at Plei Me, word had come down that Luat and his task force would not reach the embattled camp today, so Maj. Thompson, Beckwith's XO, spent the afternoon coordinating a series of vicious CAS strikes on NVA positions around Plei Me. As before, strikes near the wire sent red-hot shrapnel ripping through the camp. But with each thunderous explosion, Thompson, sometimes working two radio handsets simultaneously, excitedly called, "I like it, I like it!" The continued heavy air attacks seemed to be taking their toll. NVA harassment and interdiction fire fell off dramatically. With the lull, Beckwith decided the time had come to risk calling in slick helicopters to evacuate some of the Montagnard women and children. And, of course, there were the dead. Many of the bodies stacked inside the dispensary and on the ground outside, had lain exposed to heat and rats for days. He'd thought from his first day in camp that their presence was not just a health hazard but a drain on morale as well. It was grim work. Those charged with loading the bodies were nearly overcome with the enormity of it all. Even John Pioletti, the 5th Group's seasoned sergeant major, vomited all over one body bag as he was struggling to load it aboard a Huey.[7]

With the NVA's grip seemingly loosening, Beckwith now turned to something he'd agonized over for two days: Tom Pusser's body was still out on the north ridge. It was time to bring the young captain in. Beckwith began to organize a retrieval mission and asked for volunteers. Almost immediately, Maj. Tat, commander of the 91st Airborne Rangers, volunteered his men for the job. "The Vietnamese will get his body for you," he told Beckwith. "We want to do this." Tat gave the job to his 1st Company commander. Supporting fires from the camp were coordinated, and an Airborne Ranger recon team fanned out near the site where the NVA's machine gun positions had been discovered. The Rangers took no fire in the operation, and the follow-on carrying element managed to retrieve not just Pusser's body but also those of the other fallen. Despite Beckwith's various clashes with Tat in previous days—especially his outrage that the Rangers had abandoned Pusser's body in the first place—the DELTA commander in his after-action report praised the Airborne Rangers' operation as one conducted "in a very professional manner." Beckwith came over and looked down at the young captain he had been so fond of and shook his head. The twenty-six-year-old's body was badly bloated and deformed from two days of lying exposed to the elements. "It was," as Beckwith would later write, "a damn shame."[8]

25 OCTOBER

Following the second disastrous attempt on 23 October to clear the NVA's trench works and machine gun positions near the camp's north corner, Beckwith and the troopers had devised a new plan for dealing with the problem. Using flamethrowers, a "commando-type" squad consisting of 1st Lt. Berry and Sgt. Tafoya, the only ones who knew how to use the weapon, and seven or eight CIDG troops would assault and burn the positions out. The flamethrowers had come in on a supply drop the day before. After testing them to ensure they were in good working order, the plan was a go. Armed with flamethrowers, Berry and Tafoya would pave the way under small-arms protection from the accompanying CIDG squad, as well as machine gun and mortar supporting fires from camp. According to Berry, the plan also called for a follow-on force from camp to exploit any success the squad had in clearing the trenches. At about 0930 hours, Berry, Tafoya, and the CIDG moved out beyond the wire. At some point, the squad met with fairly intense small-arms fire. According to both Berry and Beckwith's after-action report, the commando squad was nevertheless able to knock out one machine gun position before being forced to withdraw back into camp.[9]

But Berry was livid. Where was the follow-on force he'd expected? They'd finally knocked out one of the NVA's positions, but when the opportunity came to exploit the success, there were no reinforcements to capitalize on it. The SF lieutenant dropped his equipment and went looking for Beckwith. He found the DELTA commander in the open area outside the team house at the center of camp. "We were out there, where were you?" he bellowed, storming up to the major. "Why did you leave us out there?" Berry stood there, hands on his hips, waiting for an answer. Beckwith didn't say a word but instead reared back and punched the twenty-two-year-old XO straight in the face. The men tussled for a moment before nearby troopers pulled them apart. And then, just as suddenly as it had begun, it was over. They both, in Berry's words, "adulted up" and got back to the business at hand. "There was this sense that, 'Okay, I've had my words, he hit me, and we moved away. This is not helping anything.' It was an emotional reaction to a rather tense situation. And I was like, 'Get over it, Berry. Life goes on.'"[10]

The flamethrower-commando raid would be the last of three sorties ordered by Beckwith since he'd assumed command three days earlier. Again, whether those attacks were the idea of 5th Group commander William McKean or Beckwith himself remains unclear. What is clear were their results. Tom Pusser had been killed, and Euell White and Bill DeSoto had been grievously wounded. Scores of South Vietnamese Special Forces, Airborne Rangers, and CIDG had also been killed or wounded in the attacks. All three attacks were launched in broad daylight against entrenched enemy positions. With the exception of knocking out a lone NVA machine gun position—a success, according to Berry, that was then not exploited—none of the sorties came close to accomplishing their objective. Indeed, the most notable consequence seemed to have been adding to the camp's casualty rolls. Yet, the man tasked with caring for all those additional casualties believes now, just as he did then, that something had to be done about the enemy on the north ridge.[11]

"I thought it was a good idea," says Hunter. "At night, they didn't have far to go to rush us. We couldn't just let them sit there. You have to break a siege from either inside or out. It doesn't take a military genius to figure that out."[12]

And the Special Forces doctor isn't alone. Berry, who by his own account "didn't see eye to eye with Beckwith," supports the impetus behind the sorties to this day. "When it's a stalemate situation," he says, "the only way to change the situation is to do something."[13]

Still, following the final sortie of 25 October, Berry says a consensus formed: it was now time to sit tight and wait. Word had come down that Luat's ATF was finally on the move again. More importantly, scuttlebutt had it that the 1st Cav itself would soon take a much more active role around Plei Me—and beyond.[14]

When Clark discovered late on the afternoon of 24 October that Luat had decided to spend another night in his Route 5 perimeter, the 1st Brigade commander took the opportunity to truck his artillery and cavalry element closer to the ARVN column. The new firebase at Objective FIELD GOAL SOUTH, just three kilometers north of Luat's bivouac, would allow his guns to reach even farther along the ATF's axis of approach. At the same time, Clark ordered yet another air assault, this time by two companies of the 2nd Battalion, 8th Regiment, under Lt. Col. James H. Nix, to a position about halfway between Plei Me and the armored task force. Once again, 1st Cav troopers encountered no resistance as they secured LZ SOUTH, a position that would allow the accompanying B Battery, 2/19 Artillery to cover both the ATF and the areas surrounding the Special Forces camp. Now, as the sun rose on the 25th, Clark opted to move even closer to the action. LZ SOUTH's contingent was airlifted to its new location, Position HOMECOMING, where it was joined by a second 2/19 howitzer battery and the rest of the 2/8 Cavalry. From this position east of Route 5 and about halfway between the original ambush site and Plei Me, 1st Brigade could now rain down dominating artillery fires over a kilometers-wide swath. With that, the FIELD GOAL SOUTH contingent, now relatively far from the action back up Route 5, was pulled back to Camp Holloway to act as a reaction force as the siege continued to unfold.[15]

Back at the ATF's perimeter, Luat was still in no great hurry to roll for Plei Me. No doubt exasperated, Avera finally climbed into the ATF's lead tank and began calling in arty fires all along the column's route of advance. At 1300, as great geysers of smoke and fire exploded skyward ahead of the column, Luat at last gave the order to advance. Laurence, who had been invited to ride along in Luat's command APC, bumped along the road with the armored commander. A cluttered assortment of ammunition boxes, C-ration crates, and even cases of beer was stacked here and there inside the armored track's cargo hold. To Laurence, Luat was something of an eccentric character. The journalist described him as a good-natured, stoutly built man in his midforties, with a thick neck and brown leathery skin, undoubtedly toughened from years of riding an open armored track beneath the relentless Vietnamese sun. Seated in what appeared to be a living room recliner that had been bolted to the cargo hold deck, Luat "bounced merrily along . . . like a potentate at the center of his realm." In between barking orders into his radio set, the ATF commander sipped steadily at a potent local brew called "Bierre Larue." As the day wore on, wrote Laurence, Luat's "eyes became cloudy and moist."[16]

And thus, the day passed quietly until about 1500 hours, and some five kilometers south of the original ambush site, when the ATF once again began receiving sporadic, small-arms fire, sparking fears that another ambush was imminent. Whether the harassing fire emanated from one of the 32nd's rearguard elements or local force Viet Cong was unclear. At any rate, Avera called in a heavy artillery strike to pound the jungle. This, along with renewed CAS sorties, quickly engulfed in a series of earth-shaking explosions any enemy troops lurking about. When the barrage had ceased, Luat for good measure called up a troop of M113s to blast the position with .50 caliber machine gun fire, while infantry lobbed 40mm grenades into the bush from their M79 launchers. While such recon by fire might have seemed excessive to Laurence, Luat, with memories of the 23 October ambush still fresh, was taking no chances. With the enemy fire silenced, the ATF, which had taken no casualties in the encounter, once again rolled on.

Just as the sun was setting on 25 October, the convoy finally reached Plei Me, a full five days after Luat had first been dispatched to Phu My.[17]

The heavy vehicles rumbled up to the main gate on the camp's east side. South Vietnamese and Montagnard troops stood whooping and hollering as they waved their tiger-striped boonie caps and filthy yellow scarves aloft. The tankers smiled broadly and waved back, drawing up their tracked armor into a defensive line northeast of camp. Plei Me's exhausted and depleted defenders had just spent six days fighting for their lives in conditions of nearly unimaginable filth while an entire NVA regiment had rained down fire and death at every opportunity. The cloying stench of decomposing bodies, human excrement, and decaying garbage hung like a dirty shroud, a malodorous testament to the misery they'd endured. The ground, pockmarked with mortar craters, was strewn with a mélange of war-fighting refuse: bloodstained bandages, empty ammo crates, C-ration cans, shattered glass and splintered wood, shredded sandbags, shell casings. Body lice infested the defenders, and rats, some as large as housecats, scurried amongst the debris with impunity. The beasts had fattened up on the putrefying corpses of Plei Me's fallen. The dead had been wrapped in Army blankets and later the brightly colored supply parachutes after the stock of body bags had run dry. Corpses were piled high in what was left of the medical dispensary, and then, when there was no more room, simply laid out on the bare ground outside. But now, after all the suffering and degradation, the men of Plei Me had finally been delivered. The moment's goodwill, however, was to be short lived.[18]

Luat dismounted his APC and marched confidently toward the gate, a leather swagger stick tucked under his arm. There he was met by Maj. Beckwith and a small retinue of hollow-eyed and bedraggled Special Forces troopers. Each man was befouled from days of hard fighting, encrusted from head to toe in a film of stale sweat, soot, and the red clay dust that saturated every inch of the camp. Water had been at a premium, so a wash and a shave was a luxury none of them could afford. Beckwith offered a grime-streaked hand and thanked the armored commander for coming to the camp's aid. But Laurence, who witnessed the exchange and would interview Beckwith on camera two days later, noted that the DELTA commander was in reality deeply resentful that it had taken Luat and his ATF so long to arrive. The DELTA commander wondered bitterly, *Where were they when we had really needed them?*[19]

After the pleasantries had concluded, Luat declared that he wanted to bring some of his staff and infantry inside the camp for a safe place to spend the night. Beckwith's thinly veiled frustration boiled over. "No," he said flatly. Luat and his men could not come inside. The camp was simply too crowded to admit anyone else. The task force commander and his people were to sleep outside the gates and maintain a security perimeter for the camp. The otherwise affable Luat exploded in a fit of indignation, cursing Beckwith in three languages. From Luat's perspective, he'd just spent nearly a week fighting his way to rescue the camp, losing dozens killed and wounded along the way, and several vehicles too. And now this American, this *junior* officer, was denying him access to a camp in his own country? To Luat, a lieutenant colonel, it was for him alone to decide who could enter the camp and when. Beckwith's breach of military protocol, he concluded, was nothing short of an outrage. The ATF commander collected himself and looked hard into Beckwith's face. If the American didn't obey his order, Luat said, he would shoot him. Beckwith merely stared back, his face contorted in a fierce scowl, but behind him, the three Special Forces troopers flicked their M16 select fire switches off safety. A deadly silence settled over the little group. After a few anxious moments, Luat, perhaps suddenly aware of his danger, spun on his heels and strode back to his APC without another word.[20]

Beckwith wasn't any happier to see Laurence and his fellow journalists. After hurling a series of profane epithets at those assembled, he let the newsmen know in no uncertain terms that they were, in effect, in the Army now. As with Joe Galloway and Eddie Adams a few days earlier, the reporters would be expected to pull guard duty and man the perimeter just like everyone else. Later in the evening, while Laurence chatted with some of the SF troopers, he spied Wilson and Hoan following DELTA Maj. A. J. "Bo" Baker as he led them to one of the corner bunkers. They'd volunteered to make good on Beckwith's command and were on their way to learn how to fire the M2 .50 caliber machine gun. The troopers with Laurence threw out a few good-natured jibes at the newsmen. But a short while after, all could hear as Wilson and Hoan became acquainted with the "Ma Deuce," firing several short bursts and raucously cheering themselves on. The two journalists would man the heavy machine gun position for the rest of the night.[21]

Laurence spent the next several hours hanging around the team house, listening to the back-and-forth as the troopers passed a bottle of whiskey and reflected on their ordeal. Earlier, Beckwith had racked out at the other end of the team house and left orders to wake him if something happened. Outside, all was quiet. Some of the troopers speculated that the siege might finally be over. The NVA, it appeared, had had enough. At some point, a radio operator emerged from the communications bunker housed beneath the team house. He had news he was sure no one would believe. Maj. Charles "Tommy" Thompson, Beckwith's second in command, perked up. What was going on, Thompson asked. Lyndon Baines Johnson had a message for Beckwith, came the reply. The radioman had been right, Thompson thought. It *was* unbelievable. But then Thompson remembered some of the "dumbass" requests he'd been receiving from Pleiku the past few days. Senator Edward Kennedy had arrived in-country Saturday for the stated purpose of touring refugee camps but had since been pestering MACV to fly him into Plei Me to see the action firsthand.[22] Thompson sent the radio operator to wake Beckwith. Moments later, the DELTA commander emerged, as irritable as ever. "The president of what, for fuck's sake?" he growled. Thompson smiled broadly. "The president of the United States, Charlie," Thompson replied. Beckwith grumbled. "I got better things to do than talk to that guy." Then he disappeared into the commo bunker, reemerging a half an hour later. He hadn't talked to the president but had instead received a message expressing LBJ's "concern" for the camp's defenders. But according to Laurence, the DELTA commander later confided that his attitude had changed. Beckwith had come to believe that the president's message had a deeper meaning. That the president had taken time to reach out meant that the job he and his men were doing at Plei Me must be pretty important after all. In other words: *The whole country is watching, son, so don't screw this up.*[23]

The NVA's tactic of "lure and ambush" had failed. Not only had the 32nd Regiment been unable to destroy the responding ARVN column, but it had suffered mightily under Luat's guns, and the CAS and artillery fires brought in to support him. Now, with the ATF finally breaking through to Plei Me, the rationale for keeping the 33rd Regiment, which itself had suffered tremendously from tac-air strikes over the previous six days, had disappeared. Indeed, two of the 33rd's battalion commanders had been killed, and the third severely wounded. The 2nd Battalion alone had lost 250 men, about half its strength. The 1st and 3rd battalions had also taken heavy casualties, and the regimental mortar company had lost half its men KIA, with five of its nine mortar tubes wrecked. At about 2200 hours on 25 October—right around the time Beckwith was receiving LBJ's congratulatory message—Field Front command ordered regimental commander Lt. Col. Vũ Sắc to begin withdrawing the remnants of his battered unit west toward its rally point at a place the NVA called the "village of Kro." While intelligence analysts were never able to identify that location, it was likely a waystation along the route to Field Front base areas in the Chu Pong mountain complex on the Cambodian border. The retreat was to begin the following morning, with the regiment's reinforced 3rd Battalion acting as a rearguard to cover the withdrawal. This battalion would soon demonstrate that communist forces around Plei Me still had some fight left in them.[24]

26 OCTOBER

The next morning dawned quietly. It was Tuesday, one full week after the start of the siege. Plei Me was already returning to life. CIDG cleanup crews roved here and there across the grounds, a haze of smoke hanging over the camp as the Montagnards cleared and burned the dross of seven days' worth of waste and rubble. Others ventured outside the wire to police the surrounding battlefield. The killing fields beyond the perimeter were littered with the detritus of men at war. Weapons and wallets, diaries and cigarette packs, and more. Everywhere the earth was cratered and scorched, a testament to the voluminous ordnance—thousands of tons' worth—that had fallen during the siege. And, of course, there were the bodies, maggot-riddled and bloated under the merciless Southeast Asian sun. A miasma of sickly sweet decomposition hung over the battlefield. These corpses had once been living and breathing men who'd slogged hundreds of miles down the Ho Chi Minh Trail to do the bidding of their political leaders in the North. Now, they were so much carrion littering the bomb-cratered landscape, blasted and charred by the cluster munitions, cannon fire, and flaming napalm delivered by American CAS. The ARVN dead would be flown back to Pleiku for proper burial. The Montagnards would be laid to rest here on their ancestral lands. But these NVA, so far from their homes, would simply be bulldozed into the gaping bomb craters and piled over with dirt.[25] But they and their comrades who'd survived had been busy. Trench works, some collapsed under the thunderous bombing, others still intact, snaked their way across the open fields, some as close as fifty meters from the outer perimeter. To look at the blackened and barren moonscape left in the bombing's wake, it was hard to imagine that the communists could've tunneled this close unseen. But a week ago the land beyond the wire had been a choking tangle of vegetation, a screen that had concealed the NVA's insidious work. The air strikes had since razed every bush, every tree, every blade of grass for hundreds of meters in all directions.[26]

Meanwhile, at the ATF's defensive perimeter, Luat's task force was again revving up to move. Gen. Hon had ordered Luat to take his task force and first sweep the northern slope near the camp, the same site that had hosted several NVA heavy machine gun nests over the previous week. Once the ridge was clear, the ATF commander was to continue his sweep west and then south toward the airstrip. This area, of course, had been the site of the heaviest enemy fire over the previous week. At midmorning, the ARVN moved out in two columns: the M41 tank company and the 22nd Ranger Battalion on the right, with the APCs, the 1/42nd Infantry, and what remained of the 21st Rangers covering the left flank. By about 0930 hours, Luat had swept the northern slope, and it appeared to be completely abandoned. Over the next few hours, never straying far from Plei Me's outer perimeter, the task force made its way cautiously around the triangular camp's northern apex. By about 1400 hours, the ATF had rounded the heavy bunker on Plei Me's western point and continued its sweep south.[27]

At some point south of the airstrip, the tracked vehicles found the ground too broken to negotiate. The order was given to turn the ATF around and head back the way it had come. It was a tricky maneuver given the difficult terrain and the large number of men and vehicles involved, and the movement quickly became a quagmire. Making matters worse, some of the ARVN infantry took the opportunity to break discipline and raid nearby parachute drops for supplies and water. And then the world caught fire. The NVA's reinforced 3rd Battalion, well dug in and lying in wait to cover the regiment's retreat, chose this moment of chaos to unleash its ambush. At about 1205 hours, the battalion let loose with a heavy barrage of mortar, B-40 rockets, and machine gun and recoilless rifle fire. The ARVN task force, no doubt complacent in its belief that the fighting around Plei Me had ended, was dumbfounded as NVA fire cut through the column like a murderous scythe. Some of the tankers and APC drivers, unlike during the attack on Route 5, panicked and fled in fear of communist rocket-propelled grenades. This time, the ambush was threatening to dissolve into a rout.[28]

Back in the American sector at the center of camp, Laurence and crew were just settling into an interview with a captured NVA prisoner when glowing red machine gun tracers began streaking in from the south, ripping the buildings around them. Everyone hit the dirt, clawing for cover as death-dealing rounds shrieked overhead. Beckwith and a few troopers, who'd come over to see the prisoner, dropped and then bear-crawled for the American team house nearby. Mortars had also begun to crash down into the camp. Laurence, Wilson, and Hoan dove into a nearby three-foot communication trench and scurried hunched over until they emerged near a circular mortar pit near the smaller of the two Montagnard barracks. Lined with a thick, sandbag parapet, the pit housed an 81mm mortar tube. CIDG mortar crews were trained to respond to incoming mortar volleys with rapid and continuous fire of their own. Laurence noticed that the mortar tube was pointed nearly straight up—an orientation that suggested "final protective fire"—a defensive tactic typically employed only as a last resort. Wilson dove into the pit and rolled film as the CIDG relentlessly pummeled a section of the tree line just south of camp. Unknown to the Montagnards, this was precisely where the ATF was currently being hammered by the

NVA ambush. Now, the luckless ARVN troops were likely getting a taste of their own mortars, as well.[29]

Just then, Staff Sgt. Cornelius Clark, a demolitions expert with A-217, came barreling out of the smoky haze that hung over the camp, waving his arms and hollering for a ceasefire. Clark did not speak Jarai, but the 'Yards might still not have listened if he had. They continued to load and fire in an almost trance-like state, robotically sending one heavy round after another. Finally, Clark leapt down into the pit, seized a mortar shell from the loader, and shoved him aside. The message finally got through. But then another mortar crew opened up some distance away, and Clark disappeared back into the smoke to silence that one, as well. He would end up having no luck. Like a life-and-death game of "whack-a-mole," Clark spent the next hour running from pit to pit trying to stop the crews from dropping ordnance on friendly troops. But just when he'd get them calmed down, another barrage of NVA mortars would rain down, and the 'Yards would maniacally renew their own. It was, as Clark would later say, "fucking insane."[30]

In the meantime, word had reached 1st Cav artillery at Position HOMECOMING that the ATF was heavily engaged. In response, 2/19th Artillery's two batteries of 105mm howitzers opened up with a murderous barrage, sending thunderous fireballs skyward all along the tree line south of the airstrip. Soon after, tac-air fighter-bombers roared in on strafing and napalm runs. The 2/8 Cav, also believing all was quiet at Plei Me, had planned to insert and support A Company of the 8th Engineers so it could begin repairs on the camp's heavily damaged airstrip. But with the ATF so heavily engaged near the runway, the plan was immediately scrapped. Still, with arty and CAS pounding 3rd Battalion positions, Luat was finally able to rally his task force for a limited counterattack. After an hourlong firefight, the NVA's rearguard battalion was forced to break contact and withdraw. Luat's ATF staggered back around the northwestern corner of the camp and reestablished its defensive position from the previous night. The armored commander would later be chastised both for failing "to make a proper terrain analysis prior to the sweep around Plei Me" to ensure his vehicles could negotiate the topography and for losing control of his men as they broke ranks to plunder nearby supply drops. The short, sharp clash had cost the ARVN twenty-seven dead and at least eighty wounded. How many of those casualties were due to friendly fire cannot be known. The wounded poured into camp by the score, some on foot, others splayed upon the decks of the M113s.[31]

What followed were two ugly incidents that did not cover the ARVN in glory. The ambush was surely a traumatic experience for the column's

South Vietnamese soldiers. They had just spent the better part of a week fighting their way—albeit haltingly—to relieve the camp and had already been hit with several sharp attacks. Now, just when many had no doubt started to believe the fight was over, the NVA had struck again. Hard. That the soldiers' morale had been badly shaken was made abundantly clear by their behavior during the attack—but especially after it.

It all began when an M113 came careening back into camp while the fight was still raging. Beckwith and some troopers had come out to see what had happened. They'd already had reports that the column had a lot of wounded, including American advisers who'd been caught in the ambush. But when the APC's cargo hatch swung open, it revealed nothing more than a dozen uninjured ARVN, some appearing to have abandoned their weapons during their flight from the field. No wounded had been carried out, American or otherwise. Beckwith was apoplectic. He rallied a three-man fire team of SF troopers and gathered kit and weapons. The DELTA commander then walked up to the APC driver, pulled the charging handle on his M16, and ground the muzzle to the man's temple. *Take us to the wounded Americans,* Beckwith growled. Whether the driver spoke English or no, the message seemed to have gotten through loud and clear, for moments later, the APC, Beckwith and team aboard, barreled back out the front gate. Some time later, the Americans staggered back into camp on foot carrying a wounded US adviser who would later die. Four other American advisers were also wounded in the ambush.[32]

Meanwhile, Hunter was once again flooded with casualties. He set up a makeshift medical dispensary in the safety of the deep communications bunker and spent the next several hours treating and triaging, deciding who could be saved and who would be left to fate. When it was clear that the fight was over, the SF surgeon called in a train of medevacs to pull out the worst cases. The wounded gathered around the makeshift landing pad at the center of camp and waited expectantly. As he readied the first round of the most severe casualties for extraction, Hunter cast a wary eye across the throngs of others who had assembled. He'd seen this movie only a few days earlier following one of the ill-conceived sorties against entrenched NVA machine gun positions beyond the wire. And he didn't have to wait long for the replay. The first chopper had no sooner settled onto its skids than a mob of walking wounded surged forward, pushing and shoving and climbing over one another, all trying to crowd aboard at the same time. As before, Hunter waved for help from a few of his SF comrades. Only those casualties with a red medevac tag were cleared for extraction. The troopers pushed the jostling on-rushers back, trying to maintain order. In the chaos, one of the SF soldiers spied a tagless Ranger climbing over the backs of his comrades into the cargo hold. The American tore away the soldier's suspicious-looking bandage, revealing nothing beneath but smooth, brown skin. Enraged, he flung the fraud head-over-heels into the red dirt. And there were many others: unwounded ARVN soldiers, some affixed with counterfeit bandages, forcing aside their wounded comrades in a bid for escape.[33] On it went until all the legitimately wounded—and some who weren't—finally got out. As night came on, calm finally settled over Plei Me. South of the air strip, the 3rd Battalion had gone quiet, itself badly stung by American supporting fires and Luat's counterattack. Official body count listed 148 NVA killed, but it was unclear how many of those KIA were from the previous week's siege.[34]

A few kilometers to the northeast at Position HOMECOMING, Gen. William Westmoreland, the commanding general of US forces in Vietnam, choppered in for a visit to 1st Brigade's new forward command post. Clark had moved the CP up from Camp Holloway just that morning.[35] A plan was in the works to dramatically expand the 1st Cav's role in the war, and Westmoreland wanted to confer directly with division officers. The expanded mission's theme was unmistakable: where in the past the enemy had been allowed to hit and then run away to lick his wounds, he would now be relentlessly pursued and destroyed wherever he might go.

The instrument for this new aggressive approach was to be the 1st Cavalry Division and its cutting-edge airmobile concept. It was no secret that the division's commander, Maj. Gen. Kinnard, had disapproved of the Cav's early missions under Field Force commander Maj. Gen. Larsen. Kinnard believed those limited reinforcement and reaction operations were far too restrictive and prevented his troopers from aggressively searching out and engaging enemy formations. Now, Westmoreland was prepared to loosen the reins on his cavalry general. First Cav's new area of operations would now swell to more than 2,500 square kilometers. The territory essentially represented about half of Pleiku Province, stretching from Highway 14 in the east all the way to the Cambodian border to the west. It would also encompass the ground between Highway 19 to the north, all the way down to the province's southern boundary.[36]

The first order of business was to find, fix, and kill the NVA regiments that had laid siege to Plei Me. Lt. Col. Clark's 1st Brigade, already engaged and in the area, would initially take the lead. The plan was to disperse battalions to ensure the widest possible search grid. Kinnard had faith that the mobility of his helicopters, along with superior communications capability, would not only allow his troopers to systematically scour exceptionally large swaths of territory but also respond with devastating alacrity once the enemy was found. Each battalion was to be deployed with its own artillery support and, once in its assigned sector, would disperse its companies to further widen the hunting grounds. Company-level units were to engage in extensive and "vigorous" patrols, searching for the enemy "in the villages, in the jungle, and along the stream beds." When communist formations were located, a separate rapid reaction force could be called in to swoop down by air assault and strike the enemy. Airlifted artillery, organic to the 1st Cav, along with tactical air assets, would provide supporting fires. Ultimately, this dramatically expanded mission was to be a trial-by-fire for both the airmobile concept and the new division that had been created to implement it.[37]

In its earliest stages, Clark's brigade task force would be comprised of the following units: 2nd Battalion, 8th Cav; 2nd Battalion, 12th Cav; Company B, 1st Battalion, 8th Cav; 2nd Battalion, 17th Artillery, and its 105mm towed howitzers; and the helicopter gunships of Battery B, 2nd Battalion, 20th Artillery. Additional Hueys, tasked with a reconnaissance role, would be provided by the 1st Squadron, 9th Cav. The 1st Battalion, 12 Cav, would initially act as the brigade reserve.[38]

The brigade's first task, especially in light of the latest bloody ambush of Luat's ATF, was to clear the areas surrounding Plei Me. Throughout the siege, the region south of camp had seen the highest level of enemy activity. Kinnard reasoned it made sense to start there. He issued the warning order to 1st Brigade at about 2145 hours, and staff worked all night planning the operation, scheduled for the next day. Clark decided to insert the 2/8th Cav near the camp and have the battalion sweep the vicinity. The ultimate destination was to be "Objective CHERRY" atop the four-hundred-meter Chu Don Massif, about two thousand meters due south of Plei Me. But Clark's staff faced a dilemma: where could they safely insert the battalion? Memories of the enemy's ferocious antiaircraft fires were still fresh. After all, the NVA had shot down several American aircraft during the siege and damaged many others. The NVA ambush earlier in the day near Plei Me's airstrip ruled out that location and only served to exacerbate the staff officers' fears. Of course, 1st Brigade didn't yet know that the NVA 3/33rd Regiment had already pulled out following its attack on the ATF. At any rate, the key for staff officers was to find a suitable LZ far enough away from enemy antiaircraft elements around the camp but close enough so the Cav troopers wouldn't wear themselves out reaching their objective. Nonplussed, Clark's staff finally reached out through the brigade's liaison officer to the man who they figured knew the area best—Chargin' Charlie Beckwith.[39]

Beckwith, demonstrating his puckish side, was only too happy to help. He was fairly certain that the area north of camp was now quiet. He also knew that the region was littered with hundreds of bloated NVA corpses that had been ripening under Vietnam's tropical sun for nearly a week. The stench was overwhelming. The fresh-faced cavalry troopers, most of whom had never fired a shot in anger, were new in-country. A visit to the north slope would prove an "instructive introduction" for the 1st Cav, according to Beckwith. "No better way to let them know war is hell." So that's exactly where the DELTA commander suggested the 2/8th set down.[40]

27–28 OCTOBER

At dawn, the NVA 3/33rd finally began to slink away to the west, its ultimate destination the regimental base area at a place the communists called Kro Village near the Cambodian border. It had mostly left the camp alone overnight, offering up only the occasional sniper or mortar round to harass the defenders. Still, some journalists in camp had offered to man machine guns along the perimeter so the troopers could catch up on much-needed sleep. A water resupply promised fresh coffee for the first time in a week. It also meant that the men could finally wash themselves and scrub away the grime of combat. The memories would be much harder to purge. Cleanup at Plei Me continued apace. The last of the wounded were choppered out, and Beckwith even believed things had calmed down enough to call in still others to carry out more of the dead. Loading the bodies, some of which had been festering for more than a week, was putrid work. Every jostle unleashed from the bloated, slippery corpses a rancid mix of bowel gas and the reek of rotting flesh. Once aboard, the bodies became the problem of the slick crews charged with flying them out. The aircrews would soak cotton swabs in Wintergreen cream and stick them up their noses to deal with the stench. Worse, once the chopper reached a certain altitude, the change in pressure caused the bloated bodies to release fluids. If they weren't zipped into a body bag—and many of the corpses from Plei Me weren't—the vile secretions would leak and puddle on the deck. Because the choppers were normally flown with a slightly nose-down orientation, this caused the viscous liquids to run forward and pool in the Plexiglas chin bubble at the pilots' feet. Bad for the pilots but worse for the crew chiefs whose job it was to clean the ships at day's end.[41]

At 0800, Beckwith again ordered a two-company sortie of ARVN Rangers to sweep the north ridge but postponed it when the 2/8th Cav confirmed that they would indeed insert there. The camp was abuzz with the news that the 1st Cavalry would soon arrive and take over. The consensus among the SF troopers seemed to be, *Good, let them have it*. UPI reporter Joe Galloway, who'd finagled his way into camp on Saturday the 23rd, had done several turns as one of Beckwith's impromptu machine gunners over the past few days. Galloway, too, had heard that the 1st Cav was coming. With things winding down at Plei Me, the newsman knew that the story was moving on. It was time to saddle up with the cavalry. He found Beckwith to say his goodbyes. When the DELTA commander heard that Galloway would be heading out with the Cav unarmed, he told the young reporter that that wasn't very smart.[42]

"Sir, in spite of how you've made use of me these past few days, I am, technically speaking, a civilian noncombatant," replied Galloway. Beckwith looked the newsman up and down and laughed. "There ain't no such thing in these mountains, sonny." Actually, the UPI newsman wasn't above carrying a .45 pistol or even an old M3 "grease gun" whenever he went into the field. "A combat zone," he would later say, "is no place for the philosophical arguments of journalism school." Still, neither of those short-ranged weapons would do him much good if push came to shove in a firefight. Beckwith turned to an NCO standing nearby. "Grab this man an M16 and a bag full of loaded magazines." Galloway gratefully accepted the offering and walked out the front gate of Plei Me to link up with the 1st Cav. Beckwith's gift would soon come in handy. A few weeks later, Galloway would carry that same rifle when he and the troopers of Lt. Col. Hal Moore's 1/7th Cavalry found themselves in a fight for their lives a few miles away in the Ia Drang Valley.[43]

At 1000 hours, the 2/8th Cavalry began its air assault along the north ridge. Waves of helicopter transports rolled in like massive black dragonflies, discharging the green cavalry troopers for the inaugural combat operation of the 1st Cav's new role. The troopers hit the ground ready for action. To the delight of their commanders, the landing met no opposition. Indeed, there were no NVA waiting for the 2/8th that morning—no living ones at least. Instead, Beckwith's suggested LZ had set the troopers down atop a field of rotting corpses. Some of the cavalrymen were immediately overcome, retching and vomiting as soon as they stepped off their choppers. Their "introduction" to the hell of combat, courtesy of Beckwith, made quite an impression, indeed.[44]

Nevertheless, the battalion gathered itself and worked its way along the ridge. The lush greens and yellows of the jungle-carpeted hill had been utterly denuded by a week's worth of pounding airstrikes. Now, the troopers moved through a blasted moonscape of splintered, leafless trees and scorched earth. At some point, Galloway and the troopers came upon a smashed, tripod-mounted .51 caliber heavy machine gun. The NVA had employed the DShK to deadly effect as an antiaircraft weapon over the previous week. Sprawled beside it lay the DShK's two-man crew, decomposing in the sun. The men had been chained to the weapon by their ankles. Galloway would visit Hanoi in 1990 to mark the Ia Drang battle's twenty-fifth anniversary. There, he and Moore met with Lt. Gen. Nguyen Huu An, then comman-dant of the Vietnamese army's Senior Military Academy. But twenty-five years earlier, he had been senior Lt. Col. An, deputy commander of the B3 Front who had helped coordinate the 32nd Regiment's failed ambush of Luat's ATF. He would also command the NVA's 66th Regiment in the bloody fight with Moore's troopers a few weeks after Plei Me. Galloway took the opportunity to ask the old regimental commander about the chained gun crews he had seen all those years before. According to Galloway, An told him that the 33rd Regiment had been full of draftees not yet tested in combat and so had been assigned the task of besieging Plei Me. Some of the men, said An matter-of-factly, had been chained in place to keep them from fleeing in the face of withering US air attacks. Suddenly, the previous week's antiaircraft duels between such gunners and tac-air strike planes made more sense. It was easier for a man to stand and fight against impos-sible odds when he had been given no other choice.[45]

Over the next several hours, the 2/8th swept around the entire Plei Me perimeter but met no resistance. Finally, the battalion pushed on for Objective CHERRY to the south. As Staff Sgt. Charles W. Rose of B Company was leading his squad up the hill to secure the objective, he was shot and killed by sniper fire. He was the division's first KIA in what would become known as the Pleiku Campaign. He, along with Capt. John Avera, the artillery liaison who'd coordinated support fires from the lead tank of Luat's ATF, would each be awarded the Bronze Star with "V" devices. They would be the first air cavalrymen to receive the honor. As for now, it ap-peared that the NVA had fled the field. Aside from the 2/8th, the brigade had on 26 October also inserted the 1/9th Cavalry, along with the attached 2/12th Cav, into the brigade area west of the camp to conduct screening operations. These continued into 27 October, which put nearly two thou-sand American troops in the Plei Me vicinity.[46]

Indeed, as 1st Brigade officially assumed responsibility for the areas surrounding the camp, Luat was ordered to begin withdrawing his ATF back to Pleiku. To help secure the route, II Corps commander Maj. Gen. Vinh Loc recalled Marine Task Force Alpha from its operation near Ban Ma

Thuot to the south. The task force was to deploy its two battalions—some 1,100 men—along Route 5 to secure the ATF's withdrawal. Once the last elements of Luat's ATF closed into Pleiku at 1840 hours on 29 October, Operation Dan Thang 21—the mission to rescue Plei Me—was officially terminated. Meanwhile, Beckwith and his DELTA-Ranger force was heli-lifted back to Pleiku on 28 October. Beckwith and DELTA would go on to assist—with not much success—the 1st Cavalry during the early stages of its pursuit of the NVA regiments involved in the Plei Me siege.[47]

Once the guns around Plei Me had at last fallen silent, the men of the 119th returned to bring their fallen brothers home. The bodies of Macklin, Knowlton, Racine, and McDonial had lain in the wreckage of their Croc gunship since being shot down on 20 October while providing cover for the first medivac flight into Plei Me. Losing the crew had shaken the entire unit, but enemy action around Plei Me had simply been too hot to risk a recovery mission. But now that the NVA had seemingly quit the field, company commander Maj. Charles W. Mooney called for volunteers. There could still be enemy fire in the area, and those risking their lives to attempt recovery had to do so voluntarily. And it wasn't just enemy activity that was concerning. The mission would be an especially grim one. Everyone knew that the ship had exploded and burned on impact, and what was left of their friends had been left to the elements ever since. No one was sure what they'd find once they got there or whether recovery at this point was even possible. Still, volunteers stepped forward to answer the call. One man was 1st Lt. Jerry Riches, an Alligator section leader. He'd had breakfast with Don Knowlton the morning of the shoot-down. Though the two weren't especially close, Knowlton had still been his brother-in-arms. To this day, Riches can't fully articulate why he volunteered. All he really knew was that he just wanted to bring those guys back.[48]

It would be a two-ship Alligator mission, along with a gunship es-cort. Capt. John R. "Doc" Maxwell, who was the CO of the 94th Medical Detachment and the company's flight surgeon, would come along, as would a team from Graves Registration. As the choppers drew near the crash site, Riches could see the Plei Me compound off to the north. The camp was blasted and scorched and was pockmarked by mortar craters. The bodies of the enemy—some whole, some in parts—lay broken and bloated about the battlefield. Still others hung in burnt and bloody chunks in the camp's perimeter wire. Some were clothed in the customary "black pajamas" that he and his comrades had come to expect. But many, many more wore the mustard-brown of the North Vietnamese. Riches had made an earlier supply run while the siege was still underway but had been far too busy at the time to take in the enormity of what he was seeing. Now, it was all rendered in vivid horror. Growing up, Riches had seen movies depicting the carnage of war. As a young officer candidate, he'd even sat through classes that described such scenes. But none of it had come close to capturing the butchery that now lay before him. *My God,* he thought, *this must have been a holocaust.*[49]

The choppers took no fire on the way in, so the pilots settled the Hueys onto their landing skids and shut down the engines. To presume, however, that the enemy had completely gone was ludicrous. Prudence demanded that they hurry. Every man was issued body bags and rubber gloves. Each in his own way steeled himself for what he was about to see. And then it was time to approach the wreckage. What was left of the chopper's skin had been blasted through with gaping holes, some the size of .51 caliber rounds, others even larger. Perhaps 20mm shells. It didn't matter. Both were large and powerful enough to blast a Huey from the sky. Inside, the bodies of their friends were burnt beyond recognition. *How will we ever identify them,* Riches thought. Then a glint of reflected light caught his eye. One of the men was wearing a cross. The patch of skin under the cross was the only thing that hadn't burned. It was Ron Macklin. Riches remembered that the pilot's wife, Margaret, had sent him the cross some time before, and Macklin was never without it. There was no way of telling who any of the other three were. Riches bent to lift one of his fallen comrades and zip him into a body bag. But when he grasped the body, Riches's hands simply passed through the flesh as though it were jelly. Horrified, he staggered backward as maggots began streaming up his gloves. Riches had turned twenty-four just the month before.[50]

When the worst of it was done, Riches walked the field. Here and there he plucked cigar-sized .51 caliber casings from the red dirt. Even bigger 20mm casings were scattered about as well. Then, some distance away, he spied the visor from one of the pilot's helmets that had been thrown clear. It had not burned. Instead, three neat holes had been punched through by small-arms fire. It was, in the parlance of what he'd been told in officer's basic training, a "perfect shot group." Had it been some sort of post-crash execution? No, he didn't believe it was. One glimpse of that charred wreckage told him that no one could have survived. And besides, if it *had* been an execution, the visor would've still been on the dead pilot's helmet. No, the big rounds that had punched through the chopper, and now the holes in the visor, suggested to Riches that the men had been hit and killed in midair, long before they crashed. In a way, the realization was even comforting. To know that they hadn't suffered, that they hadn't been alive to feel the flames consume their flesh. *When it's my time,* he thought, *that's how I want it. Quick. Painless. Dead.*[51]

Still, walking back to his chopper, Riches couldn't help but wonder what it had been like for them. What had been their final thoughts in those last terrible moments? But then he realized that he'd never truly be able to put himself in their shoes. He might be able to sympathize with them, but he could never empathize. He might, of course, one day suffer the same fate as his fallen brothers. Like Macklin and the others, he flew dangerous missions nearly every day. It was enough, he would later say, to sicken your stomach and wobble your knees. If dwelt upon, such thoughts could paralyze a man into inaction. And yet he, and so many like him, continued to do the job, day after day, mission after mission. "You made a commitment," he says. "And you say to yourself, 'Okay, I'm here for the duration.' I could quit, but I didn't want to. I observed my commitments, my obligations."

One of those obligations was waiting for him when he got back to Holloway that afternoon. As a commissioned officer, one of Riches's duties was to serve as a Summary Courts Officer (SCO) when called upon. The SCO is tasked with going through the personal effects of a fallen comrade, logging and packaging the items that were near and dear to the man so they could be shipped back to his grieving family. Riches had been tapped to fulfill this function for Knowlton. For the young lieutenant, it marked just one more unpleasant task to draw out the grim process of recovering his fallen brothers. But it was his duty, and he meant to perform it to the best of his ability.[52]

Part III

THE AFTERMATH

9

SEARCH AND DESTROY
(29 OCTOBER–26 NOVEMBER)

Over the next few weeks, the 1st Cavalry tried to make good on its open-ended mission of immediately and relentlessly pursuing the NVA units that had besieged Plei Me and ambushed its relief force. According to the 1st Cav's after-action report, the division's new Pleiku Campaign was designed to be the first large-scale effort to prevent the communists from executing their normal hit-and-run tactics. Rather than letting the enemy pick and choose when he would fight and when he would flee, the 1st Cav would instead hunt down and bring to battle large communist units according to its own dictates. This was to be the first true test of the army's airmobile concept, the very reason the 1st Cavalry existed in the first place. Division commander Maj. Gen. Harry Kinnard, with the full blessing of Gen. William Westmoreland, was to employ the unique capabilities of aircraft—especially helicopters—to find, fix, and kill the enemy. The campaign's initial stage was dubbed Operation Long Reach, and Kinnard tasked 1st Brigade's acting commander Lt. Col. Harlow Clark with the mission. The 1st Brigade was comprised of the 1/9th Cavalry Regiment, three infantry battalions pieced together from the 8th and 12th Cavalry Regiments, and its own dedicated artillery assets in the form of the 17th, 19th, and 20th Artillery. But other than the 1/9th, none of the units had their own dedicated helicopter assets. Therefore, two lift companies of the 227th Assault Helicopter Battalion were attached to 1st Brigade, giving the unit a total of thirty-two Huey slicks. A company of Hog gunships was also attached. Despite all of this, Kinnard and Clark would soon discover that finding the fleeing NVA regiments among a 2,500-square-kilometer expanse of dense, difficult terrain was much easier said than done.[1]

The NVA's 32nd Regiment had had the benefit of beginning its withdrawal early on the 24th. It managed to slip away virtually undetected before the first of the 1st Cav's helicopters began to scour the region west of Plei Me. The regiment reached its base area at Plei The on the Ia Drang River, just east of the Cambodian border, a few days later. The regiment's ordeal had begun with a grueling march down the Ho Chi Minh Trail beginning in late 1964. The 32nd had then spent the better part of a year fighting throughout the Western Highlands and been badly beaten up during its ill-fated attack on Duc Co in August. The morale of its sick, malnourished, and physically and psychologically battered troops was only further ravaged following the drubbing it took at the hands of Luat's armor and American airpower on 23 October. Now, as the last of its elements limped into Plei The, the regiment would finally get a respite. The 32nd's war, at least for the time being, was over.[2]

The 33rd Regiment wouldn't be so lucky. The regiment initially headed for its advance base at a village the communists called Kro, about fifteen kilometers west and slightly south of Plei Me. But since its withdrawal hadn't started until the 26th, the 33rd was more likely to be discovered by the newly arrived helicopters of Clark's 1st Brigade. For the first several days, that didn't happen. Clark and his staff surmised that enemy regiments would head northwest in a bid to escape into "neutral" Cambodia, but despite a near-frenzied search during late October, Clark's units were having a great deal of trouble locating the enemy. Other than a few minor contacts on 30 and 31 October, the communists had remained out of reach. It was later learned that the brigade had been searching too far north. Indeed, its search grids—labeled SHOE, JIM, and EARL—were all too far northeast of the enemy's true destination, the Chu Pong mountain complex. MACV's J2 intelligence section was by this time well aware that the Viet Cong and NVA had long used the Chu Pong as a substantial base area and had recently conducted a study of the region as a potential target for B-52 interdiction strikes. But when the 1st Cavalry had taken over operations in the area, its commanders either did not seek out guidance from MACV intelligence or were otherwise not read in on the accumulated knowledge about the region. Frustrated by Clark's inability to find the NVA, Kinnard ordered his deputy, Brig. Gen. Richard T. Knowles, to take a more active hand in directing the 1st Brigade's search.[3]

The brigade's fortunes changed, however, when on the morning of 1 November, scout ships from the 1/9 Squadron B Troop happened across a dozen NVA soldiers moving about twelve kilometers west and just south of Plei Me. By 0808 hours, 1/9 rifle platoons had been air landed into the area.

After a short, sharp firefight with elements of the 33rd's 1st Battalion, the troopers had captured what they soon discovered to be the carefully concealed regimental field hospital. First Battalion's retreat from Plei Me had been hampered by air strikes and by its number of wounded. The NVA had paused at the aid station to rest and see to their casualties when it was discovered. The initial fight yielded twenty enemy dead with another nineteen captured. The hospital's seizure also netted the 1st Cav troopers a substantial stockpile of medical supplies the NVA badly needed, along with a cache of captured documents. The hospital's importance was rendered evident when elements of the 33rd Regiment mounted a counterattack to reclaim it early that afternoon. Several more 1st Brigade platoons were rushed in to bolster the American perimeter. Throughout the rest of the afternoon, the communists launched a series of determined attacks to recapture the position but were repulsed each time. By early evening, the NVA had broken contact and once again disappeared into the forest. By day's end, enemy losses—the overwhelming majority from the 33rd's 1st Battalion—stood at ninety-nine dead and forty-four captured. The Cav's troopers had also seized some three

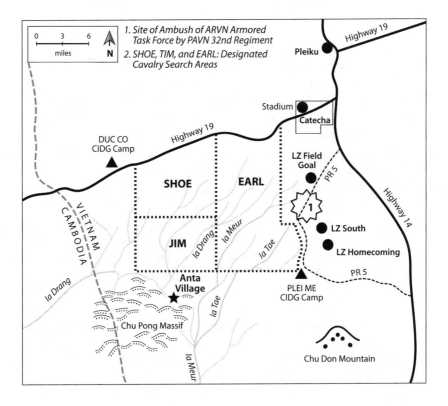

hundred pounds of rice, three 75mm recoilless rifles, an 82mm mortar, and various other weapons, including Chinese grenades, Bangalore torpedoes, and a large stock of ammunition. The battle had cost the United States eleven dead and forty-seven wounded. Seven helicopters were also hit, but none crashed. The action not only further ravaged the 33rd Regiment and denied it badly needed medical supplies but also yielded a treasure trove of intelligence in the form of prisoner interrogations and seized documents. The latter included a detailed map depicting enemy supply and march routes, all of which led to communist base areas in the Chu Pong Massif complex. The 1st Brigade, it seemed, had been looking in the wrong place.[4]

Indeed, 1st Brigade's staff was now eager to establish contact in the Chu Pong region. Over the next week, the brigade began to find its way and was involved with several more skirmishes with NVA units, most of which belonged to the fleeing 33rd Regiment. Although its initial forays into the region were still too far to the north and east of the main communist base area near Anta Village, the 1st Brigade still managed to inflict some damage on NVA units. The most successful of these skirmishes was the ambush on 2 November of an NVA company by a platoon-sized American element on the north side of the Chu Pong near the Cambodian border. The 1/9 Cavalry's C Squadron managed to catch unawares what would only later be revealed as a company of the newly infiltrated 8th Battalion of the 66th Regiment that had been moving south and east toward the Chu Pong base areas. Enemy losses during the action amounted to seventy-three dead, along with the capture of several heavy weapons and a large ammunition cache. US forces lost four KIA and thirty wounded in the fight. First Brigade on 4 to 6 November also managed to establish contact with elements of both the 1st and 3rd Battalions as the beleaguered and harried 33rd Regiment desperately tried to reach its sanctuary near Anta Village. This series of skirmishes east of the Chu Pong cost the 33rd Regiment's battalions 120 dead and five captured, along with another three 75mm recoilless rifles, two 82mm mortars, and three heavy machine guns. US casualties stood at forty-one KIA and another ninety wounded. Even though 1st Brigade had finally started to find and bring NVA units to battle, none of the enemy formations had been enveloped and forced to fight on the 1st Cav's terms. Indeed, with exceptions of the 1 November hospital capture and the 2 November ambush north of the Chu Pong, the communists—as they had for years—continued to give battle only at times and places of their choosing. Kinnard decided a change was in order. On 7 November, he ordered the 1st Brigade out, replacing it with the 3rd Brigade under Col. Thomas W. Brown. The 1st Brigade yielded formal control at 1100 hours on 9 November, but the official changeover would not be complete until 12 November.[5]

Meanwhile, if the main objective of the 1st Cav's early introduction into the Western Highlands had been to immediately pursue and destroy the NVA regiments that had attacked Plei Me and ambushed its relief force, it had largely missed its chance even before 3rd Brigade had fully taken over. The 32nd, although battered and bruised, had managed to retreat to its base area largely untouched and had been resting and recuperating for two weeks now. The 33rd's retreat had, of course, largely been a torturous ordeal. Still, even after being forced to break into ever-smaller packets to avoid further contact with the 1st Cav, it would finally succeed in pulling the last of its bedraggled elements into the regimental base area near Anta Village on 11 November. Nevertheless, the subsequent regimental muster showed that the 33rd had suffered egregiously. Its rifle battalions had lost between 33 and 50 percent KIA. The regimental antiaircraft company, which had been attached to the 32nd, saw about 60 percent of its men killed. Meanwhile some of the 33rd's support units, like its regimental medical company, had lost 80 percent killed in action. Another one hundred men were listed as missing in action. Still, now that the regiment had reached the safety of the Chu Pong, its troops no doubt hoped for a long period of convalescence, along with a replenishment of their ranks by replacement troop packets infiltrating south.[6]

The 3rd Brigade, at the behest of I Field Force, Vietnam commander Lt. Gen. Stanley "Swede" Larsen, initially concentrated its search north, south, and east of Plei Me, but nothing had come of it. By 12 November, and after finally consulting the II Corps intelligence staff, Brown realized that, like 1st Brigade before them, his men had been looking in the wrong place. Not only had the Chu Pong been a longtime no-go communist sanctuary, but intelligence staff at 24 STZ had discovered that a newly infiltrated NVA regiment—the 66th—was based there. Brown passed this information up the chain to Brig. Gen. Richard Knowles, the 1st Cav's deputy commander, who then conferred with Larsen on the morning of 13 November. If the 1st Cav was looking to get into a fight with the NVA, the Chu Pong was the place to be. Knowles got with Brown later that morning and ordered him to attack the communist base area the very next day. The job was given to Lt. Col. Harold Moore, forty-three, commander of the 3rd Brigade's 1/7 Cavalry. After weeks of searching, the 1st Cav would finally have its best to chance to find, fix, and kill a large NVA unit.[7]

Interestingly, the confusion created when the 1st Brigade pulled out and the 3rd Brigade initially concentrated its efforts east of Plei Me may have inspired communist planners to attempt to regain the Tay Nguyen Campaign's lost initiative in Western Pleiku. According to information gleaned from prisoner interrogations discussed in two official US reports on the period, Man and his B3 Front may have begun to hatch a plan on 10 November to use all three of his regiments to wage a second attack on Plei Me. This time, rather than an elaborate lure-and-ambush gambit, the goal was simply to annihilate the Special Forces camp. Though the troops of the 32nd were undoubtedly exhausted both mentally and physically by this point, the regiment had nevertheless maintained its continuity and could, at least theoretically, have been committed yet again. The 33rd had had an even rougher time of it, but according to prisoner testimony, the regiment was to be committed again. The real punch, of course, was to be delivered by the newly arrived 66th Regiment under Lt. Col. Nguyen Huu An, who also served as Man's deputy for the B3 Front. After its skirmish with the 1/9's C Squadron on 2 November, the regiment's 7th, 8th, and 9th Battalions had settled into their base area along the north banks of the Ia Drang River near the Chu Pong. An, under orders from Man, had also recently established a forward headquarters for the B3 Front on the Chu Pong Massif itself. The second attack on Plei Me would also have the help of the soon-to-arrive 120mm mortar and 14.5mm twin-barreled antiaircraft battalions that had begun their infiltration south in late August. The B3 Front set the date of attack for 16 November, and units were to spend the intervening days preparing for the assault.[8]

Whether this plan would've ever come off—indeed, whether it was ever planned in the first place—became moot when on the morning of 14 November Moore's 1/7 Cavalry began its air assault into Landing Zone Xray in the Ia Drang Valley at the foot of the Chu Pong Massif. Indeed, rather than launching a renewed attack on Plei Me, Man's B3 Front was instead faced with the urgent need to defend its own headquarters and base area. It was the first time since at least 1954 that an anticommunist unit had penetrated the Chu Pong. And it was from this longtime communist sanctuary that the 32nd and 33rd NVA Regiments had staged and ultimately moved against Plei Me in October. Ironically, Moore's battalion had launched from Plei Me at the start of the battle, and the camp would continue to play a prominent role as the bloody Ia Drang fights between elements of the 1st Cavalry and the NVA's 33rd and 66th Regiments unfolded over the next twelve days. By the time they were over, the Ia Drang battles—especially those at LZ Xray from 14 to 17 November and at nearby LZ Albany on 17 to 18 November—would cost 236 US KIA, 304 wounded in action (WIA), and four missing in action (MIA). For the communists, the toll would be even higher. By body count, the NVA lost 1,276 KIA and six captured. It must be noted, however, that the highly confused nature of these battles—especially that of the NVA ambush of the 2/7 Cavalry at LZ Albany—made thoroughly reliable body counts difficult to achieve.[9]

In the battles' aftermath the 1st Cav, exhausted and likely shocked by the ferocity of the fights and the casualties it had incurred, chose not to mount operations to search the Chu Pong itself. Instead, B-52 strikes were called in from 15 to 20 November to pulverize whatever communist units and base areas remained in the complex. By this time, however, most of the NVA had already begun their withdrawal to the sanctuary of neighboring Cambodia. On 20 November, Kinnard ordered the battle-weary 3rd Brigade to stand down and replaced it with the still-unused 2nd Brigade under Col. William R. Lynch. Lynch was ordered to continue search-and-destroy missions north of the Chu Pong and south of Duc Co. His brigade was to share search responsibilities with the South Vietnamese Airborne Brigade, which was operating out of the camp. Most of these searches turned up nothing; however, two Airborne Brigade battalions did find and engage one of the 32nd Regiment's battalions as it neared the border on 20 November. After a sharp fight, which included calling in 1st Cavalry artillery support, the South Vietnamese claimed to have killed about two hundred enemy troops. Still, it quickly became clear that NVA's main force units had by that time absconded to Cambodia. Kinnard initially gained permission from Westmoreland to pursue the enemy across the border, but the idea was nixed by Washington. President Johnson, came the reply, was not interested in widening the war. US ground units were to restrict themselves to South Vietnamese territory only. Thus, Kinnard terminated the Pleiku Campaign on 26 November.[10]

With Man's regiments now in Cambodia, the Tay Nguyen Campaign was over as well. Regardless of its objectives—whether the opening gambit in some grand scheme to split South Vietnam along the Highway 19 axis from Pleiku to Qui Nhon, or merely to capture the lion's share of Pleiku Province for its own sake—US Special Forces and airpower, ARVN ground units, and the 1st Cav had all combined in late 1965 to thwart communist aims in the Western Highlands.[11]

10

POSTLUDE

The siege of Plei Me had indeed been a bitter defeat for the communists. The camp had remained in anticommunist hands, and the ambush of Luat's Armored Task Force, while inflicting some casualties and the loss of a few transport vehicles, had been an utter failure. Meanwhile, the two NVA regiments tasked with carrying out the mission had been badly mauled and forced to flee first to their base areas near the Chu Pong and ultimately across the border into Cambodia. Interestingly, the communists' Plei Me gambit had created a conundrum that likely led to its eventual failure. South Vietnamese leaders in II Corps, along with their American advisers, were by this time well used to the communists' lure-and-ambush tactic. Indeed, B3 Front commander Maj. Gen. Chu Huy Man's strategy, however well planned and rehearsed, was simply too shopworn by that point in the war to garner the results that he and his superiors so craved. Anticommunist intelligence sections, while being taken somewhat by surprise by the siege itself, had even managed to predict within one kilometer the spot along Route 5 where the ambush would take place.

Yet, Plei Me still had to be relieved, and there were only so many assets available to do so: II Corps commander Vinh Loc, therefore, faced a Hobson's Choice on 20 October: commit the last of his corps reserve to the relief effort and risk losing Pleiku, the strategic center of GVN power in the Western Highlands, or withhold it and send a weaker version of Luat's armored task force—risking both its destruction and that of Plei Me as well. Vinh Loc's initial impulse had been to retain his corps reserve and let Luat take his chances on Route 5. Fortunately, men like Col. Ted Mataxis, deputy senior adviser for II Corps, and 24th Special Tactical Zone commander Brig. Gen. Cao Hoa Hon, had argued convincingly that more was needed. And to his credit, Vinh Loc had listened. But where would the additional forces come from?

The impasse, of course, was overcome when I Field Force, Vietnam commander Lt. Gen. Stanley Larsen pledged the 1st Cav's Task Force Ingram to Pleiku's defense. The security guarantee allowed Vinh Loc to commit sufficient force—backed by prodigious US airpower—to defeat communist aims at Plei Me. And it also precipitated the 1st Cavalry Division's early introduction into the Western Highlands. Despite its growing pains, the new US air cavalry division was an exceptionally mobile and powerful force, and its deployment had essentially sounded the death knell for Man's Tay Nguyen Campaign. For while the NVA's 32nd and 33rd Regiments had been defeated at the hands US airpower, Luat's armor, and the stout defenders of Plei Me, the 1st Cav's arrival had created a security backstop where all that could take place.

Of course, division commander Maj. Gen. Harry Kinnard had much bigger plans. Kinnard was intensely eager to demonstrate the efficacy of the new airmobile concept—and thus the *raison d'etre* for his new air cavalry division. So he immediately set about expanding the 1st Cav's role from one of support to that of an all-out offensive effort to find, fix, and destroy the NVA regiments that had attacked Plei Me. The division's subsequent pursuit of the NVA throughout the Western Highlands ultimately led the 1st Cav to the Chu Pong's doorstep and the 3rd Brigade's fateful confrontation with the 66th Regiment and what was left of the 33rd. The resulting Ia Drang battles of 14 to 20 November were indeed savage, with heavy casualties on both sides. But what of the alternative? Left unmolested in their mountain sanctuary, it seems likely that the 66th, along with the rested and replenished 32nd and 33rd Regiments, would've once more been set loose upon GVN outposts in the Western Highlands—whether at Plei Me or elsewhere. Instead, by the end of November, all three NVA regiments and their supporting units had been severely torn up and forced to flee into Cambodia to avoid further destruction. Meanwhile, the longtime communist sanctuary in the Chu Pong complex would be rocked by ninety-six strategic-level B-52 strike sorties over five days.

An even closer look at the numbers reveals a tale of woe for the NVA regiments that had fought at Plei Me. The hardest hit, of course, had been the 33rd. Tasked with laying siege to the camp, it had suffered under six days of relentless CAS strikes, as a hail of bombs, napalm, rockets, and cannon fire had rained down from on high. The camp defenders had gotten in their licks, too, as they saturated NVA assault troops and their surrounding positions with mortar, machine gun, and small-arms fire. Added to all of this, of course, was the steadily growing artillery fires of the 1st Cav's howitzers as they pushed ever closer to Plei Me. After getting a taste of this punishment, regimental commander Lt. Col. Vũ Sắc may have tried to mitigate some of the worst effects by more widely dispersing his troops around Plei Me. This might explain the relative ease with which Lt. Robert Berry's CIDG patrol on the evening of the 20th and Maj. Charlie Beckwith's DELTA-Ranger force on the morning of the 23rd were able to enter the camp.[1]

But if that had been Sac's plan, it seemed of little help to his men. Even before the last of the regiment had withdrawn after its rearguard ambush of Luat's column on the 26th, the 33rd's losses had been egregious. Of the regiment's three battalion commanders, two had been killed and the third seriously wounded. The 2nd Battalion had lost about half its strength—250 men dead and wounded—and the 1st and 3rd Battalions had also been badly battered. The regimental mortar company had lost half its personnel KIA, and five out of its nine mortar tubes were wrecked. Likewise, the 33rd's logistical and medical support units had suffered terribly. The 17th Transportation Company saw 75 of its 150 men KIA. The forty-man 18th Medical Company had thirty-two of its soldiers killed, listed as missing in action, or captured. In the days following Plei Me, of course, the 33rd's torture continued unabated. After initially avoiding the 1st Cav's frenetic searches, the regiment's casualties and misery soon began to multiply as the 1st Brigade found its footing. By 11 November, the regiment had lost approximately 890 of its estimated 2,200 men dead, wounded, missing, or captured. The 33rd's materiel losses were also heavy. In addition to the gutting of its regimental mortar company at Plei Me, the 33rd's infantry battalions had lost another six mortars and three recoilless rifles on their way to the Chu Pong. Its regimental antiaircraft company, on loan to the 32nd, had lost thirteen of its eighteen guns. While some of those losses could no doubt be attributed to the 1st Cavalry—especially during its attack and seizure of the 33rd's aid station on 1 November—it seems clear that the overwhelming majority had been incurred during nearly a week of ferocious aerial bombardment around Plei Me. Either way, the siege of Plei Me and its subsequent retreat had been an unmitigated disaster for the 33rd Regiment. The final nail in the regiment's coffin was its combat losses during the Ia Drang battles, which essentially rendered it combat ineffective for the foreseeable future.[2]

Several factors contributed to the 33rd's battering. The first—the weather—was completely beyond the control of communist planners. The monsoon season in the Central Highlands can sometimes last through October. But following the soupy conditions on the first night of the siege, the weather was largely clear over the Plei Me area for the remainder of the battle. Had the season's normal blanket of heavy rain, storms, and fog still been in place, it might've helped alleviate the effects of American close air support—though, even at the height of the monsoon, anticommunist airpower still proved deadly effective. Nevertheless, US pilots took full advantage of the relatively dry, clear conditions during Plei Me.

A second factor was entirely within the hands of NVA leadership: the distribution of antiaircraft assets. Because Man and his B3 Front staff likely viewed the 32nd's mission of ambushing and destroying the ARVN relief force as the more important, they justifiably worried that American airpower was the greatest threat to its success. To help offset, the 33rd had been stripped of its antiaircraft company, which was then paired with the 32nd's own. As American airpower pummeled NVA positions around Plei Me, that antiaircraft company was sorely missed. Nevertheless, the 33rd's gunners—albeit some of them chained to their machine guns—still managed to send up a wall of antiaircraft fire, shooting down four US aircraft and damaging many others. Lastly, in an ironic twist, the 33rd's suffering was likely drawn out because Luat's ATF had taken five full days to assemble and make its way into camp. Every day the relief force was delayed meant one more spent under the pounding of CAS.[3]

With the benefit of post-siege NVA documents and prisoner interrogations, we now know that the 33rd was not meant to overrun the camp until its sister regiment had destroyed the ARVN relief column on Route 5. While annihilating an important government stronghold in Western Pleiku was always desirable from both a military and political standpoint, the siege, of course, had merely been the "lure." Communist planners were much more interested in the "ambush," at least in the short term. The destruction of large ARVN formations was, after all, a linchpin of Le Duan's larger General Offensive–General Uprising strategy. But Plei Me's defenders didn't know that at the time. Nor, it is almost assured, did the 33rd Regiment's rank and file. While its commanders were fully briefed on the plan, the regiment's troops had not even been told that Plei Me was their target until just four days before the attack. The first days of the battle saw several massed assaults and probes in company strength on Plei Me's wire. It strains credulity to believe that those green, untested NVA sappers and assault troops—no matter how ideologically imbued—would rush headlong into the maw of the camp's defensive fires and aerial napalm attacks had they known that these charges were merely feints designed to trick Plei Me's defenders into *believing* they were about to be overrun. The scores of dead NVA soldiers hanging in the Plei Me wire were a testament to both the costliness of these pointless assaults, and to the brutal cynicism with which the 33rd's commanders had repeatedly ordered their men into the maelstrom.[4]

The 32nd Regiment had fared little better. Its ambush of the II Corps relief force had ended in failure, heavy casualties, and lost and wrecked crew-served weapons. The man chosen to lead the ATF, Lt. Col. Nguyen Luat, while overly cautious in the eyes of some observers, was nevertheless seasoned, competent, and had had previous experience with the communists' lure and ambush tactic at Duc Co. When the moment of truth arrived, Luat and his tankers and APC gunners were well prepared to meet the challenge head-on. Indeed, even communist accounts of the ambush admit that the ARVN relief force fought tenaciously and wrought considerable havoc upon the 32nd's battalions.[5] And like its sister regiment, the 32nd had been subjected to vicious aerial attack, despite its additional antiaircraft assets. Casualty numbers for the 32nd are not as well documented as those of the 33rd. One reason is the communists' penchant for dragging off their dead to hide their losses. At any rate, fifty-one dead NVA soldiers were tallied by body count immediately following the ambush of the ATF's main body on 23 October. Another twenty-five KIA were counted when a company of CIDG Nungs was helilifted on 26 October to sweep the area where the supply trains had been ambushed three days before. Official US records eventually listed the regiment as having lost 125 KIA by body count on 23 October. The 32nd's withdrawal to its Chu Pong base areas following the Route 5 ambush had been virtually unmolested. Nor had it been committed in the mid-November Ia Drang battles. One of the 32nd's battalions had, however, been caught by the South Vietnamese Airborne Brigade near the Cambodian border on 20 November. The Airborne Brigade, with help from 1st Cavalry artillery, claimed two hundred NVA killed in action that day.[6]

The importance of American airpower at Plei Me cannot be overstated—it clearly saved the day. The siege of Plei Me was without question the largest close air support operation to that point in the war. Over ten days, the US Air Force, Navy, and Marines flew 696 day and nighttime fighter-bomber sorties, along with eighteen flareship, eighty-three FAC, and forty-one reconnaissance missions. Wave after wave of B-57s, A1Es, F-100s, and Navy F-8 Crusaders unleashed upon the NVA more than 1.6 million pounds of general purpose, fragmentation, and napalm ordnance, along with voluminous rocket, cluster munitions, and cannon and machine gun fire from tac-aircraft. The 52nd Aviation Battalion flew 1,938 rotary wing sorties in a mix of transport, medevac, and helicopter gunship missions. To staunch the flow of communist assaults and their encroaching trench works, CAS strikes were sometimes brought down to within thirty-five meters of the camp's outer perimeter. All of this in the face of murderous antiaircraft fire. As noted, four aircraft were shot down in the skies over Plei Me, including Macklin's UH1B Hog, a B-57 Canberra fighter-bomber, and the two A1E Skyraiders flown by Mel Elliott and Myron Burr. Another B-57 was shot up so badly that it was forced to crash-land on its way back to Pleiku. Numerous other fixed-wing tac-aircraft, helicopters, and flare ships were also peppered with fire during the siege. These air losses were a testament to the NVA's antiaircraft tactics, tenacity, and weaponry—and to the skill and bravery of CAS pilots who repeatedly flew into the maelstrom to save the camp and its defenders.[7]

Of course, these pilots didn't work alone. They were directed and co-ordinated by equally courageous and capable forward air controllers. By day, the FACs would prowl the airspace above the battlefield in their impossibly slow and fragile 0-1 Bird Dog observation planes. Sometimes, FACs would stack flight sorties up to 40,000 feet, keeping track of everything from tac-air fighter-bombers to resupply transports to helicopter slicks with nothing more than grease-pen scrawls on their planes' Plexiglas windows. At night, there was no respite for the enemy, for the FACs simply ditched their Bird Dogs and climbed aboard C-123 flare ships to keep up the pounding by nighttime sorties. Indeed, fixed-wing and helicopter flare ships would rain thousands of illumination flares to light the way for camp defenders and tac-air. For FACs like Capt. Richard Shortridge, who flew mission after mission over Plei Me, three hours of sleep a day was a luxury. In the end, were it not for all of this relentless and brutally accurate air support, Plei Me and its defenders would not have survived.[8]

And just as CAS was vital to successfully holding the camp, so too was aerial resupply. For days on end, daring and skilled cargo pilots and crews, in both rotor and fixed-wing craft, braved a fusillade of antiaircraft fire to ensure the men of Plei Me had the food, water, medicine, and am-munition they desperately needed to keep up the fight. Between 20 and 25 October, C-7 Caribous from the 92nd Army Aviation Company and C-123 Providers from the 310th Air Commando Squadron flew forty-eight mission sorties dropping 338,300 pounds of supplies, all of which but nine thousand pounds fell inside of Plei Me's defenses. Most of the errant supply drops were destroyed by tac-air strikes before they could fall into enemy hands. Another nearly fifty thousand pounds of aerial resupply were delivered to Luat's ATF between 26 and 29 October. Two Army and two Air Force enlisted men were wounded during the resupply missions. While none of the planes were shot down, nineteen C-123s and two C-7s sustained varying levels of damage, with seven of the Providers and both Caribous so badly damaged that they were ultimately scrapped. None of this, of course, includes the badly needed supplies brought into Plei Me on helicopter slicks, usually at great peril to pilots and crew. Again, without aerial resupply, the victory at Plei Me could not have been accomplished.[9]

Of course, that victory did not come without cost. The anticommunist side had itself lost ninety-five dead, with another 222 wounded, and nineteen missing in action during the siege of Plei Me. Eleven of those who gave their last full measure were Americans. Ron Macklin, twenty-seven; Don Knowlton, twenty-four; Frank Racine, twenty-three; and Wesley McDonial, thirty, had repeatedly flown their Huey gunship into a raging maw of antiaircraft fire to help save those in the camp, for the defenders of Plei Me, strangers though they may have been, were still their brothers-in-arms, and they needed help. And when their chopper was finally shot down, Capt. Harold Moore led his team outside the wire and into the teeth of prepared NVA positions for that same reason. Sgt. 1st Class Joe Bailey, twenty-seven, gave his life trying to help the men who had tried to help him. Harold Preisendefer, twenty-five; Josef Huwyler, twenty-three; William Johnson, thirty-four; and Michael Davis, twenty-two, had all died not by the enemy's hand but by a freak mechanical accident as they flew escort for Beckwith and McKean. Special Forces medic Staff Sgt. Jimmie McBynum, twenty-six, could easily have waited out the siege in safety back in Pleiku. Instead, he frantically searched for the quickest way to rejoin his comrades fighting in the field. He was killed before he could climb off the chopper. DELTA Capt. Tom Pusser, twenty-six, was due to DEROS in a month but nevertheless led his company of ARVN Rangers to clear the northern ridge. He died there in a hail of automatic weapons fire. Meanwhile, Dan Shea, Bill DeSoto, Harold Moore, Euell White, Bob Sloan, and Lanny Hunter had all suffered wounds—some terrible. All would recover. Each man—dead, wounded, or unscratched—had sacrificed. Each had been afraid. Each had fought for his own life—and for the lives of his brothers. And in the end, when the red dust had settled, the men of Plei Me had held their ground.[10]

EPILOGUE

A Walk in the Sun

One by one, the Hueys settled on to their landing skids along the dirt runway south of camp—something that NVA gunners would not have allowed just a week before. The 119th had once again been called to Plei Me, this time to support the 1st Cav as it hunted the enemy regiments that had attacked the camp. A wave of anxiety washed over 1st Lt. Chuck Oualline as his chopper came to rest in the red laterite. He felt vulnerable, exposed, as if at any moment a mortar shell would come crashing down. But things were quiet around Plei Me now, so Oualline and his fellow chopper pilots were given the okay to shut down their engines and settle in for a long wait. Oualline figured he may as well take the opportunity to get a closer look at the scorched and blasted terrain. Bulldozers had earlier piled over most of the NVA's trenches—and the dead right along with them. But a few remained. Oualline soon happened upon an intact slit trench, no more than five feet deep. At the bottom, he spied a spider hole no bigger than his head. *No way could an American have fit through there*, he thought. The pilot surmised that it probably led to a tunnel or cave below, someplace a gunner might take shelter from air attack. Oualline wondered about how they'd managed to tunnel this close to the wire, right under the noses of camp defenders. And where had they put all the dirt they'd excavated?[1]

He continued his wander. After a while, he came upon a body that the burial crews had missed. It was that of an NVA soldier, propped against one of the few bushes not incinerated in the tac-air strikes. The man had been hit in the lower leg. The shin bone jutted through what was left of his skin in broken, ugly shards. It looked as if the soldier might have pulled himself up against the bramble to wait out life's final moments, the last of his blood leaching into the soil. But something about the man's face seemed off. It was *moving*. Oualline peered closer. All at once the horrifying realization hit. It was no longer the face of a man at all—but a writhing swarm of maggots. For some reason, they'd started on the soldier's face and not his leg wound. Another of war's little atrocities. Nearly overcome, the pilot staggered backward. When he'd gathered himself, he crept closer and saw the brass belt buckle with a red star at its center, marking the man as a soldier of the North Vietnamese Army. This was a prized war souvenir. But Oualline wanted no part of it. He left the man alone and continued his survey.

All manner of the usual war refuse littered the battlefield. A soldier's cap here. A few ceramic rice bowls there. Even a pith helmet or two. And then he happened upon something truly unusual. In the red dirt, he found what amounted to a makeshift gunsight that the NVA had crafted out of *jungle vines*. The sight was about six inches long and could be affixed to a rifle muzzle. The vines had been twisted and worked into concentric circles, each serving as a lead line that would allow a gunner to estimate the speed and distance of an overflying aircraft. Though such a device had been crafted to kill men such as himself, Oualline couldn't help but marvel at the brutal ingenuity of it all. In the distance, he could see his fellow pilots climbing aboard their helicopters. Pocketing his souvenir, Oualline brushed the dirt from his hands and walked back to his Huey. The work with the 1st Cav was about to begin.[2]

POSTSCRIPT

What became of the men of Plei Me? **Capt. R. Lanny Hunter** earned the Distinguished Service Cross—second only to the Medal of Honor as our nation's highest award for valor—for his actions at Plei Me. Following the war, Hunter went on to enjoy a successful medical practice. He eventually penned several books about his experiences in Vietnam, including his haunting, beautifully rendered 2004 memoir *My Soul to Keep: A Journey of Faith*. Now in his eighties, Hunter continues to write and think about what Vietnam meant to him. **Capt. Richard "Dick" Shortridge** earned the Silver Star for his efforts in the skies above Plei Me. Shortridge left Vietnam in July 1966, flying home to his wife and three children alone in the belly of a cargo plane hauling used airplane tires back to the States. Two weeks earlier than expected, Shortridge walked into the house with a simple, "I'm home, dear." It was the first time the two had seen each other since Shortridge shipped out for Vietnam a year before. Although he could have made lieutenant colonel, Shortridge would instead retire as a major in 1974. The promotion would've meant more time away from Beverly, and he'd been away from his wife too long. Now in their eighties, the Shortridges live a quiet life together in a small town in the Pacific Northwest. Tragically, Richard and Beverly lost their son Richard in 2008, but their six grandkids and six great-grandkids help keep their lives full of love.

Maj. Charles Beckwith earned the Silver Star for valor at Plei Me. He would be grievously wounded during Operation Masher a few months later in early 1966. Beckwith would make full colonel and in November 1977 go on to become the first commander of America's elite counterterrorism unit colloquially known as DELTA Force. His dream of having a Special Air Service equivalent in the United States Army had finally been realized.

Beckwith went on to oversee DELTA's participation in Operation Eagle Claw, the ill-fated Iran hostage rescue attempt in 1980. Beckwith died in 1994 at the age of sixty-five.

Capt. Euell White ended up doing three tours in Vietnam. Just as he was wounded and awarded a Bronze Star at Plei Me, so too would he be wounded and awarded a Bronze Star a second time during 1968's Tet Offensive. White retired as a major from the army in 1972. With only an eighth-grade education when he'd enlisted at seventeen, White went on to earn a PhD in counseling, eventually serving in Christian ministry as a pastor and youth counselor. Following the war, White returned to his small North Alabama hometown and has lived there with his wife, Euna, ever since.

First Lt. Robert Berry earned the Silver Star for his actions during the siege. After stints at the Special Forces camps at Mang Buk and Dak To, Berry left Vietnam in 1967. He would go on to attend law school while still in the army, eventually becoming a judge advocate general at Fort Knox, Kentucky, until 1980. From there, he was recruited to become the first legal adviser to the new Joint Special Operations Command, formed in late 1980 to better coordinate special operations in the wake of the failed Iran hostage rescue. There, Berry would reteam with Col. Charles Beckwith to help get the nascent special operations command up and running. Berry retired from the army in 1984 as a lieutenant colonel. He then went to work as a civilian attorney for the Defense Intelligence Agency, retiring in 2017. Today, he lives with his wife in Virginia.

Capt. Dale Potter was awarded the Distinguished Flying Cross for his rescue of downed Skyraider pilot Mel Elliott. Potter would retire in 1977 as a lieutenant colonel after twenty years with the Air Force. Now in his eighties, Potter divides his time between several avocations. He continues his work with the Bien Hoa Eagles and their efforts to publicize the heroism of pararescue jumper William Pitsenbarger. Thanks in part to the Bien Hoa Eagles, a movie about Pitsenbarger's life, *The Last Full Measure*, was released in theaters in October 2019. Potter conducts research as an amateur anthropologist on the Nez Perce Indians of the Pacific Northwest and is also an aficionado of the game of cock fighting, a sport that Potter argues has gotten a bad rap over the years. And when he's not engaged in all of that, he's logging thousands of miles driving around the country with his girlfriend to visit his many friends. Potter still keeps in touch with old chums Dick and Beverly Shortridge. In fact, he lives right next door to one of their daughters in Oregon.

For actions in support of Plei Me, **Capt. Bob Wright**, along with the rest of the 119th Aviation Company, was awarded the Valorous Unit

Award, equivalent to the Silver Star for individuals. Wright went on to do a second tour in Vietnam before returning stateside to attend the Command and General Staff College from 1972 to 1973 in Fort Leavenworth, Kansas. Afterward, Wright was due to take over a battalion at Fort Rucker, Alabama, but the flying bug was still with him. When an Iranian general asked him to come help establish his country's own Army Aviation Program, Wright jumped at the chance. He would retire from the army a lieutenant colonel in 1977. He and his wife, Joy, had one son, Robert Jr., who gave the couple two grandchildren. Today, they all live in Tennessee, where in October 2019 they were standing by to welcome their first great-grandchild.

First Lt. Charles Oualline did two tours in Vietnam. He retired from the army in 1982 as a lieutenant colonel. Oualline, ever the Aggie, returned home to his native Texas, where he lives today with his family. He stays in touch with his friends from the 119th to this day and usually attends the annual reunion. In 2004, Oualline published *Flying Alligators and Silver Spurs: The Dangers, Tragedies, and Comradeship of the Vietnam War*, a book based on his experiences as a helicopter pilot.

First Lt. Jerry Riches left Vietnam in May 1966. By then, Riches had decided he'd seen enough of war. He separated from the army as a captain in September of that same year. But he never gave up on his love of flying. From then on, he would just do it without people shooting at him. In 1972, Riches obtained his certified flight instructor certificate and has been helping others experience the joy of flight ever since. One of those he helped would become his wife, Susan. Two kids, three houses, a Cesna 172, and half a century later, they're still together and living in Tennessee.

WO Dean Christensen left Vietnam just a few weeks after the Plei Me siege ended. He left active duty in 1967 but remained in the army reserves until retiring as a WO4 in 1986. Christensen would make his living for years as a commercial helicopter pilot in the Northwest, flying the likes of Carrie Fisher, John Wayne, and even Ted and Robert Kennedy through the mountains of Idaho's Chamberlain Basin. He and his wife of fifty-three years would eventually own a seventy-nine-foot fishing trawler in Alaska before settling down on their ranch in Utah. These days, Christensen spends his time tending his spread, his faithful Blue Heeler cattle dog always at his side.

NOTES

PROLOGUE

1. WO4 Dean Christensen (US Army Ret.), interview by J. Keith Saliba, March 20, 2019, transcript 1.
2. Christensen interview, transcript 1.
3. Christensen interview, transcript 1.
4. Christensen interview, transcript 1.
5. Christensen interview, transcript 1.
6. Christensen interview, transcript 1.
7. Christensen interview, transcript 1.
8. Christensen interview, transcript 1.
9. Christensen interview, transcript 1.

CHAPTER 2

1. Col. Francis J. Kelly, "U.S. Army Special Forces, 1961–1971," Vietnam Studies, 3–4, Department of the Army, Washington DC, 2004; Shelby L. Stanton, *Green Berets at War: U.S. Special Forces in Southeast Asia, 1956–1975*, (Novato, CA: Presidio Press, 1985).
2. Stanton, *Green Berets*, 2–3; http://www.specialforcesassociation.org/about/sf-history/.
3. Kelly, "U.S. Army Special Forces," 3; Stanton, *Green Berets*, xi–xii; http://www.specialforcesassociation.org/about/sf-history/.
4. Stanton, *Green Berets*, xii; http://www.specialforcesassociation.org/about/sf-history/.
5. Stanton, *Green Berets*, 3–4.
6. Stanton, *Green Berets*, xii–xiii, 11–12; Kelly, "U.S. Army Special Forces," 4–5; http://www.specialforcesassociation.org/about/sf-history/.

7. Stanley Karnow, *Vietnam: A History* (New York: Viking Press, 1983), 198–204.

8. Stanton, *Green Berets*, 16–17; Kevin Generous, "Irregular Forces in Vietnam," in *The World Almanac of the Vietnam War*, ed. John S. Bowman, 451 (New York: Bison Books, 1985); https://www.globalsecurity.org/military/systems/aircraft/c-123.htm; https://www.globalsecurity.org/military/world/vietnam/rvn-lldb.htm; Karnow, *Vietnam*, 198–204.

9. Virginia Morris and Clive Hills, *Ho Chi Minh's Blueprint for Revolution, in the Words of Vietnamese Strategists and Operatives* (Jefferson, NC: McFarland & Company, 2018), 126, 202; Generous, "Irregular Forces in Vietnam," 460.

10. Stanton, *Green Berets*, 16–18.

11. Stanton, *Green Berets*, 17–22; Generous, "Irregular Forces in Vietnam," 451.

12. Stanton, *Green Berets*, 22–23.

13. Stanton, *Green Berets*, 23–24.

14. Stanton, *Green Berets*, 30; Generous, "Irregular Forces in Vietnam," 460.

15. Stanton, *Green Berets*, 30–32.

16. John S. Bowman, ed., *The World Almanac of the Vietnam War* (New York: Pharos Books, 1986), 33–43.

17. Bowman, *The World Almanac of the Vietnam War*, 33–43.

18. Kelly, "U.S. Army Special Forces," 4; Stanton, *Green Berets*, 35; https://www.globalsecurity.org/military/world/vietnam/rvn-lldb.htm.

19. Kelly, "U.S. Army Special Forces," 4; Stanton, *Green Berets*, 52; Generous, "Irregular Forces in Vietnam," 452.

CHAPTER 3

1. Shelby L. Stanton, *Green Berets at War: U.S. Special Forces in Southeast Asia, 1956–1975* (Novato, CA: Presidio Press, 1985), 38, https://www.stripes.com/martha-raye-1965-1.41349; https://www.thefirearmblog.com/blog/2018/08/31/type-70-anti-tank-launcher/; http://www.tpub.com/1ase2/47.htm; https://www.cc.gatech.edu/~tpilsch/AirOps/sar-penetrator.html.

2. Kevin Generous, "Irregular Forces in Vietnam," in *The World Almanac of the Vietnam War*, ed. John S. Bowman (New York: Bison Books, 1985), 451; https://www.globalsecurity.org/military/systems/aircraft/c-123.htm; https://www.globalsecurity.org/military/world/vietnam/rvn-lldb.htm; Stanton, *Green Berets*, 37–38.

3. Stanton, *Green Berets*, 37–38.

4. Stanton, *Green Berets*, 38–41.

5. J. P. Harris, *Vietnam's High Ground: Armed Struggle for the Central Highlands, 1954–1965* (Lawrence: University Press of Kansas, 2016), 66–68, 91.

6. Harris, *Vietnam's High Ground*, 66–74.

7. Harris, *Vietnam's High Ground*, 69–71.

8. Harris, *Vietnam's High Ground*, 70–74.

9. Harris, *Vietnam's High Ground*, 70–74.

10. Harris, *Vietnam's High Ground*, 76.

11. Harris, *Vietnam's High Ground*, 76–77.

12. Harris, *Vietnam's High Ground*, 77, 90.

13. Harris, *Vietnam's High Ground*, 84, 91–92.

14. Francis J. Kelly, "U.S. Army Special Forces, 1961–1971," Vietnam Studies, 3–4, Department of the Army, Washington DC, 2004; Harris, *Vietnam's High Ground*, 91–92.

15. Harris, *Vietnam's High Ground*, 104–5.

16. Harris, *Vietnam's High Ground*, 102–6; Stanton, *Green Berets*, 51–52; Kelly, "U.S. Army Special Forces," 34.

17. Kelly, "U.S. Army Special Forces," 30.

18. Kelly, "U.S. Army Special Forces," 37; Generous, "Irregular Forces in Vietnam," 454.

19. Kelly, "U.S. Army Special Forces," 37, 54–57; Generous, "Irregular Forces in Vietnam," 454; Harris, *Vietnam's High Ground*, 148; "Teamwork Saves the Day at Nam Dong," *VFW Magazine*, August 2014, http://digitaledition.qwinc.com/article/Teamwork+Saves+The+Day+At+Nam+Dong/1749270/215523/article.html.

20. Kelly, "U.S. Army Special Forces," 37, 54–57; Generous, "Irregular Forces in Vietnam," 454; Harris, *Vietnam's High Ground*, 148; J. D. Coleman, *Pleiku: The Dawn of Helicopter War in Vietnam* (New York: St. Martin's Press, 1988), 58.

21. Harris, *Vietnam's High Ground*, 146.

22. Harris, *Vietnam's High Ground*, 208–9.

23. Kelly, "U.S. Army Special Forces," 63–64.

CHAPTER 4

1. Merle L. Pribbenow, *Victory in Vietnam: The Official History of the People's Army of Vietnam, 1954–1975* (Lawrence: University Press of Kansas, 2002), 124–25 (Pribbenow translated from original Vietnamese); Lien-Hang Nguyen, *Hanoi's War: An International History of the War for Peace in Vietnam* (Chapel Hill: University of North Carolina Press, 2012), 62–66.

2. J. P. Harris, *Vietnam's High Ground: Armed Struggle for the Central Highlands, 1954–1965* (Lawrence: University Press of Kansas, 2016), 177–78.

3. William P. Boyle and Maj. Robert Samabria, "The Lure and the Ambush: An Account of the Opening Battle of Phase Three in the Struggle for the Highlands 19 October 1965–26 October 1965," 2; Harris, *Vietnam's High Ground*, 221–22.

4. Harris, *Vietnam's High Ground*, 217; Theodore Mataxis, Sr., ARMY—War in The Highlands: Attack and Counterattack on Highway 19, October 1965, Box 01, Folder 01, Theodore Mataxis, Sr. Collection, Vietnam Center and Archive, Texas Tech University, https://www.vietnam.ttu.edu/virtualarchive/items.php?item=1390101001, accessed 02 Aug 2019.

5. Pribbenow, *Victory in Vietnam,* 142–44; Mark Moyar, *Triumph Forsaken: The Vietnam War, 1954–1965* (New York: Cambridge University Press, 2006), 365.

6. "Monsoon Offensive in The Highlands," No Date, Box 01, Folder 01, Theodore Mataxis, Sr. Collection, Vietnam Center and Archive, Texas Tech University, https://www.vietnam.ttu.edu/virtualarchive/items.php?item=1390101003, accessed 08 Jun 2019.

7. Mataxis, "Monsoon Offensive," 7–14; J. D. Coleman, *Pleiku: The Dawn of Helicopter Warfare in Vietnam* (New York: St. Martin's Press, 1988), 54–55.

8. Mataxis, "Monsoon Offensive," 20–21.

9. Mataxis, "Monsoon Offensive," 3–4.

10. Mataxis, "Monsoon Offensive," 40; Kelly, "U.S. Army Special Forces," 50, 69; Coleman, *Pleiku,* 53.

11. Mataxis, "Monsoon Offensive," 40–41; Coleman, *Pleiku,* 55; Harris, *Vietnam's High Ground,* 294.

12. Mataxis, "Monsoon Offensive," 41–49; Coleman, *Pleiku,* 54–55; Harris, *Vietnam's High Ground,* 294–97.

13. Mataxis, "Monsoon Offensive," 49–52.

14. Mataxis, "Monsoon Offensive," 52–55; Stanton, *Green Berets,* 110.

15. Mataxis, "Monsoon Offensive," 36, 57–59; Harris, *Vietnam's High Ground,* 301.

16. Harris, *Vietnam's High Ground,* 286–87.

17. Boyle and Samabria, "The Lure and the Ambush," 3; John M. Carland, *Stemming the Tide: May 1965 to October 1966* (Washington, DC: Center of Military History, United States Army, 2000), 95.

18. Coleman, *Pleiku,* 55; Harris, *Vietnam's High Ground,* 174, 196, 216.

19. For more on this interpretation, see Boyle and Samabria, "The Lure and Ambush," 3; Coleman, *Pleiku,* 55–57.

20. For more on this interpretation, see Harris, *Vietnam's High Ground,* 305; North Vietnamese history quoted in: Publication, People's Army Publishing House, Hanoi—English Translation by Merle Pribbenow—304th Division, Volume II, March–December 1965, 16900105001, 1990, Box 01, Folder 05, Merle Pribbenow Collection, Vietnam Center and Archive, Texas Tech University, accessed 10 April 2019; Lt. Gen. Harold G. Moore (Ret.) and Joseph L. Galloway, *We Were Soldiers Once . . . and Young: Ia Drang—The Battle That Changed the War in Vietnam* (New York: Harper Collins, 1992), 23–24.

21. Coleman, *Pleiku,* 55–57; Boyle and Samabria, "The Lure and the Ambush," 2–3.

22. Coleman, *Pleiku,* 62; Harris, *Vietnam's High Ground,* 310; "The Lure and the Ambush," 2–3.

23. Coleman, *Pleiku,* 62; Harris, *Vietnam's High Ground,* 310; "The Lure and the Ambush," 2–3.

24. Boyle and Samabria, "The Lure and the Ambush," 2–3, 5; Moore and Galloway, *We Were Soldiers,* 126.

25. Boyle and Samabria, "The Lure and the Ambush," 13; Moore and Galloway, *We Were Soldiers*, 68–69.

26. Coleman, *Pleiku*, 61–62.

27. Kelly, "U.S. Army Special Forces," 50, 70; Maj. Gen. Nguyen Van Hieu, ARVN, "Operation Relief of Pleime Camp Dân Thắng 21," http://www.general hieu.com/pleime-danthang21-2.htm; Coleman, *Pleiku*, 63, 76; http://www.special forcesbooks.com/A255.htm.

28. Harris, *Vietnam's High Ground*, 307; Coleman, *Pleiku*, 64; Lt. Col. Robert Berry (Ret.), executive officer at Plei Me during the siege, provided a description of the camp's layout and fortifications in an email exchange with the author on January 21, 2019.

29. Boyle and Samabria, "The Lure and the Ambush," 2–3; Harris, *Vietnam's High Ground*, 306.

30. Boyle and Samabria, "The Lure and the Ambush," 4; Intelligence Report, MACV J-2 Report—Intelligence Aspect of Plei Me/Chu Pong Campaign, 24990309001, 20 November 1965, Box 03, Folder 09, Dale W. Andrade Collection, Vietnam Center and Archive, Texas Tech University, accessed 10 April 2019.

31. Intelligence Report—Intelligence Aspect of Plei Me/Chu Pong Campaign, 4; Archie D. Hyle, "Combat Operations After Action Report." Headquarters, Special Tactical Zone 24, Advisory Detachment (MACV/RCS/J3/32) Operation Dan Thang 21, 5 December 1965; Harris, *Vietnam's High Ground*, 307.

32. Boyle and Samabria, "The Lure and the Ambush," 5; Coleman, *Pleiku*, 76.

CHAPTER 5

1. Archie D. Hyle, "Combat Operations After Action Report," Headquarters, Special Tactical Zone 24, Advisory Attachment (MACV/RCS/J3/32) Operation Dan Thang 21, 5 December 1965; Intelligence Report, MACV J-2, Intelligence Report—Intelligence Aspect of Plei Me/Chu Pong Campaign, 6, 24990309001, 20 November 1965, Box 03, Folder 09, Dale W. Andrade Collection, Vietnam Center and Archive, Texas Tech University, accessed 10 April 2019.

2. Hyle, "Combat Operations Action Report," 4; Nguyen Van Hieu, "Operation Relief of Pleime Camp Dân Thắng 21," http://www.generalhieu.com/pleime-danthang21-2.htm.

3. Inclosure 1 (CIDG in Camp Defense) to Quarterly Command Report for Period Ending 31 December 1965, HQ, 5th SFG (Abn), 1st SF, 10 January 1966, 27; Russell Lanny Hunter, *My Soul to Keep: A Journey of Faith* (St. Louis, MO: Chalice Press, 1997), 147–48; for more information on A-217 personnel at Plei Me, see http://www.specialforcesbooks.com/A255.htm.

4. Inclosure 1 (CIDG in Camp Defense), 27; Hunter, *My Soul to Keep*, 147–48; http://www.specialforcesbooks.com/A255.htm; J. D. Coleman, *Pleiku: The Dawn of Helicopter War in Vietnam* (New York: St. Martin's Press, 1988), 76; William P. Boyle

and Robert Samabria, "The Lure and the Ambush: An Account of the Opening Battle of Phase Three in the Struggle for the Highland 19 October 1965—26 October 1965 (December 1965), Box 16, 74/053, RG 319, National Archives and Records Administration, 5.

5. Lt. Col. Robert K. Wright (US Army Ret.), interview by J. Keith Saliba, April 24, 2019, transcript 1; ARMY 1965 52nd Cmbt Avn Bn History Part 1, 168300010053, No Date, Box 00, Folder 01, Bud Harton Collection, Vietnam Center and Archive, Texas Tech University, accessed 10 April 2019; History of the 119th Aviation Company (Air Mobile Light), 1 January 1965–31 December 1965, No Date, Box 05, Folder 13, Vietnam Helicopter Pilots Association (VHPA) Collection: Unit Histories—1st Aviation Brigade, Vietnam Center and Archive, Texas Tech University, https://www.vietnam.ttu.edu/virtualarchive/items.php?item=3030513001, accessed 15 May 2019; Van Hieu, "Operation Relief of Pleime Camp Dân Thắng 21."

6. Wright interview, transcript 1; Dean Christensen (WO4, US Army Ret.), interview by J. Keith Saliba, March 20, 2019, transcript 1.

7. Wright interview, transcript 1; Christensen interview, transcript 1.

8. Wright interview, transcript 1; Lt. Col. Charles Oualline (US Army Ret.), interview by J. Keith Saliba, April 5, 2019, transcript 1; see http://www.virtualwall.org/dr/RacineFD01a.htm; https://www.vvmf.org/Wall-of-Faces/28481/DON-G-KNOWLTON/; https://www.vvmf.org/Wall-of-Faces/36547/WESLEY-MCDONIAL/.

9. Wright interview, transcript 1; Oualline interview, transcript 1; http://www.virtualwall.org/dr/RacineFD01a.htm; https://www.vvmf.org/Wall-of-Faces/28481/DON-G-KNOWLTON/; https://www.vvmf.org/Wall-of-Faces/36547/WESLEY-MCDONIAL/.

10. Wright interview, transcript 1; Oualline interview, transcript 1; http://www.virtualwall.org/dr/RacineFD01a.htm; https://www.vvmf.org/Wall-of-Faces/28481/DON-G-KNOWLTON/; https://www.vvmf.org/Wall-of-Faces/36547/WESLEY-MCDONIAL/.

11. Wright interview, transcript 1.

12. Wright interview, transcript 1; History of the 119th, Aviation Company (Air Mobile Light); ARMY 1965, 52nd Cmbt Avn Bn History, Part 1.

13. Boyle and Samabria, "The Lure and the Ambush," 3; Wright interview, transcript 1; "History of the 119th"; ARMY 1965, 52nd Cmbt Avn Bn History, Part 1.

14. Project CHECO Southeast Asia Report #160—Special Report: The Siege of Plei Me—19–29 October 1965, F031100010279, 24 February 1966, Box 0001, Folder 0279, Vietnam Center and Archive, Texas Tech University, accessed 10 April 2019; Coleman, *Pleiku*.

15. Maj. Richard Shortridge (USAF Ret.), interview by J. Keith Saliba, October 3, 2018, transcript 1.

16. Shortridge interview, transcript 1.

17. Shortridge interview; https://www.stripes.com/martha-raye-1965-1.413 492; interview with Col. Ed Manning, 27700415005, 15 July 1965, Box 4, Folder

15, J. D. Coleman Collection, Vietnam Center and Archive, Texas Tech University, accessed 03 April 2019.

18. Shortridge interview, transcript 1; Richard Shortridge, interview with Veterans History Project Oral History.

19. Shortridge interview, transcript 1; Shortridge, interview with Veterans History Project Oral History.

20. Shortridge interview, transcript 1; Shortridge, interview with Veterans History Project Oral History.

21. Shortridge interview, transcript 1; Shortridge, interview with Veterans History Project Oral History.

22. Shortridge interview, transcript 1; Shortridge, interview with Veterans History Project Oral History.

23. Shortridge interview, transcript 1; Beverly Shortridge, interview by J. Keith Saliba, October 12, 2018; Shortridge, interview with Veterans History Project; https://www.aopa.org/news-and-media/all-news/2011/june/01/cessna-l -19-bird-dog-a-soldiers-best-friend; https://www.militaryfactory.com/aircraft/ detail.asp?aircraft_id=751.

24. Shortridge, interview with Veterans History Project.

25. Wright interview, transcript 1.

26. Wright interview, transcript 1.

27. Capt. Russell L. Hunter (US Army Ret.), interview by J. Keith Saliba, April 25, 2019, transcript 2.

28. Capt. Russell L. Hunter, interview by J. Keith Saliba, April 23, 2019, transcript 1; Hunter interview, transcript 2; Hunter, *My Soul to Keep*, 103–4.

29. Hunter interview, transcripts 1 and 2; Shelby L. Stanton, *Green Berets at War: U.S. Special Forces in Southeast Asia 1956–1975* (Novato, CA: Presidio Press, 1985), 110.

30. Hunter interview, transcripts 1 and 2; Hunter, *My Soul to Keep*, 33–35, 42.

31. Hunter interview, transcripts 1 and 2; Hunter, *My Soul to Keep*, 33–35, 42.

32. Hunter interview, transcript 1; Hunter, *My Soul to Keep*, 45–46; Russell Hunter, "Vietnam Journal," *Horizons—A Vietnam Journal,* September 1966, Folder 54, Box 3, J. D. Coleman Collection, Vietnam Center and Archive, Texas Tech University, accessed 26 April 2018.

33. Hunter interview, transcript 1.

34. Hunter, *My Soul to Keep*, 45–46.

35. Hunter interview, transcript 1; Hunter, *My Soul to Keep*, 3–4, 9–12.

36. Hunter interview, transcript 1; Hunter, *My Soul to Keep*, 3–4, 9–12.

37. Wright interview, transcript 1; https://www.aircav.com/huey/m5.html; https://apps.dtic.mil/docs/citations/AD0417908.

38. Inclosure 1 (CIDG in Camp Defense), 27; Coleman, *Pleiku*, 76–77.

39. Inclosure 1 (CIDG in Camp Defense), 27; Coleman, *Pleiku*, 76–77; Wallace Beene, "Plei Me Fight Stands as War Turning Point," *Stars and Stripes*, December 27, 1965.

40. Inclosure 1 (CIDG in Camp Defense), 27; Coleman, *Pleiku*, 76–77; Wallace Beene, "Plei Me Fight Stands as War Turning Point," *Stars and Stripes*, December 27, 1965.

41. Wright interview, transcript 1; Project CHECO, "The Siege of Plei Me."

42. Richard Burgess and Rausa Rosario, *US Navy A-1 Skyraider Units of the Vietnam War* (Oxford, UK: Osprey Publishing, 2009).

43. Don Holloway, "How the low, slow A-1 Skyraider earned its place in the hearts of US troops in Vietnam," *Military Times*, December 15, 2017, https://www.militarytimes.com/off-duty/2017/12/15/how-the-low-slow-a-1-skyraider-earned-its-place-in-the-hearts-of-us-troops-in-vietnam/.

44. Holloway, "How the low, slow A-1 Skyraider earned its place."

45. Dan Alex, "Douglas A-1 Skyraider," Militaryfactory.com, Last modified October 16, 2018, https://www.militaryfactory.com/aircraft/detail.asp?aircraft_id=144.

46. Coleman, *Pleiku*, 78; Project CHECO, "The Siege of Plei Me," 2; Shortridge interview, transcript 1; Gen. Nguyen Van Hieu, *"Roll Call at Pleime-Chupong-Iadrang Battlefront,"* http://www.generalhieu.com/pleime_names-2.htm.

47. Wright interview, transcript 1; Wallace Beene, "Plei Me Fight Stands as War Turning Point," *Stars and Stripes*, December 27, 1965.

48. Inclosure 1 (CIDG in Camp Defense), 27; https://www.thefirearmblog.com/blog/2018/08/31/type-70-anti-tank-launcher/; Coleman, *Pleiku*, 78; Beene, "Plei Me Fight Stands as War Turning Point."

49. Hunter interview, transcript 2; Louis Mizell, Letter to J. D. Coleman and Attachment—re: 50th Medical Detachment at Plei Me, 27700415019, 10 October 1985, Box 4, Folder 15, J. D. Coleman Collection, Vietnam Center and Archive, Texas Tech University, accessed 03 April 2019; 498th Medical Company, No Date, Box 01, Folder 20, Vietnam Helicopter Pilots Association (VHPA) Collection: Unit Histories—Medical Units, Vietnam Center and Archive, Texas Tech University, https://www.vietnam.ttu.edu/virtualarchive/items.php?item=3090120001, accessed 26 May 2019.

50. 1st Lt. Jerry Riches, interview by J. Keith Saliba, April 8, 2019, transcript 1; Wright interview, transcript 1.

51. 1st Lt. Jerry Riches, interview by J. Keith Saliba, July 20, 2019, transcript 2.

52. Riches interview, transcript 1; Wright interview, transcript 1.

53. Shortridge interview, transcript 1; Hunter interview, transcript 2; Coleman, *Pleiku*, 78.

54. Shortridge interview, transcript 1.

55. Shortridge interview, transcript 1; Maj. Richard Shortridge, USAF—Interview re: FAC Missions at Plei Me, 27700415001, No Date, Box 4, Folder 15, J. D. Coleman Collection, Vietnam Center and Archive, Texas Tech University, accessed 03 April 2019; Hunter interview, transcript 1; Hunter, *My Soul to Keep*, 141.

56. Hunter interview, transcript 2; Hunter, *My Soul to Keep*, 141; Wright interview; Mizell, Letter to Coleman.

57. Hunter interview, transcript 2; Hunter, *My Soul to Keep*, 141–42; Mizell, Letter to Coleman.

58. Hunter interview, transcript 2; Wright interview, transcript 1; Hunter, *My Soul to Keep*, 141–42; Mizell, Letter to Coleman.

59. Wright interview, transcript 1.

60. Wright interview, transcript 1.

61. Wright interview, transcript 1.

62. Wright interview, transcript 1; Shortridge interview, transcript 1.

63. Wright interview, transcript 1; see https://www.virtualwall.org/dm/MacklinRW01a.htm; https://www.virtualwall.org/dk/KnowltonDG01a.htm; https://www.vvmf.org/Wall-of-Faces/36547/WESLEY-MCDONIAL/; http://www.virtualwall.org/dr/RacineFD01a.htm.

64. Wright interview, transcript 1: Riches interview, transcript 1; "History of the 119th," 8–11.

65. Riches interview, transcript 1.

66. Hunter interview, transcript 2; Hunter, *My Soul to Keep*, 147–48; Mizell, Letter to Coleman; http://www.copters.com/pilot/max_takeoff.html.

67. Hunter interview, transcript 2; Hunter, *My Soul to Keep*, 145–46.

68. Beene, "Plei Me Fight Stands as War Turning Point"; Hunter interview, transcript 2; Hunter, *My Soul to Keep*, 145–46.

69. Beene, "Plei Me Fight Stands as War Turning Point"; Hunter interview, transcript 2; Hunter, *My Soul to Keep*, 145–46; Shea described the attempt to reach the downed chopper in this filmed interview, https://www.efootage.com/stock-footage/42838/Gi_Describes_The_Plei_Me_Battle_-_1965/.

70. Beene, "Plei Me Fight Stands as War Turning Point"; Hunter interview, transcript 2; Hunter, *My Soul to Keep*, 145–46; https://www.efootage.com/stock-footage/42838/Gi_Describes_The_Plei_Me_Battle_-_1965/.

71. Hunter interview, transcript 2; Hunter, *My Soul to Keep*, 146; https://www.vvmf.org/Wall-of-Faces/1969/JOSEPH-D-BAILEY/.

72. Hunter interview, transcript 2; Hunter, *My Soul to Keep*, 146.

73. Hunter interview, transcript 2.

74. Hunter interview, transcript 2.

75. Hunter interview, transcript 2; Hunter, *My Soul to Keep*, 147.

76. Hunter interview, transcript 2.

77. 1st Lt. Robert H. Berry, interview by J. Keith Saliba, August 8, 2018, and August 31, 2018, transcripts 1 and 2; Col. Nguyen Van Hieu, II Corps Chief of Staff, Pleiku 1966, *"Operation Dan Thang 21,"* http://www.generalhieu.com/pleime-danthang21-2.htm.

78. Berry interview, transcripts 1 and 2.

79. Berry interview, transcript 2.

80. Berry interview, transcript 2; Hyle, "Combat Operations After Action After Report," 7.

81. Inclosure 1 (CIDG in Camp Defense), 28; Stanton, *Green Berets at War,* 194–97; Van Hieu, "Roll Call at Pleime-Chupong-Iadrang Battlefront," http://www.generalhieu.com/pleime_names-2.htm.

82. B-52 (Project Delta) After Action Report—Operation 19-65, After Action Report to OPORD 19-65 (II Corps Than Phong Five and Six), 10 November 1965.

83. Charlie A. Beckwith and Donald Knox, *Delta Force: A Memoir by the Founder of the U.S. Military's Most Secretive Special-Operations Unit* (New York: Harper Collins, 71–72; Hunter, *My Soul to Keep,* 159; http://www.specialforcesbooks.com/B52S .htm.

84. Beckwith and Knox, *Delta Force,* 65–68; Inclosure 22 (Sequence of Events for Plei Me Operation for Period 20–28 October 1965) to Quarterly Command Report for Period Ending 31 December 1965, HQ, 5th SFG (Abn), 1st SF, 10 January 1966, 112; Coleman, *Pleiku,* 80; https://fas.org/man/dod-101/sys/ac/c-130 .htm; https://www.globalsecurity.org/military/systems/aircraft/c-123.htm.

85. "Distinguished Member of the Special Forces Regiment," https://web. archive.org/web/20161221090013/http://www.soc.mil/SWCS/Regimental Honors/_pdf/sf_beckwith.pdf; Beckwith and Knox, *Delta Force,* 19, 56; "Special Forces History: Operation White Star," http://www.specialforceshistory.info/opns/ white-star.html.

86. Beckwith and Knox, *Delta Force,* 19; "Distinguished Member of the Special Forces Regiment."

87. Beckwith and Knox, *Delta Force,* 30.

88. Beckwith and Knox, *Delta Force,* 31–36; https://www.cdc.gov/leptospirosis /infection/index.html.

89. Beckwith and Knox, *Delta Force,* 38–39; Viscount William Slim, *Defeat into Victory: Battling Japan in Burma and India, 1942–1945* (New York: Cooper Square Press, 2000).

90. Beckwith and Knox, *Delta Force,* 40–52.

91. Beckwith and Knox, *Delta Force,* 52–54.

92. Beckwith and Knox, *Delta Force,* 56–57; Stanton, *Green Berets at War,* 194–95; Col. Francis J. Kelly, "U.S. Army Special Forces: 1961–1971," Vietnam Studies, Department of the Army, Washington, DC, 2004, 53–54.

93. Beckwith and Knox, *Delta Force,* 56–57; Stanton, *Green Berets at War,* 194–95; Kelly, *U.S. Army Special Forces,* 53-54; Beckwith and Knox, *Delta Force,* 60–61.

94. Van Hieu, "Roll Call at Pleime-Chupong-Iadrang Battlefront"; Kelly, U.S. Army Special Forces, 140; Stanton, *Green Berets at War,* 194–95; Beckwith and Knox, *Delta Force,* 60–61.

95. Major Euell T. White (US Army Ret.), interview by J. Keith Saliba, February 15, 2019, transcript 1; Euell White, *The Siege of Plei Me: My Combat with the Green Berets* (self-pub., 2012), 9.

96. White interview, transcript 1.

97. White interview, transcript 1.

98. White interview, transcript 1.

99. White interview, transcript 1.

100. White interview, transcript 1.

101. White interview, transcript 1; White, *Siege of Plei Me*, 18–19.

102. White interview, transcript 1; White, *Siege of Plei Me*, 18–20.

103. J. P. Harris, *Vietnam's High Ground: Armed Struggle for the Central Highlands, 1954–1965* (Lawrence: University Press of Kansas, 2016), 325–26; Coleman, *Pleiku,* 80–81; John M. Carland, *Stemming the Tide: May 1965 to October 1966* (Washington, DC: Center of Military History, United States Army, 2000), 101; Van Hieu, "Operation Relief of Pleime Camp Dân Thắng 21."

104. Hyle, "Combat Operations After Action Report"; Harris, *Vietnam's High Ground,* 294, 326; Coleman, *Pleiku,* 80.

105. Hyle, "Combat Operations After Action Report," 6; Inclosure 22 (Sequence of Events for Plei Me Operation), 112; Van Hieu, "Operation Relief of Pleime Camp Dân Thắng 21."

106. Beckwith and Knox, *Delta Force,* 69; Inclosure 22 (Sequence of Events for Plei Me Operation), 1.

107. Beckwith and Knox, *Delta Force,* 69; Inclosure 22 (Sequence of Events for Plei Me Operation), 1.

108. Beckwith and Knox, *Delta Force,* 69–70; Inclosure 22 (Sequence of Events for Plei Me Operation), 1.

CHAPTER 6

1. Unit History, 155th Aviation Company—Stage Coach, History of the 155th Aviation Company (AML), 19, 24 February 1966, Box 01, Folder 03, Les Davison Collection, Vietnam Center and Archive, Texas Tech University, https://www.viet nam.ttu.edu/virtualarchive/items.php?item=28550103001, accessed 22 April 2019; J. D. Coleman, *Pleiku: The Dawn of Helicopter War in Vietnam* (New York: St. Martin's Press, 1988), 84.

2. Charlie A. Beckwith and Donald Knox, *Delta Force: A Memoir by the Founder of the US Military's Most Secretive Special-Operations Unit* (New York: Harper Collins, 1983), 70; Inclosure 22 (Sequence of Events for Plei Me Operation for Period 20–28 October 1965) to Quarterly Command Report for Period Ending 31 December 1965, HQ, 5th SFG (Abn), 1st SF, 10 January 1966, 2; Unit History, 155th Aviation Company, 19.

3. Beckwith and Knox, *Delta Force,* 70; Inclosure 22 (Sequence of Events for Plei Me Operation), 1; Unit History, 155th Aviation Company, 19; Shortridge explained his CAS for Beckwith's task force in a letter to his wife, Beverly, 28 October 1965, a copy of which was provided to the author.

4. Beckwith and Knox, *Delta Force,* 70; Inclosure 22 (Sequence of Events for Plei Me Operation), 2.

5. Beckwith and Knox, *Delta Force,* 70–71.

6. Beckwith and Knox, *Delta Force*, 70–71; Inclosure 22 (Sequence of Events for Plei Me Operation), 2.

7. Beckwith and Knox, *Delta Force*, 70–71; Inclosure 22 (Sequence of Events for Plei Me Operation), 2; Shortridge letter to wife, Beverly, 28 October 1965.

8. Euell White, *The Siege of Plei Me: My Combat with the Green Berets* (self-pub., 2012), 20–21.

9. White, *The Siege of Plei Me*, 20–21.

10. White, *The Siege of Plei Me*, 20–21; Major Euell T. White (US Army Ret.), interview by J. Keith Saliba, February 15, 2019, transcript 1; White, *The Siege of Plei Me*, 21.

11. J. P. Harris, *Vietnam's High Ground: Armed Struggle for the Central Highlands, 1954–1965* (Lawrence: University of Kansas Press, 2016), 326–27; John M. Carland, *Stemming the Tide: May 1965 to October 1966* (Washington, DC: Center of Military History, United States Army, 2000), 101.

12. Beckwith and Knox, *Delta Force,* 72; Inclosure 22 (Sequence of Events for Plei Me Operation), 2; John Laurence, *The Cat from Hue: A Vietnam War Story* (New York: PublicAffairs, 2002), 259; White, *The Siege of Plei Me*, 21.

13. Beckwith and Knox, *Delta Force*, 72.

14. Beckwith and Knox, *Delta Force*, 72; Laurence, *The Cat from Hue,* 259–60; Inclosure 22 (Sequence of Events for Plei Me Operation), 2.

15. Melvin C. Elliott, "Bailout at Plei Me," *The Intake—Journal of the Super Sabre Society,* no. 4 (2007): 28; Harris, *Vietnam's High Ground*, 316.

16. Elliott, Bailout at Plei Me.

17. R. Lanny Hunter, *My Soul to Keep: A Journey of Faith* (St. Louis, MO: Chalice Press, 1997), 150.

18. Elliott, "Bailout at Plei Me."

19. Elliott, "Bailout at Plei Me"; Shortridge recounted the napalm strike and body count in a letter to wife, Beverly, 28 October 1965, a copy of which was provided to the author.

20. Elliott, "Bailout at Plei Me"; Shortridge letter to wife, 28 October 1965.

21. Elliott, "Bailout at Plei Me"; R. W. Apple, "US Pilot Tells How He Eluded the Vietcong," *New York Times*, October 24, 1965.

22. Elliott, "Bailout at Plei Me"; Apple, "US Pilot Tells How He Eluded the Vietcong."

23. Elliott, "Bailout at Plei Me"; Apple, "US Pilot Tells How He Eluded the Vietcong."

24. Inclosure 1 (CIDG in Camp Defense), 27.

25. Hunter interview, transcript 2.

26. Hunter interview, transcript 2; Inclosure 1 (CIDG in Camp Defense), 27; Project CHECO Southeast Asia Report #16—Special Report: The Siege of Plei Me—19–29 October 1965, F031100010279, 24 February 1966, Box 0001, Folder 0279, Vietnam Archive Collection, Vietnam Center and Archive, Texas Tech University, accessed 10 April 2019.

27. Hunter interview, transcript 2.

28. Hunter, *My Soul to Keep*; Hunter interview, transcript 1.

29. Hunter, *My Soul to Keep*, 150; Inclosure 1, "CIDG in Camp Defense," 4.

30. Harris, *Vietnam's High Ground*, 307; "History of the 310th Air Commando Squadron (Troop Carrier), 1 July 1965–31 December 1965," prepared by Captain Donald B. Foisy and edited by Captain Douglas W. Hawkins, 1; Robert Berry provided a description of the camp's layout and fortifications in an email exchange on January 21, 2019.

31. "History of the 310th Air Commando Squadron," 2, 7.

32. "History of the 310th Air Commando Squadron"; Hunter interview, transcript 2; Project CHECO Southeast Asia Report #16; Inclosure 1 (CIDG in Camp Defense), 27–28; Joseph Galloway, interview by J. Keith Saliba, September 19, 2018, transcript 1.

33. Hunter, *My Soul to Keep*, 150; "Douglas AC-47 Spooky," Militaryfactory.com, last modified February 26, 2018, https://www.militaryfactory.com/aircraft/detail.asp?aircraft_id=1225.

34. Hunter interview, transcript 2; Project CHECO Southeast Asia Report #16, 1–3.

35. Elliott, "Bailout at Plei Me," 28.

36. Elliott, "Bailout at Plei Me."

37. "History of the 310th Air Commando Squadron," 7.

38. Elliott, "Bailout at Plei Me"; Hunter, *My Soul to Keep*, 157; Lt. Col. Robert Berry (US Army Ret.), interview by J. Keith Saliba, August 6, 2018, interview transcripts 1 and 2; Apple, "US Pilot Tells How He Eluded the Vietcong."

39. Elliott, "Bailout at Plei Me"; Hunter, *My Soul to Keep*, 157; Berry interview, transcripts 1 and 2; Apple, "US Pilot Tells How He Eluded the Vietcong."

40. Berry interview, transcripts 1 and 2; Hunter, *My Soul to Keep*, 157–58.

41. Capt. Dale Potter (USAF Ret.), interview by J. Keith Saliba, December 12, 2018, transcript 1; History of 38th Air Rescue Squadron, Air Rescue Service (MATS), Tan Son Nhut AB, Republic of Vietnam, 1 July–31 December 1965.

42. Potter interview, transcript 1; see https://www.nationalmuseum.af.mil/Visit/Museum-Exhibits/Fact-Sheets/Display/Article/196061/kaman-hh-43b-huskie/; http://www.tpub.com/1ase2/47.htm; https://www.cc.gatech.edu/~tpilsch/AirOps/sar-penetrator.html.

43. See https://www.military.com/military-fitness/air-force-special-operations/usaf-pararescue-jumper-fact-sheet; https://www.pjassociation.com/vietnam.

44. Potter interview, transcript 1.

45. Potter interview, transcript 1.

46. Potter interview, transcript 1; https://www.nationalmuseum.af.mil/Visit/Museum-Exhibits/Fact-Sheets/Display/Article/196061/kaman-hh-43b-huskie/; "Local Airmen See Action in Vietnam Jungle Fighting," *The Oregonian*, Sunday, October 24, 1965.

47. Potter interview, transcript 1.

48. Elliott, "Bailout at Plei Me"; "Downed Pilot Tells of Harrowing Escape" and "Pilot Covers Himself With Mud to Elude VC" at http://skyraider.org/skyassn/warstor/pleime.htm.

49. Elliott, "Bailout at Plei Me"; "Downed Pilot Tells of Harrowing Escape" and "Pilot Covers Himself With Mud to Elude VC" at http://skyraider.org/skyassn/warstor/pleime.htm.

50. Elliott, "Bailout"; History of 38th Air Rescue Squadron.

51. Charlie Beckwith and Donald Knox, *Delta Force: A Memoir by the Founder of the U.S. Military's Most Secretive Special-Operations Unit* (New York: William Morrow, 1983), 72–73; Inclosure 22 (Sequence of Events for Plei Me Operation), 2; Euell White, *The Siege of Plei Me*, 22.

52. White interview, transcript 1.

53. Beckwith and Knox, *Delta Force,* 73.

54. White, *The Siege of Plei Me*, 22.

55. Inclosure 22 (Sequence of Events for Plei Me Operation), 3; Harris, *Vietnam's High Ground,* 318; Beckwith, *Delta Force,* 72–73.

56. Beckwith and Knox, *Delta Force,* 73.

57. John Laurence, *The Cat from Hue: A Vietnam War Story* (New York: PublicAffairs, 2002), 260; Hunter, *My Soul to Keep*, 158–59; Coleman, *Pleiku*, 85.

58. Carland, *Stemming the Tide,* 54, 101; Coleman, *Pleiku*, 82; Kinnard obituary, https://www.nytimes.com/2009/01/11/us/11kinnard.html.

59. Harris, *Vietnam's High Ground,* 327–28; Van Hieu, "Roll Call"; Gen. William C. Westmoreland, *A Soldier Reports* (New York: Dell, 1976), 201.

60. Archie D. Hyle, "Combat Operations After Action Report," Headquarters, Special Tactical Zone 24, Advisory Detachment (MACV/RCS/J3/32) Operation Dan Thang 21, 5 December 1965, 14.

61. After Action Report, 1st Cavalry Division Airmobile—Pleiku Campaign, 23 October to 26 November 1965, 4 March 1966, Box 03, Folder 14, Company C, 2nd Battalion, 5th Cavalry, 1st Cavalry Division Collection, Vietnam Center and Archive, Texas Tech University, 10, 18, https://www.vietnam.ttu.edu/virtualarchive/items.php?item=24050314001, accessed 21 May 2019; Coleman, *Pleiku*, 86–87.

62. Beckwith and Knox, *Delta Force,* 73; White interview, transcript 1.

63. Beckwith and Knox, *Delta Force,* 73; White interview, transcript 1; Laurence, The *Cat from Hue*, 260; Hunter, *My Soul to Keep,* 159; Hunter interview, transcripts 1 and 2.

64. Hunter interview, transcripts 1 and 2.

65. "History of the 310th Air Commando Squadron."

66. "History of the 310th Air Commando Squadron"; Inclosure 1 (CIDG in Camp Defense), 4.

67. "History of the 310th Air Commando Squadron"; Inclosure 1 (CIDG in Camp Defense), 4.

68. *Newsweek* reporter Bill Cook was aboard Martin's 0-1 and witnessed Burr's shoot-down. The full account of what he witnessed can be found here: https://vimeo.com/52259114.

69. See https://vimeo.com/52259114.

70. Unit History, 155th Aviation Company, 19; https://vimeo.com/52259114; https://veteransfuneralcare.com/obituary/myron-myke-burr.

71. Beckwith and Knox, *Delta Force*, 73–74; Inclosure 22 (Sequence of Events for Plei Me Operation), 3.

72. Beckwith and Knox, *Delta Force*, 74; White interview, transcript 1.

73. White, *Siege of Plei Me*, 27–28.

74. White, *Siege of Plei Me*, 25–26; White interview, transcript 1; email correspondence with Euell T. White, July 3, 2019; https://army.togetherweserved.com/army/servlet/tws.webapp.WebApp?cmd=ShadowBoxProfile&type=Person&ID=59536.

75. White, *Siege of Plei Me,* 28–29; White interview, transcript 1; for more on Chinese advisers, see Charles Mohr, "3 Prisoners Tell of Aid from China," *New York Times*, November 17, 1965, 3.

76. White, *Siege of Plei Me,* 29–30; White interview, transcript 1; Shelby L. Stanton, *Green Berets at War: U.S. Special Forces in Southeast Asia, 1956–1975* (Novato, CA: Presidio Press, 1985), 114; Coleman, *Pleiku*, 85.

77. White, *Siege of Plei Me*, 29–30; White interview, transcript 1.

78. White, *Siege of Plei Me*, 29–30; White interview, transcript 1.

79. White, *Siege of Plei Me*, 32–33; White interview, transcript 1.

80. White, *Siege of Plei Me*, 34; White interview, transcript 1.

81. Inclosure 1 (CIDG in Camp Defense), 3.

82. White interview, transcript 1; White, *The Siege of Plei Me*, 35–37.

83. Beckwith and Knox, *Delta Force,* 74–75.

84. Joe Galloway, interview by J. Keith Saliba, September 9, 2018, transcript 1; Joe Galloway, "'If You Want a Good Fight . . .' UPI Correspondent Joins the Cavalry," *Soldier of Fortune Magazine,* September 1983, 23.

85. Oualline interview, transcript 1.

86. Galloway interview, transcript 1; Joe Galloway, "A Combat Reporter Remembers the Siege at Plei Me," https://www.projectdelta.net/plei_mei.htm.

87. Galloway interview, transcript 1; Galloway, "A Combat Reporter Remembers the Siege at Plei Me"; Galloway, "If You Want a Good Fight," 23.

88. Galloway interview, transcript 1.

89. Galloway interview, transcript 1.

90. Hunter interview, transcript 2; Hunter, *My Soul to Keep*, 160.

91. Hunter interview, transcript 2; Hunter, *My Soul to Keep*, 160.

92. Hunter interview, transcript 2; Hunter, *My Soul to Keep*, 160; Beckwith and Knox, *Delta Force,* 74–75.

CHAPTER 7

1. Dale Potter, interview by J. Keith Saliba, December 12, 2018, transcript 1; Email correspondence with Lt. Col. Charles Oualline (US Army Ret.). Oualline

explained the challenges and particulars of flying helicopters at night and by instruments only, May 21, 2019; 1st Lt. Jim Huebner, *My Life* (Tecumseh, MI: DiggyPOD, Inc., 2016). Huebner was an aircraft commander with the 52nd Aviation Battalion based at Camp Holloway from 1965 to 1966.

2. Potter interview, transcript 1; Email correspondence with Lt. Col. Charles Oualline; Huebner, *My Life.*

3. Potter interview, transcript 1; Email correspondence with Lt. Col. Charles Oualline; Huebner, *My Life.*

4. Potter interview, transcript 1; Email correspondence with Lt. Col. Charles Oualline, https://www.aopa.org/training-and-safety/air-safety-institute/accident-analysis/featured-accidents/epilot-asf-accident-reports-sucker-hole.

5. Potter interview, transcript 1.

6. Melvin C. Elliott, "Bailout at Plei Me," *The Intake: Journal of the Super Sabre Society*, no. 4 (2007): 28.

7. Elliott, "Bailout at Plei Me."

8. Elliott, "Bailout at Plei Me."

9. Elliott, "Bailout at Plei Me"; Maj. Richard "Dick" Shortridge (USAF Ret.), interview by J. Keith Saliba, October 3, 2018, transcript 1; Excerpt from Draft of 21 TASS History 1 July–31 December 1965—Support Document from Project CHECO Report #160, F031100010268, No Date, Box 0001, Folder 0268, Vietnam Archive Collection, Vietnam Center and Archive, Texas Tech University, accessed 10 April 2019.

10. Potter interview, transcript 1; Shortridge interview, transcript 1.

11. Potter interview, transcript 1; Shortridge interview, transcript 1; Unit History, 155th Aviation Company—Stage Coach, History of the 155th Aviation Company (AML), 24 February 1966, Box 01, Folder 03, Les Davison Collection, Vietnam Center and Archive, Texas Tech University, https://www.vietnam.ttu.edu/virtualarchive/items.php?item=28550103001, accessed 22 April 2019.

12. Shortridge interview, transcript 1.

13. Potter interview, transcript 1; Elliott "Bailout at Plei Me."

14. Potter interview; Elliott, "Bailout at Plei Me"; History of 38th Air Rescue Squadron, Air Rescue Service (MATS), Tan Son Nhut AB, Republic of Vietnam, 1 July–31 December 1965; Excerpt from Draft of 21 TASS History, 1 July–31 December 1965.

15. Potter interview, transcript 1.

16. Potter interview, transcript 1; Elliott, "Bailout at Plei Me"; Excerpt from Draft of 21 TASS History."

17. Potter interview, transcript 1.

18. Elliott, "Bailout at Plei Me."

19. Potter interview, transcript 1; Elliott, "Bailout at Plei Me"; Shortridge interview, transcript 1.

20. Potter interview, transcript 1.

21. Potter interview, transcript 1.

22. Potter interview, transcript 1.

23. Potter interview, transcript 1.

24. Potter interview, transcript 1.

25. See   https://archive.is/20121212203754/http://www.af.mil/informa-tion/heritage/person.asp?dec=&pid=123006523;   https://www.washingtonpost.com/archive/lifestyle/magazine/1989/05/28/on-the-perimeter-of-hell/2a9bc028-5277-486f-9171-e4e329868ca4/?noredirect=on&utm_term=.bd4cfbc13734; Potter interview, transcript 1.

26. See   https://archive.is/20121212203754/http://www.af.mil/informa-tion/heritage/person.asp?dec=&pid=123006523;   https://www.washingtonpost.com/archive/lifestyle/magazine/1989/05/28/on-the-perimeter-of-hell/2a9bc028-5277-486f-9171-e4e329868ca4/?noredirect=on&utm_term=.bd4cfbc13734; Potter interview, transcript 1.

27. See https://archive.is/20121212203754/http://www.af.mil/information/heritage/person.asp?dec=&pid=123006523; Potter interview, transcript 1.

28. Beverly Shortridge, interview by J. Keith Saliba, October 12, 2018, transcript 1; https://cherrieswriter.com/2017/11/10/calling-home-during-the-vietnam-war/.

29. Beverly Shortridge interview, transcript 1.

30. Beverly Shortridge interview, transcript 1.

31. Euell T. White, interview by J. Keith Saliba, February 15, 2019, transcript 1; Euell T. White, *The Siege of Plei Me: My Combat with the Green Berets* (self-pub., 2012), 40–41, 44.

32. White, *The Siege of Plei Me,* 55–56.

33. White interview, transcript 1; White, *The Siege of Plei Me,* 61–62.

34. Robert H. Berry, interview by J. Keith Saliba, August 6, 2018, transcript 1; Robert H. Berry, interview by J. Keith Saliba, August 31, 2018, transcript 2; Robert H. Berry, Silver Star citation, Headquarters United States Army Vietnam, 17 May 1966; John Laurence, *The Cat from Hue: A Vietnam War Story* (New York: PublicAf-fairs, 2002), 261; Charlie A. Beckwith and Donald Knox, *Delta Force: A Memoir by the Founder of the US Military's Most Secretive Special-Operations Unit* (New York: Harper Collins, 1983), 75; Russell L. Hunter, *My Soul to Keep: A Journey of Faith* (St. Louis, MO: Chalice Press, 1997), 161.

35. Berry interview, transcript 1; Hunter, *My Soul to Keep,* 161.

36. Hunter, *My Soul to Keep,* 161–63; Hunter interview, transcript 2; Letter from Louis Mizell to J. D. Coleman and Attachment—re: 50th Medical Detachment at Plei Me, 5, 27700415019, 10 October 1985, Box 4, Folder 15, J. D. Coleman Col-lection, Vietnam Center and Archive, Texas Tech University, accessed 03 April 2019.

37. Letter from Louis Mizell, 5.

38. Hunter, *My Soul to Keep,* 161–63; Hunter interview, transcript 2.

39. Berry interview, transcripts 1 and 2; Inclosure 22, Sequence of Events, 4.

40. Inclosure 22 (Sequence of Events for Plei Me Operation), 4; Oualline inter-view, transcript 1.

41. Oualline interview, transcript 1.

42. Qualline interview, transcript 1.

43. Nguyen Van Hieu, "Roll Call at Pleime-Chupong-Iadrang Battlefront," http://www.generalhieu.com/pleime_names-2.htm; https://veteransfuneralcare.com/obituary/myron-myke-burr; J. P. Harris, *Vietnam's High Ground: Armed Struggle for the Central Highlands, 1954–1965* (Lawrence: University Press of Kansas, 2016), 328–29; Archie D. Hyle, "Combat Operations After Action Report," Headquarters, Special Tactical Zone 24, Advisory Detachment (MACV/RCS/J3/32) Operation Dan Thang 21, 5 December 1965; Combat After Operations Report for Pleiku Campaign—Lessons Learned: Report 3-66, 10 March 1966, Box 04, Folder 22, Glenn Helm Collection, Vietnam Center and Archive, Texas Tech University, 27, https://www.vietnam.ttu.edu/virtualarchive/items.php?item=1070422001, accessed 21 May 2019.

44. Harris, *Vietnam's High Ground*, 329–30; J. D. Coleman, *Pleiku: The Dawn of Helicopter War in Vietnam* (New York: St. Martin's Press, 1988), 83; John M. Carland, *"Stemming the Tide: May 1965 to October 1966* (Washington, DC: Center of Military History, United States Army, 2000), 102–3; Translated copy of the 32nd NVA Regiment Combat Order for an Ambush, prepared at 32nd NVA Regiment Headquarters on 12 October 65, in William P. Boyle and Robert Samabria, "The Lure and the Ambush: An Account of the Opening Battle of Phase Three in the Struggle for the Highlands 19 October 1965–26 October 1965."

45. Maj. William P. Boyle and Maj. Robert Samabria, "The Lure and the Ambush: An Account of the Opening Battle of Phase Three in the Struggle for the Highlands 19 October 1965–26 October 1965," 2–4.

46. Harris, *Vietnam's High Ground,* 304–12; Translated copy of the 32nd NVA Regiment Combat Order for an Ambush; Boyle and Samabria, "The Lure and the Ambush," 7.

47. Boyle and Samabria, "The Lure and the Ambush," 4–5; Translated copy of the 32nd NVA Regiment Combat Order for an Ambush; Coleman, *Pleiku,* 83.

48. Boyle and Samabria, "The Lure and the Ambush," 4–5; Translated copy of the 32nd NVA Regiment Combat Order for an Ambush; Coleman, *Pleiku,* 83; Harris, *Vietnam's High Ground,* 311–12; Laurence, *The Cat from Hue,* 250.

49. Boyle and Samabria, "The Lure and the Ambush," 4–5; Translated copy of the 32nd NVA Regiment Combat Order for an Ambush; Coleman, *Pleiku,* 83; Harris, *Vietnam's High Ground,* 311–12; Laurence, *The Cat from Hue,* 250.

50. After Action Report, 1st Cavalry Division Airmobile—Pleiku Campaign, 23 October to 26 November 1965, 4 March 1966, Box 03, Folder 14, Company C, 2nd Battalion, 5th Cavalry, 1st Cavalry Division Collection, Vietnam Center and Archive, Texas Tech University, 10, 18, https://www.vietnam.ttu.edu/virtualarchive/items.php?item=24050314001, accessed 21 May 2019; Laurence, *The Cat from Hue,* 235–37; ARMY 1965 52nd Cmbt Avn Bn History Part 1, 168300010053, No Date, Box 00, Folder 01 Bud Harton Collection, Vietnam Center and Archive, Texas Tech University, accessed 10 April 2019.

51. After Action Report, 1st Cavalry Division Airmobile—Pleiku Campaign, 28; Laurence, *The Cat from Hue*, 235–37.

52. After Action Report, 1st Cavalry Division Airmobile—Pleiku Campaign, 28; Laurence, *The Cat from Hue*, 235–37.

53. After Action Report, 1st Cavalry Division Airmobile—Pleiku Campaign, 28; Laurence, *The Cat from Hue*, 235–37.

54. Laurence, *The Cat from Hue,* 238–40, 249.

55. Maj. Gen. Vinh Loc, II Corps commander, "Why Pleime," Army of the Republic of Vietnam, Pleiku: South Vietnam, 1966, 56–57; Carland, *Stemming the Tide,* 101–2; Coleman, *Pleiku,* 83, 89; Harris, *Vietnam's High Ground,* 330–31.

56. Coleman, *Pleiku,* 83, 89–90; Hyle, "Combat Operations After Action Report," 8; After Action Report, 1st Cavalry Division Airmobile—Pleiku Campaign, 27.

57. Hyle, "Combat Operations After Action Report," 6–7; Coleman, *Pleiku,* 90–91; After Action Report, 1st Cavalry Division Airmobile—Pleiku Campaign, 27.

58. Harris, *Vietnam's High Ground,* 333; Coleman, *Pleiku,* 83, 90–91; Carland, *Stemming the Tide,* 103; After Action Report, 1st Cavalry Division Airmobile—Pleiku Campaign, 27; Hyle, "Combat Operations After Action Report," 7; Boyle and Samabria, "The Lure and the Ambush," 9; Project CHECO Southeast Asia Report #160—Special Report: The Siege of Plei Me—19–29 October 1965, F031100010279, 24 February 1966, Box 0001, Folder 0279, Vietnam Archive Collection, Vietnam Center and Archive, Texas Tech University, accessed 10 April 2019.

CHAPTER 8

1. J. D. Coleman, *Pleiku: The Dawn of Helicopter War in Vietnam* (New York: St. Martin's Press, 1988), 88; William P. Boyle and Robert Samabria, "The Lure and the Ambush: An Account of the Opening Battle of Phase Three in the Struggle for the Highlands 19 October 1965–26 October 1965" (December 1965), Box 16, 74/053, RG 319, National Archives and Records Administration, 8–9; Translated copy of the 32nd NVA Regiment Combat Order for an Ambush, prepared at 32nd NVA Regiment Headquarters on 12 October 65, in William P. Boyle and Robert Samabria, "The Lure and the Ambush: An Account of the Opening Battle of Phase Three in the Struggle for the Highlands 19 October 1965–26 October 1965."

2. Translated copy of the 32nd NVA Regiment Combat Order for an Ambush; John Laurence, *The Cat from Hue: A Vietnam War Story* (New York: PublicAffairs, 2002), 243, 246–47; Charles Mohr, "Vietcong Drive on Outpost Appears to Ease," *New York Times,* October 25, 1965, 1.

3. Laurence, *The Cat from Hue,* 249–50.

4. For claims that Luat wanted to abandon relief effort following the ambush, see Coleman, *Pleiku,* 91, and Laurence, *The Cat from Hue,* 254–55.

5. Coleman, *Pleiku*, 86, 91; After Action Report, 1st Cavalry Division Airmobile—Pleiku Campaign, 23 October to 26 November 1965, 4 March 1966, Box 03, Folder 14, Company C, 2nd Battalion, 5th Cavalry, 1st Cavalry Division Collection, Vietnam Center and Archive, Texas Tech University, 33, https://www.vietnam.ttu.edu/virtualarchive/items.php?item=24050314001, accessed 21 May 2019; John M. Carland, *Stemming the Tide: May 1965 to October 1966* (Washington, DC: Center of Military History, United States Army, 2003), 103; Archie D. Hyle, "Combat Operations After Action Report," Headquarters, Special Tactical Zone 24, Advisory Detachment (MACV/RCS/J3/32) Operation Dan Thang 21, 5 December 1965, 7; Letter from Col. Edward Smith, Jr. (Pleiku Sector Adviser detailed to the 24th Special Tactical Zone as relief effort's Operations Officer) to J. D. Coleman—re: Resupplying Operations at Plei Me, 27700356011, 9 December 1985, Box 3, Folder 56, J. D. Coleman Collection, Vietnam Center and Archive, Texas Tech University, accessed 03 April 2019.

6. After Action Report, 1st Cavalry Division Airmobile—Pleiku Campaign, 21; Coleman, *Pleiku*, 92.

7. Charlie A. Beckwith and Donald Knox, *Delta Force: A Memoir by the Founder of the US Military's Most Secretive Special-Operations Unit* (New York: Harper Collins, 1983), 77.

8. Beckwith and Knox, *Delta Force*, 77; Inclosure 22 (Sequence of Events for Plei Me Operation for Period 20–28 October 1965) to Quarterly Command Report for Period Ending 31 December 1965, HQ, 5th SFG (Abn), 1st SF, 10 January 1966, 4.

9. Robert H. Berry, interview by J. Keith Saliba, August 6, 2018, transcript 1; Robert H. Berry, interview by J. Keith Saliba, August 31, 2018, transcript 2; Inclosure 22 (Sequence of Events for Plei Me Operation), 4.

10. Berry interview, transcripts 1 and 2.

11. Russell L. Hunter, interview by J. Keith Saliba, April 25, 2019, transcript 2.

12. Hunter interview, transcript 2.

13. Berry interviews, transcripts 1 and 2.

14. Berry interviews, transcripts 1 and 2.

15. After Action Report, 1st Cavalry Division Airmobile—Pleiku Campaign, 24; Coleman, *Pleiku*, 92; Nguyen Van Hieu, "Roll Call at Pleime-Chupong-Iadrang Battlefront," http://www.generalhieu.com/pleime_names-2.htm.

16. Coleman, *Pleiku*, 93; Laurence, *The Cat from Hue*, 254–55.

17. Coleman, *Pleiku*, 93; *The Cat from Hue*, 254–55.

18. Laurence, *The Cat from Hue*, 256–57, 270–71; Russell L. Hunter, *My Soul to Keep: A Journey of Faith* (St. Louis, MO: Chalice Press, 1997), 155; Mohr, "The Siege at Pleime: Americans Marvel at Toughness of Foe," *New York Times*, October 27, 1965, 1.

19. Laurence, *The Cat from Hue*, 256–57.

20. Laurence, *The Cat from Hue*, 256–57; Inclosure 22 (Sequence of Events for Plei Me Operation), 5.

21. Laurence, *The Cat from Hue*, 266.

22. Special to the *New York Times*, "Edward Kennedy's Copter Escort under Fire," *New York Times*, October 27, 1965.

23. Laurence, *The Cat from Hue*, 267–68; Joseph Galloway, interview by J. Keith Saliba, September 19, 2018, transcript 1.

24. Boyle and Samabria, "The Lure and the Ambush," 10.

25. Hunter, *My Soul to Keep*, 166.

26. Laurence, *The Cat from Hue*, 272–73.

27. After Action Report, 1st Cavalry Division Airmobile—Pleiku Campaign, 41; Hyle, "Combat Operations After Action Report"; Mohr, "The Siege at Pleime," October 27, 1965; Inclosure 1, "CIDG in Camp Defense"; Inclosure 22 (Sequence of Events for Plei Me Operation), 5.

28. Mohr, "The Siege at Pleime"; Inclosure 1 (CIDG in Camp Defense); Inclosure 22 (Sequence of Events for Plei Me Operation), 5.

29. Laurence, *The Cat from Hue*, 275–76; Hyle, "Combat Operations After Action Report."

30. Laurence, *The Cat from Hue*, 277, 279; Hyle, "Combat Operations After Action Report."

31. After Action Report, 1st Cavalry Division Airmobile—Pleiku Campaign, 41; Hyle, "Combat Operations After Action Report," 9.

32. Hyle, "Combat Operations After Action Report"; Laurence, *The Cat from Hue*, 279; Mohr, "The Siege at Pleime," 3.

33. Mohr, "The Siege at Pleime," 3.

34. Hunter, *My Soul to Keep*, 162, 164; Laurence, *The Cat from Hue*, 280–81; Hyle, "Combat Operations After Action Report."

35. Coleman, *Pleiku*, 99.

36. After Action Report, 1st Cavalry Division Airmobile—Pleiku Campaign, 42; Carland, *Stemming the Tide*, 104; Coleman, *Pleiku*, 99–100.

37. After Action Report, 1st Cavalry Division Airmobile—Pleiku Campaign, 42; Carland, *Stemming the Tide*, 104; Coleman, *Pleiku*, 99–100.

38. Carland, *Stemming the Tide*, 105.

39. After Action Report, 1st Cavalry Division Airmobile—Pleiku Campaign, 41; Coleman, *Pleiku*, 96–97; Beckwith, *Delta Force*, 78.

40. Beckwith, *Delta Force*, 78.

41. Inclosure 22 (Sequence of Events for Plei Me Operation), 5; Laurence, *The Cat from Hue*, 284; Coleman, *Pleiku*, 96; Jim Huebner, *My Life* (Tecumseh, MI: DiggyPOD, Inc., 2016), 182.

42. Inclosure 22 (Sequence of Events for Plei Me Operation), 5; Laurence, *The Cat from Hue*, 284; Coleman, *Pleiku*, 96; Galloway interview, transcript 1; Joe Galloway, "'If You Want a Good Fight . . .' UPI Combat Correspondent Joins the Cavalry," *Soldier of Fortune*, 23 September 1983.

43. Inclosure 22 (Sequence of Events for Plei Me Operation), 5; Laurence, *The Cat from Hue*, 284; Coleman, *Pleiku*, 96; Galloway interview, transcript 1; Galloway, "If You Want a Good Fight."

44. Inclosure 22 (Sequence of Events for Plei Me Operation), 5; Laurence, *The Cat from Hue,* 284; Coleman, *Pleiku,* 96; Galloway interview, transcript 1; Galloway, "If You Want a Good Fight."

45. Galloway interview, transcript 1; Galloway, "A Combat Reporter Remembers the Siege at Plei Me," https://www.projectdelta.net/plei_mei.htm; Galloway, "If You Want a Good Fight."

46. After Action Report, 1st Cavalry Division Airmobile—Pleiku Campaign, 45; Coleman, *Pleiku,* 96–97.

47. Hyle, "Combat Operations After Action Report"; Inclosure 22 (Sequence of Events for Plei Me Operation), 5.

48. First Lt. Jerry Riches, interview by J. Keith Saliba, April 8, 2019, transcript 1; Letter that Riches later wrote about the recovery mission, a copy of which was provided to the author.

49. Riches interview, transcript 1; Riches letter.

50. Riches interview, transcript 1; Riches letter.

51. Riches interview, transcript 1; Riches letter.

52. Riches interview, transcript 1.

CHAPTER 9

1. After Action Report, 1st Cavalry Division Airmobile—Pleiku Campaign, 23 October to 26 November 1965, 4 March 1966, Box 03, Folder 14, Company C, 2nd Battalion, 5th Cavalry, 1st Cavalry Division Collection, Vietnam Center and Archive, Texas Tech University, https://www.vietnam.ttu.edu/virtualarchive/items.php?item=24050314001, accessed 21 May 2019.

2. After Action Report, 1st Cavalry Division Airmobile—Pleiku Campaign; William P. Boyle and Robert Samabria, "The Lure and the Ambush: An Account of the Opening Battle of Phase Three in the Struggle for the Highlands 19 October 1965–26 October 1965," December 1965, Box 16, 74/053, RG 319, National Archives and Records Administration, 10.

3. After Action Report, 1st Cavalry Division Airmobile—Pleiku Campaign, 36–45; Intelligence Report, MACV J-2, Report—Intelligence Aspect of Plei Me/Chu Pong Campaign, 24990309001, 20 November 1965, Box 03, Folder 09, Dale W. Andrade Collection, Vietnam Center and Archive, Texas Tech University, accessed April 10, 2019.

4. After Action Report, 1st Cavalry Division Airmobile—Pleiku Campaign, 45.

5. After Action Report, 1st Cavalry Division Airmobile—Pleiku Campaign, 51–66.

6. Boyle and Samabria, "The Lure and the Ambush," 10–11; After Action Report, 1st Cavalry Division Airmobile—Pleiku Campaign, 69–70.

7. After Action Report, 1st Cavalry Division Airmobile—Pleiku Campaign, 72–82; John M. Carland, *Stemming the Tide: May 1965 to October 1966* (Washington,

DC: Center of Military History, United States Army, 2000), 113–14; Lt. Gen. Harold G. Moore (Ret.) and Joseph L. Galloway, *We Were Soldiers Once . . . and Young: Ia Drang—The Battle That Changed the War in Vietnam* (New York: Harper Collins, 1992), 83; J. D. Coleman, *Pleiku: The Dawn of the Helicopter War in Vietnam* (New York: St. Martin's Press, 1988), 181.

8. After Action Report, 1st Cavalry Division Airmobile—Pleiku Campaign, 72–75; Boyle and Samabria, "The Lure and the Ambush," 11–12.

9. After Action Report, 1st Cavalry Division Airmobile—Pleiku Campaign, 84–120; Carland, *Stemming the Tide*, 150.

10. After Action Report, 1st Cavalry Division Airmobile—Pleiku Campaign, 84–120; Carland, *Stemming the Tide*, 150.

11. After Action Report, 1st Cavalry Division Airmobile—Pleiku Campaign, 123; Carland, *Stemming the Tide*, 146–50.

CHAPTER 10

1. William P. Boyle and Robert Samabria, "The Lure and the Ambush: An Account of the Opening Battle of Phase Three in the Struggle for the Highlands 19 October 1965–26 October 1965," 5–12, December 1965, Box 16, 74/053, RG 319, National Archives and Records Administration.

2. Boyle and Samabria, "The Lure and the Ambush," 5–12.

3. Boyle and Samabria, "The Lure and the Ambush," 6; for information on weather conditions: see Intelligence Report, MACV J-2, Report—Intelligence Aspect of Plei Me/Chu Pong Campaign, 24990309001, 20 November 1965, Box 03, Folder 09, Dale W. Andrade Collection, Vietnam Center and Archive, Texas Tech University, accessed 10 April 2019.

4. Boyle and Samabria, "The Lure and the Ambush," 6; Intelligence Report, Intelligence Aspect of Plei Me/Chu Pong Campaign.

5. Boyle and Samabria, "The Lure and the Ambush," 9.

6. Archie D. Hyle, "Combat Operations After Action Report," Headquarters, Special Tactical Zone 24, Advisory Detachment (MACV/RCS/J3/32) Operation Dan Thang 21, 5 December 1965, 9–11; Boyle and Samabria, "The Lure and the Ambush," 10.

7. Project CHECO Southeast Asia Report #160, Special Report: The Siege of Plei Me—19–29 October 1965, F031100010279 24, February 1966, Box 0001, Folder 0279, Vietnam Archive Collection, Vietnam Center and Archive, Texas Tech University, accessed 10 April 2019, 1; Hyle, "Combat Operations After Action Report," 2.

8. Information on FACs: Manning was air liaison officer with the Air Force Support Center at II Corps during the siege. See Notes—re: Interview with Col. Ed Manning, 27700415005, 15 July 1965, Box 4, Folder 15, J. D. Coleman Collection, Vietnam Center and Archive, Texas Tech University, accessed 3 April 2019; Shortridge interview, transcript 1.

9. History of the 310th Air Commando Squadron (Troop Carrier), 1 July 1965–31 December 1965, Air Force Historical Research Agency, 1–11, Prepared by Captain Donald B. Foisy and edited by Captain Douglas W. Hawkins; "Inclosure 1 (CIDG in Camp Defense) to Quarterly Command Report for Period Ending 31 December 1965," 30, HQ, 5th SFG (Abn), 1st SF, 10 January 1966.

10. The sentiments expressed in this paragraph are derived from author interviews with Plei Me combat veterans. Each was asked why men at war make such sacrifices for each other. Two recurring themes in their answers were "doing their duty" and "helping their brothers in arms."

EPILOGUE

1. Charles Oualline, interview by J. Keith Saliba, April 5, 2019, transcript 1.

2. Qualline interview, transcript 1.

BIBLIOGRAPHY

SELECTED BIBLIOGRAPHY

After Action Report, 1st Cavalry Division Airmobile—Pleiku Campaign. 23 October to 26 November 1965. 4 March 1966. Box 03, Folder 14, Company C, 2nd Battalion, 5th Cavalry, 1st Cavalry Division Collection. Vietnam Center and Archive, Texas Tech University, 10, 18. https://www.vietnam.ttu.edu/virtual archive/items.php?item=24050314001. Accessed 21 May 2019.

Alex, Dan. "Douglas A-1 Skyraider." Militaryfactory.com. Last modified October 16, 2018. https://www.militaryfactory.com/aircraft/detail.asp?aircraft_id=144.

Apple, R. W. "US Pilot Tells How He Eluded the Vietcong." *New York Times*, October 24, 1965.

ARMY 1965 52nd Cmbt Avn Bn History, Part 1. 168300010053. No Date. Box 00, Folder 01, Bud Harton Collection. Vietnam Center and Archive, Texas Tech University. Accessed 10 April 2019.

Beckwith, Charlie A., and Donald Knox. *Delta Force: A Memoir by the Founder of the U.S. Military's Most Secretive Special-Operations Unit.* New York: Harper Collins, 1983.

Beene, Wallace. "Plei Me Fight Stands as War Turning Point." *Stars and Stripes*, December 27, 1965.

Berry, Robert H. Interview by J. Keith Saliba. August 6, 2018, transcript 1.

Berry, Robert H. Interview by J. Keith Saliba. August 31, 2018, transcript 2.

Berry, Robert H. Silver Star citation, Headquarters United States Army Vietnam. 17 May 1966.

B-52 (Project Delta) After Action Report. Operation 19-65, After Action Report to OPORD 19-65 (II Corps Than Phong Five and Six). 10 November 1965.

Bowman, John S. (ed.). *The World Almanac of the Vietnam War.* New York: Pharos Books, 1986.

Boyle, William P., and Robert Samabria. "The Lure and the Ambush: An Account of the Opening Battle of Phase Three in the Struggle for the Highlands. 19 October 1965–26 October 1965. December 1965. Box 16, 74/053, RG 319, National Archives and Records Administration.

Burgess, Richard, and Zip Rausa. *US Navy A-1 Skyraider Units of the Vietnam War* (Osprey Combat Aircraft #77). Oxford, UK: Osprey Publishing, 2009.

Carland, John M. *Stemming the Tide: May 1965 to October 1966.* Washington, DC: Center of Military History, United States Army, 2000.

Christensen, Dean (WO4, US Army Ret.). Interview by J. Keith Saliba. March 20, 2019, transcript 1.

Coleman, J. D. *Pleiku: The Dawn of Helicopter War in Vietnam.* New York: St. Martin's Press, 1988.

Combat After Operations Report for Pleiku Campaign. Lessons Learned: Report 3-66. 10 March 1966. Box 04, Folder 22, Glenn Helm Collection. Vietnam Center and Archive, Texas Tech University, 27. https://www.vietnam.ttu.edu/virtualarchive/items.php?item=1070422001. Accessed 21 May 2019.

Cook, Bill. https://vimeo.com/52259114.

"Distinguished Member of the Special Forces Regiment." https://web.archive.org/web/20161221090013/http://www.soc.mil/SWCS/RegimentalHonors/_pdf/sf_beckwith.pdf.

"Douglas AC-47 Spooky." Militaryfactory.com. Last modified February 26, 2018. https://www.militaryfactory.com/aircraft/detail.asp?aircraft_id=1225.

"Downed Pilot Tells of Harrowing Escape" and "Pilot Covers Himself with Mud to Elude VC." http://skyraider.org/skyassn/warstor/pleime.htm.

Dyhouse, Tim. "Teamwork Saves the Day at Nam Dong." *VFW Magazine*, August 2014. http://digitaledition.qwinc.com/article/Teamwork+Saves+The+Day+At+Nam+Dong/1749270/215523/article.html.

Elliott, Melvin C. "Bailout at Plei Me." *The Intake—Journal of the Super Sabre Society*, no. 4 (2007): 28.

Excerpt from Draft of 21 TASS History 1 July–31 December 1965. Support Document from Project CHECO Report #160. F031100010268. No Date. Box 0001, Folder 0268, Vietnam Archive Collection. Vietnam Center and Archive, Texas Tech University. Accessed 10 April 2019.

498th Medical Company. No Date. Box 01, Folder 20, Vietnam Helicopter Pilots Association (VHPA) Collection: Unit Histories—Medical Units. Vietnam Center and Archive, Texas Tech University. https://www.vietnam.ttu.edu/virtualarchive/items.php?item=3090120001. Accessed 26 May 2019.

Galloway, Joseph L. "A Combat Reporter Remembers the Siege at Plei Me." https://www.projectdelta.net/plei_mei.htm.

Galloway, Joseph L. "'If You Want a Good Fight . . . .'" UPI Correspondent Joins the Cavalry," *Soldier of Fortune Magazine*, 1983.

Galloway, Joseph L. Interview by J. Keith Saliba. September 19, 2018, transcript 1.

Generous, Kevin. "Irregular Forces in Vietnam." In *The World Almanac of the Vietnam War*, ed. John S. Bowman. New York: Bison Books, 1985.

Harris, J. P. *Vietnam's High Ground: Armed Struggle for the Central Highlands, 1954–1965.* Lawrence: University Press of Kansas, 2016.

Hieu, Nguyen Van. Operation Relief of Pleime Camp, Dân Thắng 21. http://www.generalhieu.com/pleime-danthang21-2.htm.

Hieu, Nguyen Van. Roll Call at Pleime-Chupong-Iadrang Battlefront. http://www.generalhieu.com/pleime_names-2.htm.

History of the 119th Aviation Company (Air Mobile Light). 1 January 1965–31 December 1965. No Date. Box 05, Folder 13, Vietnam Helicopter Pilots Association (VHPA) Collection: Unit Histories—1st Aviation Brigade. Vietnam Center and Archive, Texas Tech University, https://www.vietnam.ttu.edu/virtualarchive/items.php?item=3030513001. Accessed 15 May 2019.

History of the 310th Air Commando Squadron (Troop Carrier). 1 July 1965–31 December 1965. Air Force Historical Research Agency. Prepared by Captain Donald B. Foisy and edited by Captain Douglas W. Hawkins, 1.

History of 38th Air Rescue Squadron, Air Rescue Service (MATS). Tan Son Nhut AB, Republic of Vietnam. 1 July–31 December 1965.

Holloway, Don. "How the Low, Slow A-1 Skyraider Earned Its Place in the Hearts of US Troops in Vietnam." *Military Times*, December 15, 2017. https://www.mili tarytimes.com/off-duty/2017/12/15/how-the-low-slow-a-1-skyraider-earned -its-place-in-the-hearts-of-us-troops-in-vietnam/.

Huebner, Jim. *My Life*. Tecumseh, MI: DiggyPOD, Inc., 2016.

Hunter, Russell L. Interview by J. Keith Saliba. April 23, 2019, transcript 1.

Hunter, Russell L. Interview by J. Keith Saliba. April 25, 2019, transcript 2.

Hunter, Russell, L. *My Soul to Keep: A Journey of Faith*. St. Louis, MO: Chalice Press, 1997.

Hunter, Russell L. "Vietnam Journal." *Horizons: A Vietnam Journal*. September 1966. Folder 54, Box 3, J. D. Coleman Collection. Vietnam Center and Archive, Texas Tech University. Accessed 26 April 2018.

Hyle, Archie D. "Combat Operations After Action Report." Headquarters, Special Tactical Zone 24, Advisory Detachment, (MACV/RCS/J3/32). Operation Dan Thang 21. 5 December 1965.

Inclosure 1 (CIDG in Camp Defense) to Quarterly Command Report for Period Ending 31 December 1965. HQ, 5th SFG (Abn), 1st SF. 10 January 1966.

Inclosure 22 (Sequence of Events for Plei Me Operation for Period 20–28 October 1965) to Quarterly Command Report for Period Ending 31 December 1965. HQ, 5th SFG (Abn), 1st SF. 10 January 1966, 112.

Intelligence Report. MACV J-2, Report—Intelligence Aspect of Plei Me/Chu Pong Campaign. 24990309001. 20 November 1965. Box 03, Folder 09, Dale W. Andrade Collection. Vietnam Center and Archive, Texas Tech University. Accessed 10 April 2019.

Interview Transcript. Interview with Maj. Richard Shortridge, USAF—re: FAC Missions at Plei Me. 27700415001. No Date. Box 4, Folder 15, J. D. Coleman Collection. Vietnam Center and Archive, Texas Tech University. Accessed 03 April 2019.

Karnow, Stanley. *Vietnam: A History*. New York: Viking Press, 1983.

Kelly, Francis J. "U.S. Army Special Forces, 1961–1971." Vietnam Studies, Department of the Army, Washington DC, 2004.

Kinnard, Harry. Obituary. https://www.nytimes.com/2009/01/11/us/11kinnard.html.

Laurence, John. *The Cat from Hue: A Vietnam War Story*. New York: PublicAffairs, 2002.

Letter from Col. Edward Smith, Jr. (Pleiku Sector Advisor detailed to 24 Special Tactical Zone as relief effort's Operations Officer) to J. D. Coleman—re: Resupplying Operations at Plei Me. 27700356011. 9 December 1985. Box 3, Folder 56, J. D. Coleman Collection. Vietnam Center and Archive, Texas Tech University. Accessed 03 April 2019.

Letter from Louis Mizell to J. D. Coleman and Attachment—Re: 50th Medical Detachment at Plei Me. 27700415019. 10 October 1985. Box 4, Folder 15, J. D. Coleman Collection. Vietnam Center and Archive, Texas Tech University. Accessed 03 April 2019.

Lien-Hang, Nguyen. *Hanoi's War: An International History of the War for Peace in Vietnam.* Chapel Hill: University of North Carolina Press, 2012.

"Local Airmen See Action in Vietnam Jungle Fighting." *The Oregonian,* Sunday, October 24, 1965.

Mataxis, Theodore Sr. Monsoon Offensive in the Highlands. No Date. Box 01, Folder 01, Theodore Mataxis, Sr. Collection. Vietnam Center and Archive, Texas Tech University. https://www.vietnam.ttu.edu/virtualarchive/items.php?item=1390101003. Accessed 08 June 2019.

Mataxis, Theodore Sr. ARMY—War in The Highlands: Attack and Counter-Attack on Highway 19. October 1965. Box 01, Folder 01, Theodore Mataxis, Sr. Collection. Vietnam Center and Archive, Texas Tech University. https://www.vietnam.ttu.edu/virtualarchive/items.php?item=1390101001. Accessed 02 August 2019.

Mohr, Charles. "3 Prisoners Tell of Aid from China." *New York Times,* November 17, 1965, 3.

Mohr, Charles. "Vietcong Drive on Outpost Appears to Ease." *New York Times,* October 25, 1965, 1.

Mohr, Charles. "The Siege at Pleime: Americans Marvel at Toughness of Foe." *New York Times,* October 27, 1965, 1.

Moore, Harold G., and Joseph L. Galloway. *We Were Soldiers Once . . . and Young: Ia Drang—The Battle That Changed the War in Vietnam.* New York: Harper Collins, 1992.

Morris, Virginia, and Clive Hills. *Ho Chi Minh's Blueprint for Revolution, In the Words of Vietnamese Strategists and Operatives.* Jefferson, NC: McFarland & Company, 2018.

Morton, George C. Foreword. In Shelby L. Stanton, *Green Berets at War: U.S. Special Forces in Southeast Asia, 1956–1975.* Novato, CA: Presidio Press, 1985.

Moyar, Mark. *Triumph Forsaken: The Vietnam War, 1954–1965.* New York: Cambridge University Press, 2006.

Notes–re: Interview with Col. Ed Manning. 27700415005. 15 July 1965. Box 4, Folder 15, J. D. Coleman Collection. Vietnam Center and Archive, Texas Tech University. Accessed 03 April 2019.

Oualline, Charles. Interview by J. Keith Saliba. April 5, 2019, transcript 1.

Potter, Dale. Interview by J. Keith Saliba. December 12, 2018, transcript 1.

Pribbenow, Merle. 304th Division, Volume II, March–December 1965. 16900105001. 1990. Box 01, Folder 05, Merle Pribbenow Collection. Vietnam Center and Archive, Texas Tech University. Accessed 10 April 2019.

Pribbenow, Merle L. *Victory in Vietnam: The Official History of the People's Army of Vietnam, 1954–1975.* Lawrence: University Press of Kansas, 2002.

Project CHECO Southeast Asia Report #160. Special Report: The Siege of Plei Me—19–29 October 1965. F031100010279. 24 February 1966. Box 0001, Folder 0279, Vietnam Archive Collection. Vietnam Center and Archive, Texas Tech University. Accessed 10 April 2019.

Riches, Jerry. Interview by J. Keith Saliba. April 8, 2019, transcript 1.

Riches, Jerry. Interview by J. Keith Saliba. July 20, 2019, transcript 2.

Shortridge, Beverly. Interview by J. Keith Saliba. October 12, 2018, transcript 1.

Shortridge, Richard. Letter to his wife, Beverly. 28 October 1965.

Shortridge, Richard. Interview by J. Keith Saliba. October 3, 2018, transcript 1.

Shortridge, Richard. Interview. Veterans History Project Oral History.

Slim, William. *Defeat into Victory: Battling Japan in Burma and India, 1942–1945.* New York: Cooper Square Press, 1956.

"Special Forces History: Operation White Star." http://www.specialforceshistory .info/opns/white-star.html.

Special to the *New York Times*. "Edward Kennedy's Copter Escort under Fire," October 27, 1965.

Stanton, Shelby L. *Green Berets at War: U.S. Special Forces in Southeast Asia, 1956–1975.* Novato, CA: Presidio Press, 1985.

Translated copy of the 32nd NVA Regiment Combat Order for an Ambush. Prepared at 32nd NVA Regiment Headquarters on 12 October 65. In William P. Boyle and Robert Samabria, "The Lure and the Ambush: An Account of the Opening Battle of Phase Three in the Struggle for the Highlands 19 October 1965–26 October 1965."

Unit History, 155th Aviation Company. Stage Coach, History of the 155th Aviation Company (AML). 24 February 1966. Box 01, Folder 03, Les Davison Collection. Vietnam Center and Archive, Texas Tech University, https://www.vietnam.ttu .edu/virtualarchive/items.php?item=28550103001. Accessed 22 April 2019.

Vinh Loc, Nguyen. "Why Pleime." Army of the Republic of Vietnam. Pleiku: South Vietnam, 1966.

Westmoreland, William C. *A Soldier Reports.* New York: Dell, 1976.

White, Euell T. Interview by J. Keith Saliba. February 15, 2019, transcript 1.

White, Euell T. *The Siege of Plei Me: My Combat with the Green Berets.* Self-published, 2012.

Wright, Robert K. Interview by J. Keith Saliba. April 24, 2019, transcript 1.

WEB SOURCES

"Cessna L-19 Bird Dog: A Soldier's Best Friend," https://www.aopa.org/news-and -media/all-news/2011/june/01/cessna-l-19-bird-dog-a-soldiers-best-friend

"Cessna 0-1 Bird Dog (L-19)," https://www.militaryfactory.com/aircraft/detail .asp?aircraft_id=751

"C-123 Provider," https://www.globalsecurity.org/military/systems/aircraft/c-123.htm

"C-130 Hercules," https://fas.org/man/dod-101/sys/ac/c-130.htm

"Don Glenn Knowlton," https://www.vvmf.org/Wall-of-Faces/28481/DON-G -KNOWLTON/

"Fire Control for UH-1B Helicopter Armament Subsystem XM3," https://apps .dtic.mil/docs/citations/AD0417908

"Forest Penetrator and Flotation Collar," http://www.tpub.com/1ase2/47.htm

"Franklin Douglas Racine," http://www.virtualwall.org/dr/RacineFD01a.htm

"GI Describes the Plei Me Battle—1965," https://www.efootage.com/videos /42838/gi-describes-plei-me-battle-1965

"Harry W.O. Kinnard, Who said One Word Would Do, Dies at 93," https://www .nytimes.com/2009/01/11/us/11kinnard.html

"History of 38th Air Rescue Squadron, Air Rescue Service (MATS), Tan Son Nhut AB, Republic of Vietnam, 1 July–31 December 1965," https://archive.org/details /38thAirRescueSquadron1965JulSep

"Joseph Daniel Bailey," https://www.vvmf.org/Wall-of-Faces/1969/JOSEPH-D -BAILEY/

"Jungle Penetrator (Forest Penetrator)," https://www.cc.gatech.edu/~tpilsch/Air Ops/sar-penetrator.html

"Kaman HH-43B Huskie," https://www.nationalmuseum.af.mil/Visit/Museum -Exhibits/Fact-Sheets/Display/Article/196061/kaman-hh-43b-huskie/

"Leptospirosis," https://www.cdc.gov/leptospirosis/infection/index.html

"Martha Raye Visits the Troops in Vietnam, 1965," https://www.stripes.com/blogs -archive/archive-photo-of-the-day/archive-photo-of-the-day-1.9717/martha -raye-visits-the-troops-in-vietnam-1965-1.171238#.XvUZdihKhPY

"Maximum Performance Takeoff," http://www.copters.com/pilot/max_takeoff.html

"McBynum, Jimmie Lloyd, SSG," https://army.togetherweserved.com/army/servlet /tws.webapp.WebApp?cmd=ShadowBoxProfile&type=Person&ID=59536

"M5 Armament Subsystem," https://www.aircav.com/huey/m5.html

"Myron (Myke) Burr," https://veteransfuneralcare.com/obituary/myron-myke-burr

"On the Perimeter of Hell," https://www.washingtonpost.com/archive/lifestyle/ magazine/1989/05/28/on-the-perimeter-of-hell/2a9bc028-5277-486f-9171-e4 e329868ca4/?noredirect=on

"Pararescuemen Overview," https://www.military.com/military-fitness/air-force -special-operations/usaf-pararescue-jumper-fact-sheet

"Ronald Wayne Macklin," https://www.virtualwall.org/dm/MacklinRW01a.htm

"SF History," http://www.specialforcesassociation.org/about/sf-history/

"Southeast Asia—Vietnam," https://www.pjassociation.com/vietnam

"South Vietnam—Special Forces—Luc Luong Dac Biet (LLDB)," https://www .globalsecurity.org/military/world/vietnam/rvn-lldb.htm

"Staff Sgt. William Pitsenbarger," https://archive.is/20121212203754/http://www .af.mil/information/heritage/person.asp?dec=&pid=123006523

"Sucker Hole," https://www.aopa.org/training-and-safety/air-safety-institute/ accident-analysis/featured-accidents/epilot-asf-accident-reports-sucker-hole

"Type-70 Anti-tank Launcher: The Untold Story of the Chinese L.A.W.," https:// www.thefirearmblog.com/blog/2018/08/31/type-70-anti-tank-launcher/

"Wesley McDonial," https://www.vvmf.org/Wall-of-Faces/36547/WESLEY -MCDONIAL/

"Who's Who from Detachment A-255 (Plei Me)," http://www.specialforcesbooks .com/A255.htm

"Who's Who from Detachment B-52 (Project DELTA)," http://www.specialforces books.com/B52S.htm

ACKNOWLEDGMENTS

I extend my sincerest appreciation to all those who helped bring this book to fruition. First and foremost, my profound gratitude goes out to those veterans of the Siege of Plei Me who took the time to speak with me—often for hours at a time—about their experiences from that time and place. Without that gracious willingness on the part of R. Lanny Hunter, Dick Shortridge, Robert Berry, Dale Potter, Euell White, Bob Wright, Chuck Oualline, Jerry Riches, Dean Christensen, Bill Willoughby, Jim Bierlein, and Jim Huebner, this work would not have been possible. I also thank Lee Komich, Bob Blankenship, and Francisco Moreno for allowing me to interview them as well. Although not directly involved at Plei Me, these helicopter pilots fought in the Ia Drang battles that followed, and their various insights proved extremely helpful in broadening my understanding of those events. Joe Galloway was another invaluable interviewee. Joe related not just his personal experiences at Plei Me but his profound understanding of where it fit in the big picture. I would also like to thank Beverly Shortridge for sharing her memories of waiting anxiously for her husband's return from war. Beverly also provided invaluable personal artifacts from that time, including letters, clippings, and photos that greatly enriched my understanding.

Several archivists and research specialists deserve special recognition. Sheon Montgomery and Kelly Crager at Texas Tech University's Vietnam Center and Archive; Barry Spink and Tammy Horton at the Air Force Historical Research Agency at Maxwell Air Force Base; the Public Inquiries Team at the US Army Center of Military History; Megan Harris with the Veterans History Project at the Library of Congress; Aaron Arthur, Lauren Theodore, and Martin Gedra at the National Archives; Alisa Whitley, Fred Allison, and Susan Brubaker with the USMC History Division; and

R. Medley Gatewood at the Super Sabre Society all stand out for their helpfulness, professionalism, and responsiveness in dealing with my sometimes frantic requests for documents and information. I'm also grateful to the legendary S. Vaughn Binzer. Vaughn's own work on the story of Plei Me over the years continues to be a source of both information and inspiration to us all.

Special thanks go to Dave Reisch, Stephanie Otto, Elaine McGarraugh, and David Lampo at Stackpole Books for all their help shepherding this project to completion. My gratitude to Jacksonville University for granting the sabbatical that allowed me to make significant progress on this work. Thanks also to my friend and fellow "Elder" Ted Geltner. He's been here and done this. Those early discussions at The Swamp and elsewhere about the possibility of making this happen were invaluable. Sentences to paragraphs to pages, buddy. A big thank you is also due to Steve Sherman. His encyclopedic knowledge of Special Forces and Vietnam overall has risen to a level few could ever hope to match. I am extremely grateful to him for sharing some of that knowledge with me over the years and for his sage counsel regarding this project. Last, but certainly not least, I want to thank my wife, Vivian, and my son, Luke. Thank you, family, for your patience, understanding, and support over these many months. I love you both dearly.

INDEX

The photo section is indexed as *p1, p2, p3* etc. since there are no actual page numbers.

ABOUT THE AUTHOR

J. Keith Saliba is an associate professor of journalism and mass communication at Jacksonville (Florida) University, where he teaches narrative nonfiction and media theory. He has written about military affairs and the Vietnam War for twenty years, first as a reporter and columnist for two daily newspapers, and later as an academic at the University of Florida and JU. His master's thesis explored *Esquire* magazine's coverage of the Vietnam War, and he is a contributing author to the Indochina book series published by Radix Press. In 2018, Saliba presented his research on the psychological effects of the 1968 Tet Offensive to the annual conference of Texas Tech University's Vietnam Center & Sam Johnson Vietnam Archive. He continues to work closely with members of the Special Forces Association and Vietnam Veterans for Factual History. Saliba lives with his family in St. Johns County, Florida. This is his first book.